LACE: Living the Archive

<u>Introduction</u>

When LACE was founded in 1978, it was one
of a handful of artist-run organizations
in Los Angeles committed both to present-
ing the work of Los Angeles artists and
to highlighting the experimentation that
was taking place in contemporary art,
including performance art, video, installation and conceptual art that were, at
the time, new developments. Central to
the premise of LACE, and to others like
it across the country, was that artists
made the decisions about what was shown.
The rationale for artist-run organizations
was based on a fundamental re-thinking of
the role of artists and arts organizations
within a purportedly democratic society.
To a great extent, the organization itself
has thus been a creative practice, a
realization of the principles of engaged,
collective action.

Physical archives, with their fingerprint
smudges and notations, remain the most
comprehensive sites for accessing the
past, understanding its relationship to
this moment and to the future. It is for
this reason that LACE is embracing primary
materials and the notion of its archive
as a living public record of the art and
artists presented here.

<u>Living The Archive</u>, volume one of *LACE
in Print*, draws upon LACE's archive and
history in Southern California spanning
three decades, 1978–2008. It features
invitations, posters, letters, images and
crucial texts which continue to be in
demand, such as Branda Miller and Deborah
Irmas' essays from <u>Surveillance</u> (1987).
However, many more pieces featured on
these pages might be all that remain as
evidence of a given event or exhibition.

LACE's approach to its archive is what
archivists affectionately term "schizo,"
or in random order. With no preordained
theme, <u>Living the Archive</u> parallels the
creative process, drawing randomly from
a collection of ideas and reminiscences.

We embrace the notion of the archive as a
"town hall" (from the Greek, *arkheion*), a
place for public gathering and discussion,
because an archive only lives when experienced by the living.

We are indebted to the many people who have
made this publication a reality. First and
foremost, Mark Owens, designer, and Lisa
Carlson, independent curator, have both
worked tirelessly to ensure that <u>Living
the Archive</u> be materialized. They were
joined by Michael Ned Holte, Jane McFadden
and Glenn R. Phillips who all advised LACE
on the format and content of this volume.

Amy Adler, Michael Ned Holte, Steve Roden,
Irene Tsatsos and Jeffrey Vallance gave us
permission to publish hidden "back story"
correspondence. Liz Kotz, Weba Garretson,
Mr. Keedy, Michael Ned Holte, and Jane
McFadden and Glenn R. Phillips contributed
interstitial essays and commentary. Teresa
Carmody and Vanessa Place with Stephanie
Taylor; Harry Gamboa Jr.; the intergenera-
tional team of Suzanne Lacy, Barbara T.
Smith, Felis Stella and Tenecia Terrell;
and Liz Young created portfolio projects
exclusively for <u>Living the Archive: Box
Edition</u>.

A special thanks to our publication funders,
the Peter Norton Family Foundation and The
Andy Warhol Foundation for the Visual Arts,
as well as Lawrence Barth, Gary & Tracy
Mezzatesta and Elinor & Ruben Turner.

LACE staff Robert Crouch, Shoghig Halajian,
Geneva Skeen and Jennifer Flores Sternad,
volunteers Zemula Barr, Ingrid Cruz, Ann
Libby, Joanne Mitchell and trusted ally
Andrea Grover, all helped behind the scenes.
Finally, to everyone involved in LACE
since 1978, there are literally thousands
of you and each deserves our most heartfelt
appreciation.

Carol A. Stakenas
Executive Director
Los Angeles Contemporary Exhibitions

Archiving LACE
Liz Kotz

The question of the archive and the construction of a history for current art
practice has animated contemporary art for
some time now. Previously, a certain set
of archival methods were more commonly
used by scholars—digging through boxes of
documents, retrieving letters and other
ephemera, conducting interviews. The
generation of contemporary art historians
that I am part of, people who completed
their dissertations since the early 1990s,
were part of a larger return to archival
and historical methods. Because we had
not lived through the legendary postwar
art movements so many of us were writing
on—Fluxus, Minimalism, Happenings,
Conceptual Art, and so forth—it was almost
inevitable that we would take up a kind of
historical research that had partly been
bypassed or sidelined in, say, the more
critically and theoretically-driven art
criticism of the 1980s. If at one time a
kind of hip academic practice might have
fetishized reading Lacan in the original
French or going to Paris to participate
in seminars with the masters, for us it
was more likely to be tracking down that
obscure letter from La Monte Young or finding that unpublished version of a piece
from 1965 that had languished in an
artist's file for decades.

Of course, this kind of archival turn is
in no way unprecedented. Much of the so-
called "new art history" of the 1970s and
1980s revolved not only on incorporating
new critical models, but in reconstructing
effaced and marginalized histories, and in
finding ways to place artistic production
in relation to larger historical contexts.
Part of the pleasure of reading Thomas Crow
or T.J. Clark on French art of the 18th
and 19th centuries was immersing oneself
in the complexity and detail of narratives
constructed from press accounts, letters
and all kinds of other documents. The
guiding inspiration for this seemed to be
Walter Benjamin's legendary *Arcades Project*

of the 1930s, where he sought to reconstruct the emergence of modernity through
a series of detailed fragmentary notes on
the 19th-century Paris arcades—and, to a
perhaps secondary degree, the archivally-
based rewriting of western modernity
conducted by Michel Foucault in the 1960s
and 1970s. The archive was a lure, an
enormous site of desire, and—in ways that
are touchier and more problematic, also
the site of a kind of professionalization.
To do extensive archival work is
extraordinarily time-consuming and
expensive. All that travel to archives
and collections, all those days and weeks
spent reading and taking notes at little
tables somewhere—it is nearly impossible
without the kinds of financial support
provided by major academic institutions
and a handful of foundations. I wonder
now, in the current economic downturn, how
this type of archival project will fare,
since for many of us, especially those who
teach at public universities, that level
of research funding will be impossible for
quite some time.

The return to the archive that LACE has
been conducting is related to this more
scholarly project, but also quite
different. For the past decade or two—
again, it seems to be something that has
emerged since the early 1990s—artists have
been constructing their own histories of
artmaking, and of cultural politics, of
the postwar and more recent eras. A kind
of mania for collecting animates a lot of
recent art, and even artists whose own
work takes vastly different forms are
often deeply engaged in retrieving lost or
under-known figures or projects. While a
handful of university presses, like MIT,
have made a commitment to collecting and
republishing artists' writings, really it
has been projects organized by artists,
from ubuweb to Primary Information, that
have played the crucial role in releasing
historical documents, artworks and
materials into the present. The haphaz-
ard, selective and subjective nature of
this kind of archival unearthing is part

of its logic. Of course, institutions like LACE don't have the budgets to republish or recirculate more than a tiny selection of their ephemera or historical materials. After all, there is so much that accumulates over time: all those announcement cards, programs, posters, booklets and catalogues, not to mention the private correspondence and documents that must be filed away somewhere. To be exhaustive or complete would be logistically impossible, and probably sort of ridiculous. Because the very nature of this history is that our interests in it are partial and diverse—depending on whether we want to rediscover the history of LA-based performance or video or the earlier career of this or that artist. Maybe this very selection generates a desire for more. A show at the New York nonprofit White Columns earlier this year, *From the Archives*, presented forty projects, one each from every year of the 40-year history of 112 Green Street and White Columns. It was a great show, completely fascinating, and part of its power was that it made you wonder about all the other stuff that they'd had to leave out. So the show became like the tip of this iceberg that made you wish you could take the time and spend hours in the back rooms opening boxes and pouring over documents— and I bet some people have. This project, <u>Living the Archive</u>, is a lot like that— a selective sampling that hopefully will make you want more.

It almost goes without saying that work and activities that happened in Los Angeles and California have for a very long time been sidelined from histories of postwar and contemporary art. And in museum and scholarly cultures that are, far more than we would like to admit, enormously driven by the art market, it is almost inevitable that the nonprofit sphere, performance, video and so forth would likewise be neglected. Now, it seems like any number of artists, historians, curators and others are working to retrieve, re-use and reconstruct these histories—though what forms that might take are still unclear. However necessary, the museum retrospective works poorly for performance or film or video. And while scholarly writing usually aims to generate coherent and convincing narratives, that coherence tends to efface the fragmentary, random and excessive qualities that are integral not only to archives, but also to the histories and events and social networks they document. Behind each flier and announcement card and catalogue cover assembled here, there are so many stories and memories and also art practices and models, some well-known and some nearly forgotten. Part of the beauty of this project and similar efforts is that no one can really foresee or predict what will be most useful or interesting or provocative, as these materials again go out into the world.

1978—2008

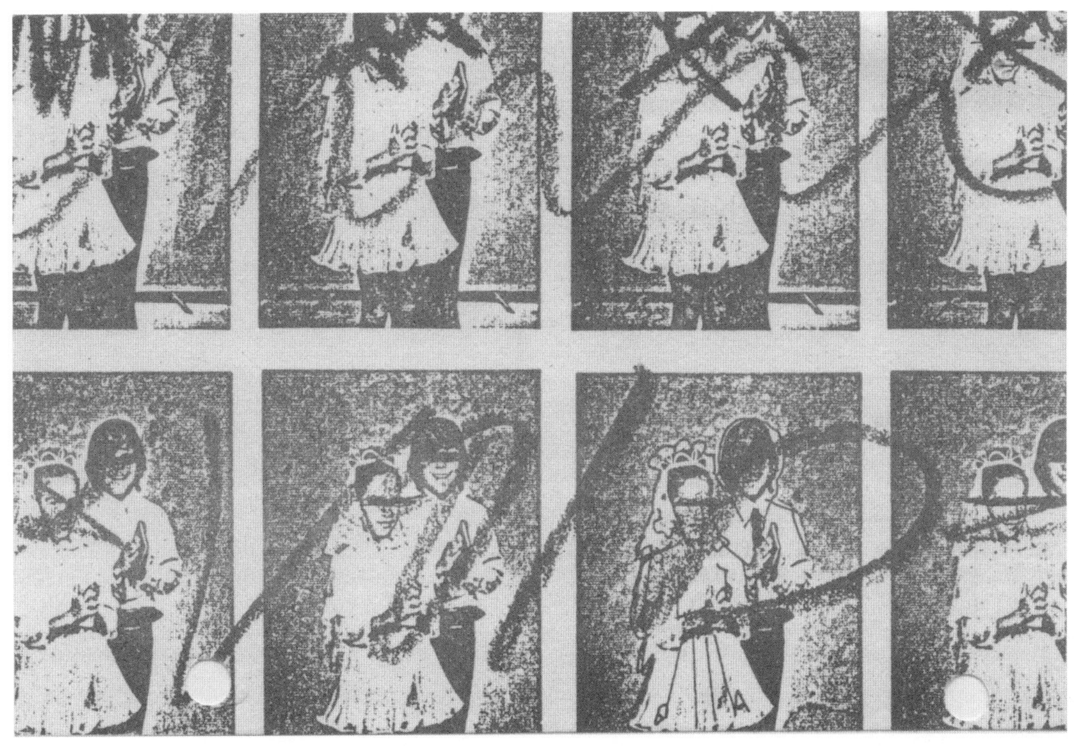

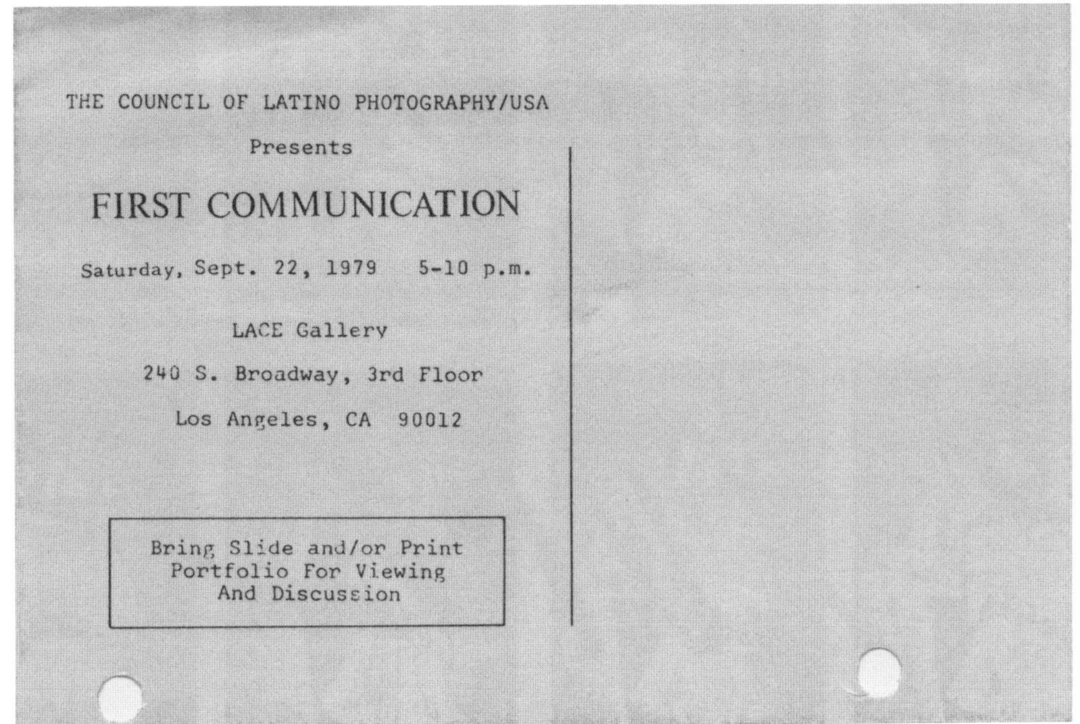

1979.01 <u>First Communication</u>, Postcard

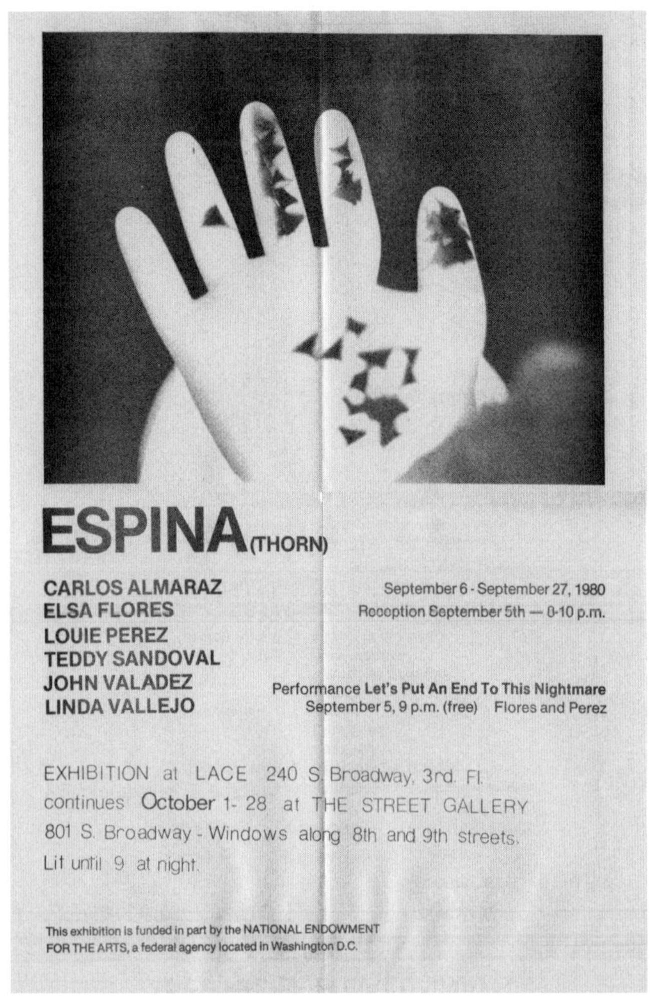

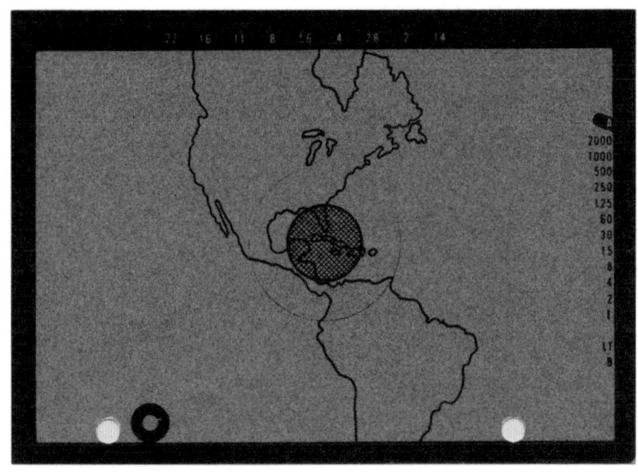

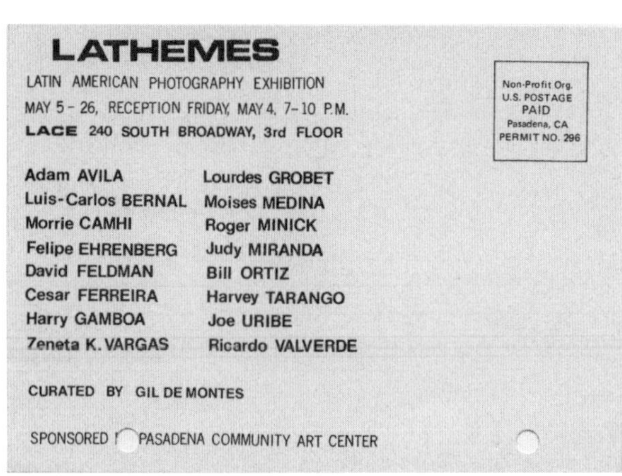

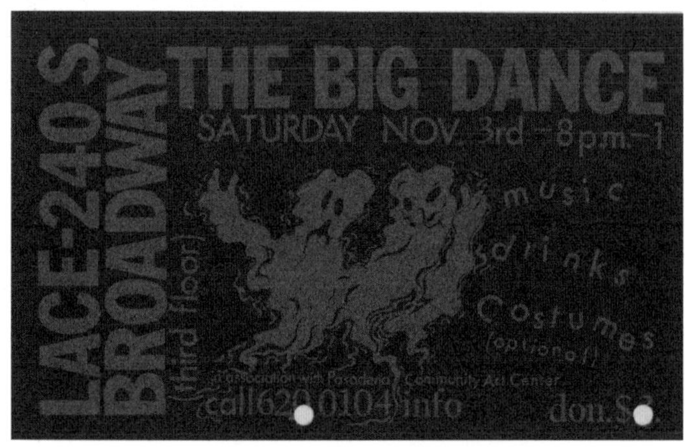

1980.01 <u>Espiña (Thorn)</u>, Flyer   1979.02 <u>LA Themes</u>, Postcard
                                              1979.03 <u>The Big Dance</u>, Postcard

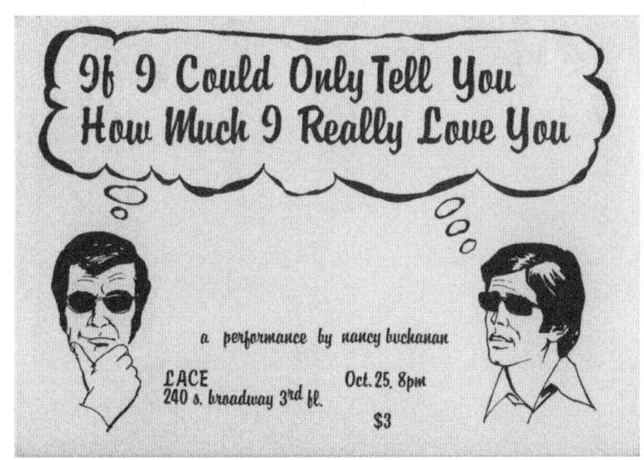

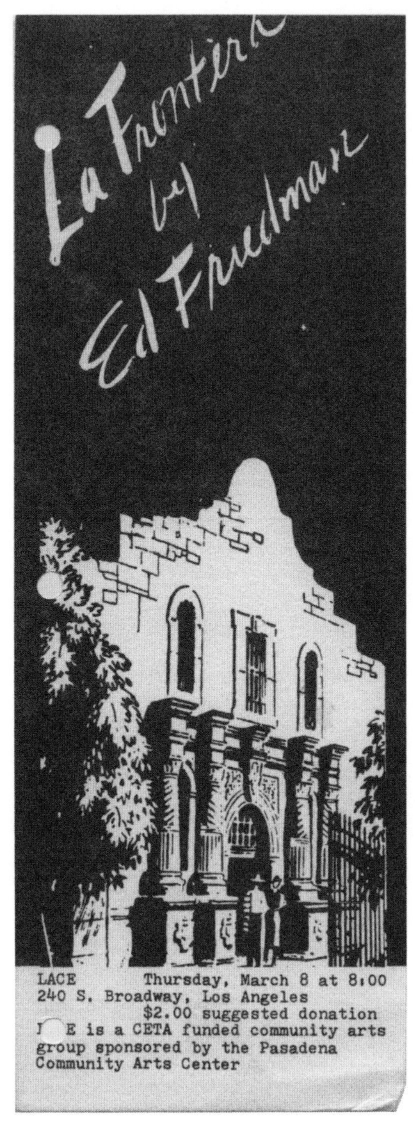

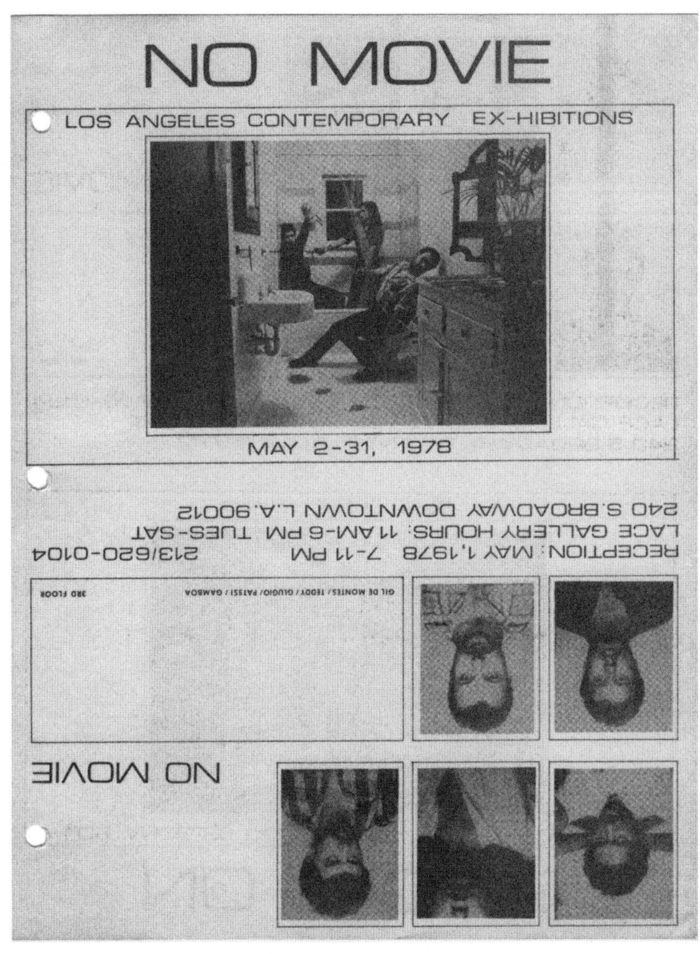

1980.02 Nancy Buchanan, <u>If I Could Only Tell You How Much I Really Love You</u>, Postcard

1979.04 <u>La Frontera by Ed Friedman</u>, Postcard

1978.01 ASCO, <u>No Movie</u>, Postcard

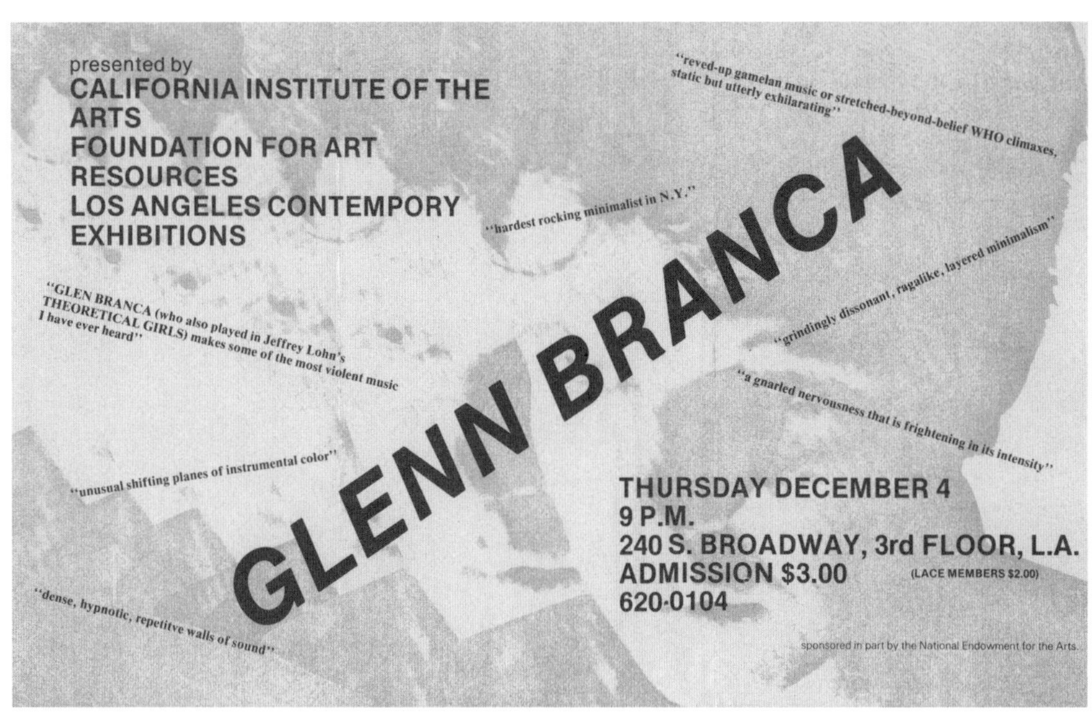

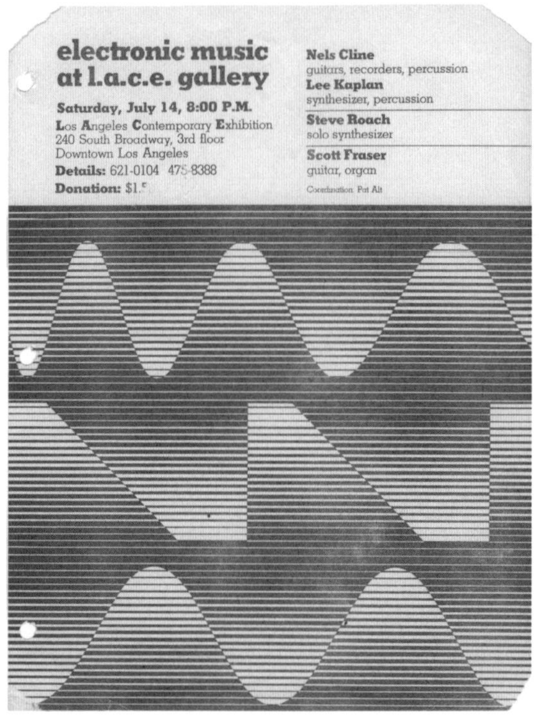

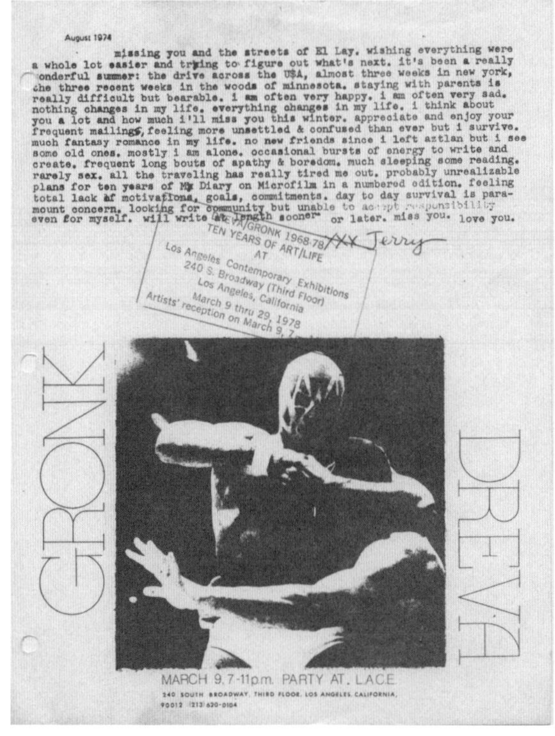

1979.05 <u>Glenn Branca</u>, Flyer
1979.06 <u>An Evening of Electronic Music</u>, Flyer

1978.02 <u>DREVA/GRONK 1968-1978/Ten Years of Art and Life</u>, Flyer

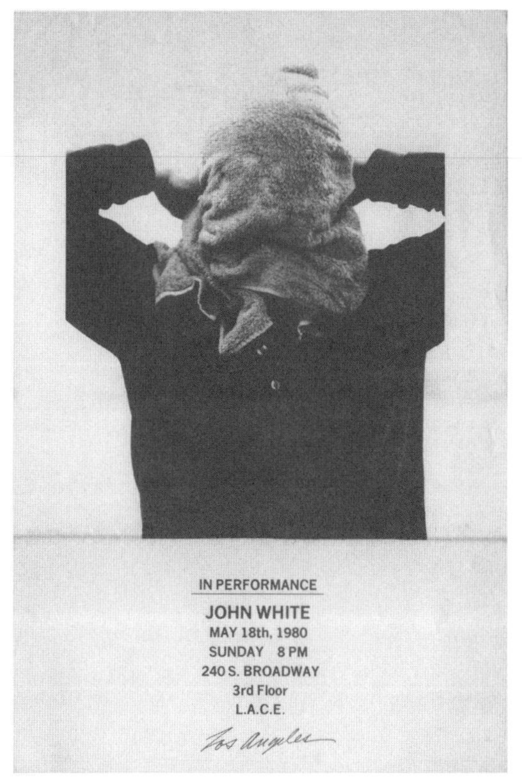

IN PERFORMANCE
JOHN WHITE
MAY 18th, 1980
SUNDAY 8 PM
240 S. BROADWAY
3rd Floor
L.A.C.E.

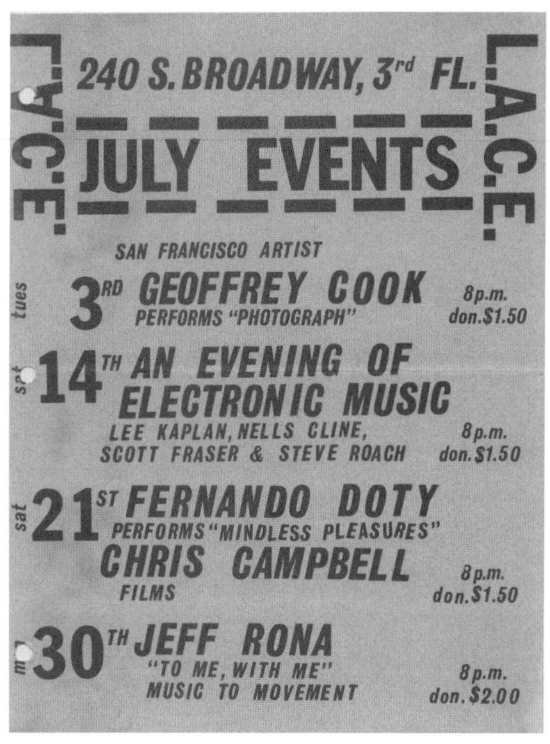

L.A.C.E.
240 S. BROADWAY, 3RD FL.
L.A.C.E.
JULY EVENTS
SAN FRANCISCO ARTIST
tues
3RD GEOFFREY COOK
PERFORMS "PHOTOGRAPH"
8 p.m.
don. $1.50
sat
14TH AN EVENING OF
ELECTRONIC MUSIC
LEE KAPLAN, NELLS CLINE,
SCOTT FRASER & STEVE ROACH
8 p.m.
don. $1.50
sat
21ST FERNANDO DOTY
PERFORMS "MINDLESS PLEASURES"
CHRIS CAMPBELL
FILMS
8 p.m.
don. $1.50
30TH JEFF RONA
"TO ME, WITH ME"
MUSIC TO MOVEMENT
8 p.m.
don. $2.00

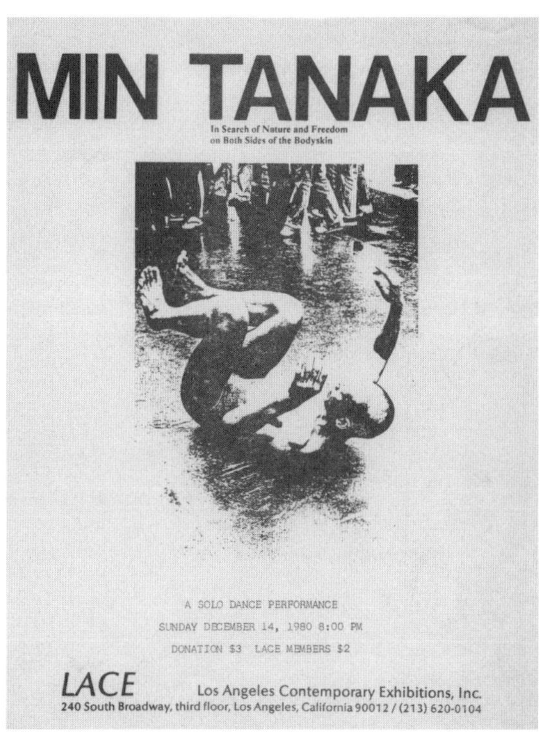

MIN TANAKA
In Search of Nature and Freedom
on Both Sides of the Bodyskin
A SOLO DANCE PERFORMANCE
SUNDAY DECEMBER 14, 1980 8:00 PM
DONATION $3 LACE MEMBERS $2
LACE
Los Angeles Contemporary Exhibitions, Inc.
240 South Broadway, third floor, Los Angeles, California 90012 / (213) 620-0104

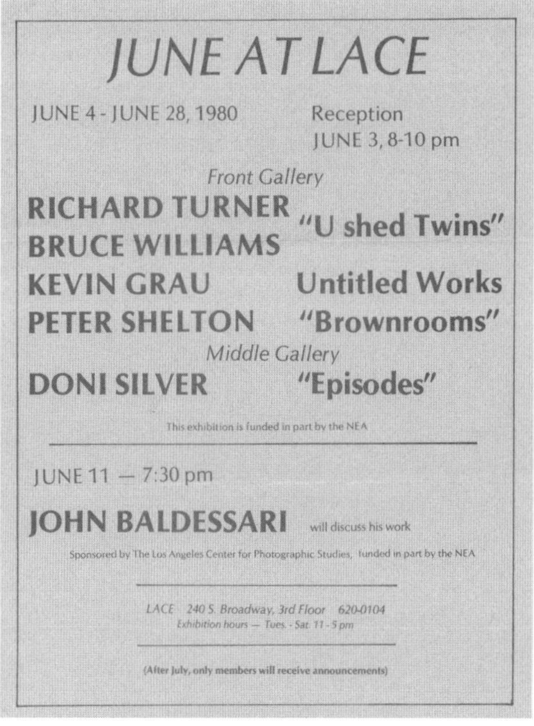

JUNE AT LACE
JUNE 4 - JUNE 28, 1980
Reception
JUNE 3, 8-10 pm
Front Gallery
RICHARD TURNER
BRUCE WILLIAMS
"U shed Twins"
KEVIN GRAU
Untitled Works
PETER SHELTON
"Brownrooms"
Middle Gallery
DONI SILVER
"Episodes"
This exhibition is funded in part by the NEA
JUNE 11 — 7:30 pm
JOHN BALDESSARI
will discuss his work
Sponsored by The Los Angeles Center for Photographic Studies, funded in part by the NEA.
LACE · 240 S. Broadway, 3rd Floor · 620-0104
Exhibition hours — Tues - Sat 11 - 5 pm
(After July, only members will receive announcements)

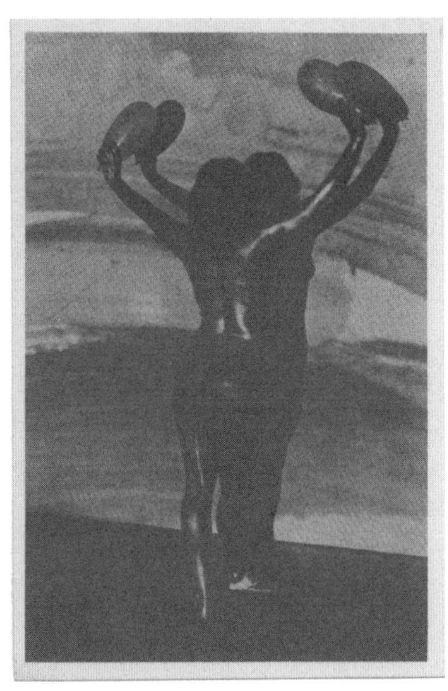

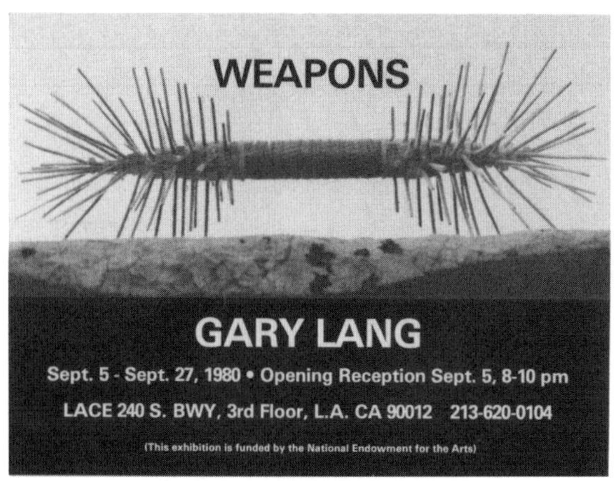

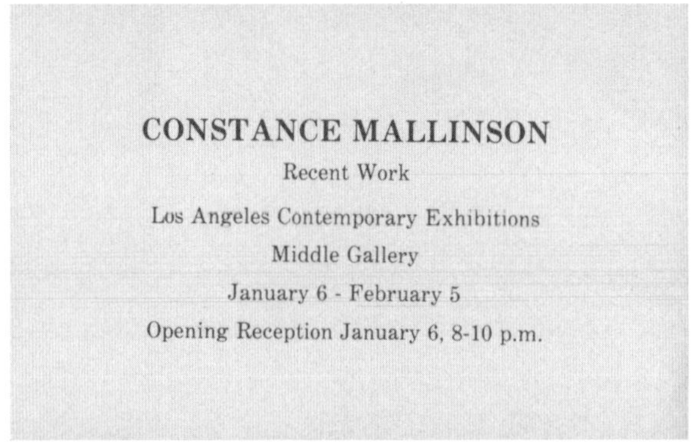

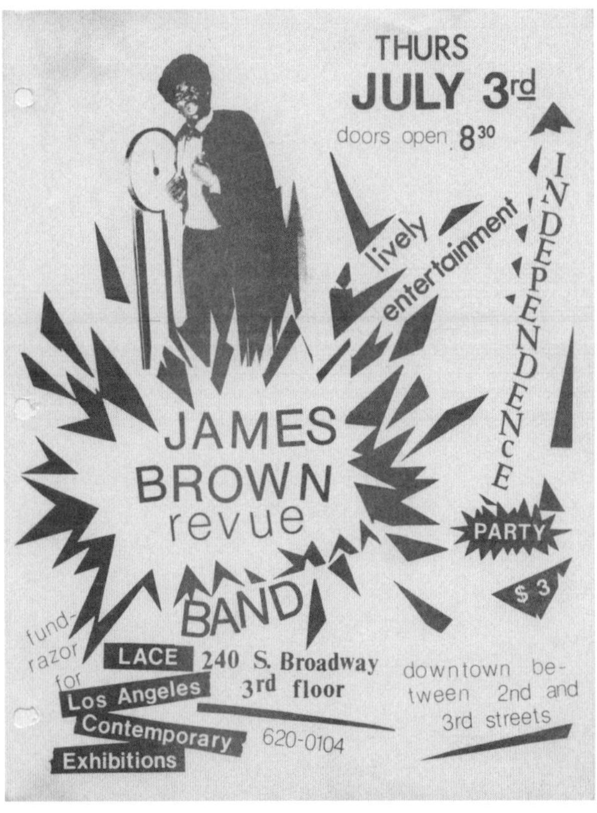

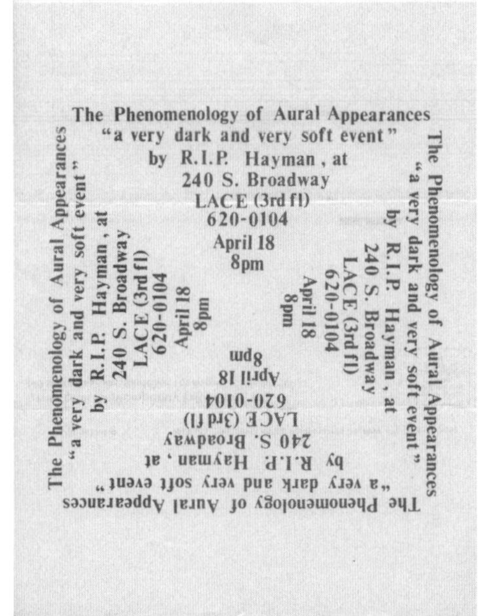

1980.06 Anne Mavor, <u>Venus on the Half Shell and Other Poses</u>, Postcard

1980.07 <u>James Brown Revue Band Fundraiser</u>, Flyer

1980.08 Gary Lang, <u>Weapons</u>, Postcard

1981.01 <u>Constance Mallinson, Recent Work</u>, Postcard

1982.01 <u>R.I.P. Hayman, The Phenomenology of Aural Appearances</u>, Flyer

LACE   Los Angeles Contemporary Exhibitions

LACE invites you to a fund-raising spectacular
and closing festivities of "The Animal Show"
featuring a buffet of animal-shaped food-art
and musical entertainment

Food-Art by

Lita Albuquerque	S. Kooter
Nancy Buchanan	Deborah Krall-Cohen
Jan Cook	Leslie Labowitz
Dan Cytron	Suzanne Lacey
Diane Destiny	Jan Lester
Marguerite Elliott	John Mandel
Joe Fay	Rick Oginz
Simone Gad	Gayle Partlow
Harry Gamboa	Patricia Patterson
Robert Gil de Montes	Margaret Paz-Partlow
Gronk	Sheila Pinkel
Larry Hathaway	Ann Preston
Willie Herron	Alexandra Sauer
Shiro Ikegawa	Maura Sheehan
Allen Kaprow	Suzanne Siegel
Wayna Kato	Laura Silagi
Mike Kelly	Nancy Youdelman

Saturday, July 28, 1979 at 7:30 P.M.
Tickets $25.00 each, suggested, tax deductible
Seating is limited, please RSVP early
Telephone 620-0104
or
Send check to LACE
240 S. Broadway
Los Angeles, California 90012

Your contribution will help LACE serve exhibiting artists better by
improving the physical facilities and installing a burglar detection
system to enable LACE to purchase insurance covering exhibited art.

1979.08 <u>Food-Art</u> for <u>The Animal Show</u>, Flyer

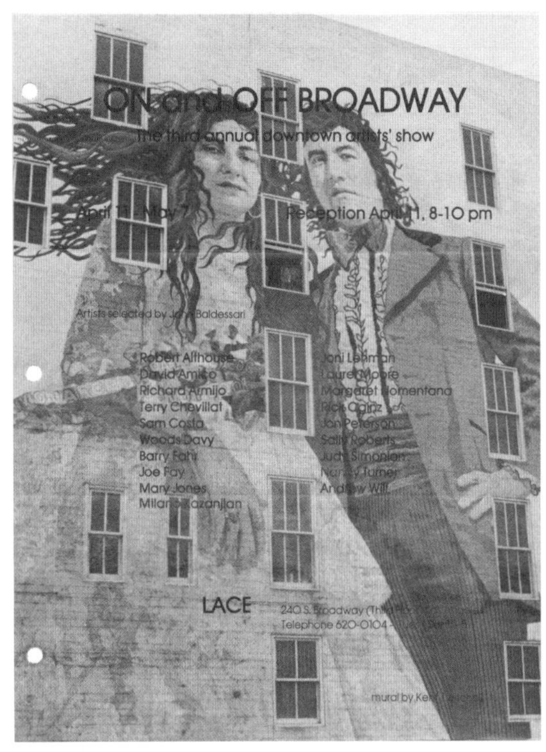

ON and OFF BROADWAY
The third annual downtown artists' show
Reception April 11, 8-10 pm
Artists selected by John Baldessari
Robert Althouse
David Amico
Richard Armijo
Terry Chevillat
Sam Costa
Woods Davy
Barry Fahr
Joe Fay
Mary Jones
Milan Mazanjian
Joni Lerman
Lauren Moore
Margaret Nomentana
Rick Oginz
Jay Peterson
Sally Roberts
Judy Simonian
Nancy Turner
Andrew Wilf
LACE
240 S. Broadway (Third fl.)
Telephone 620-0104

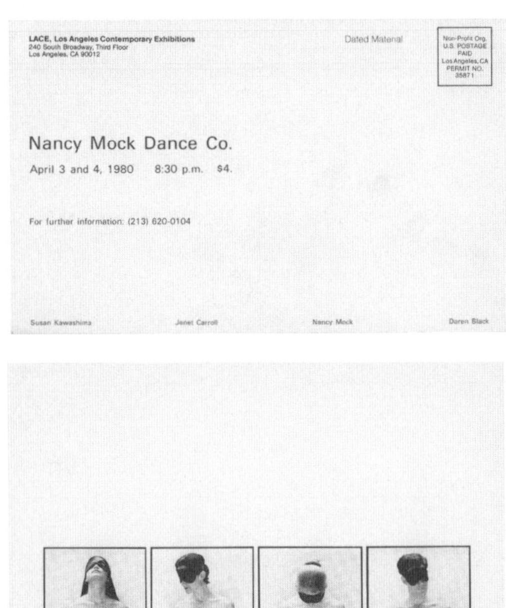

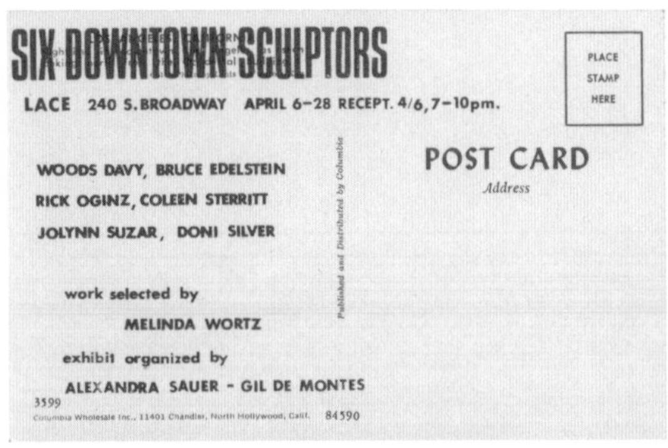

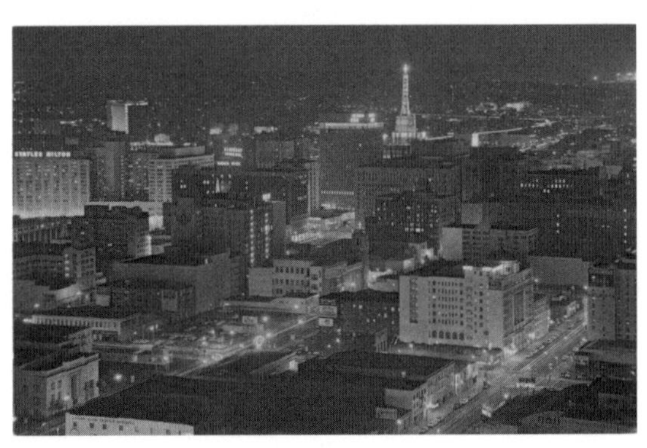

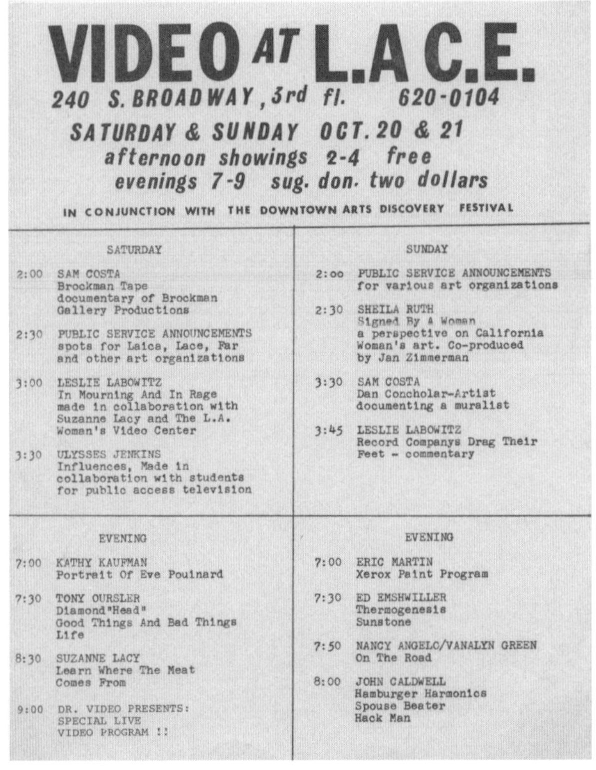

VIDEO AT L.A.C.E.
240 S. BROADWAY, 3rd fl.   620-0104
SATURDAY & SUNDAY OCT. 20 & 21
afternoon showings 2-4 free
evenings 7-9 sug. don. two dollars
IN CONJUNCTION WITH THE DOWNTOWN ARTS DISCOVERY FESTIVAL

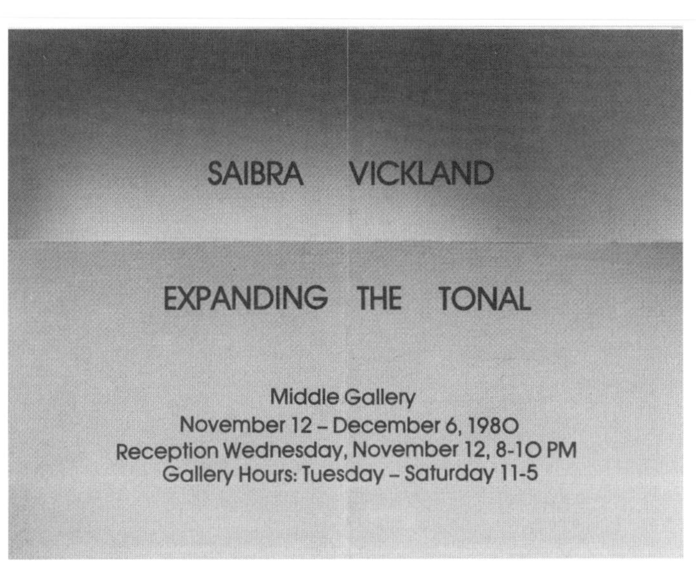

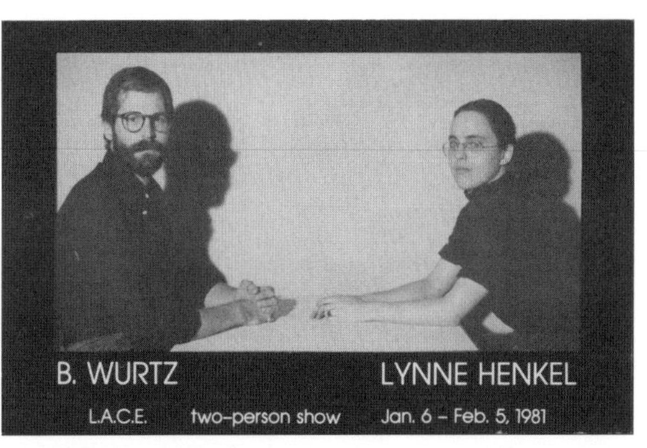

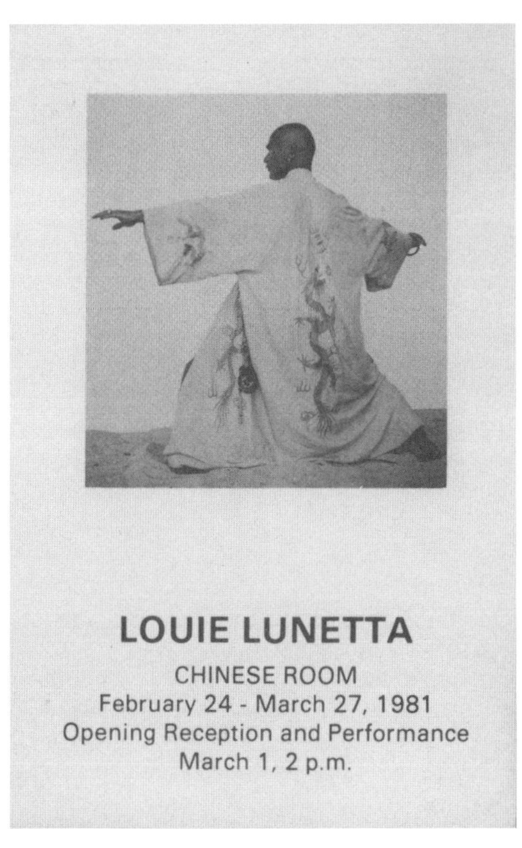

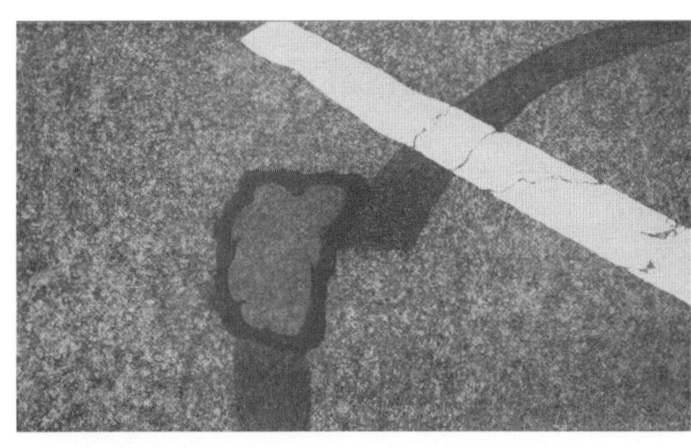

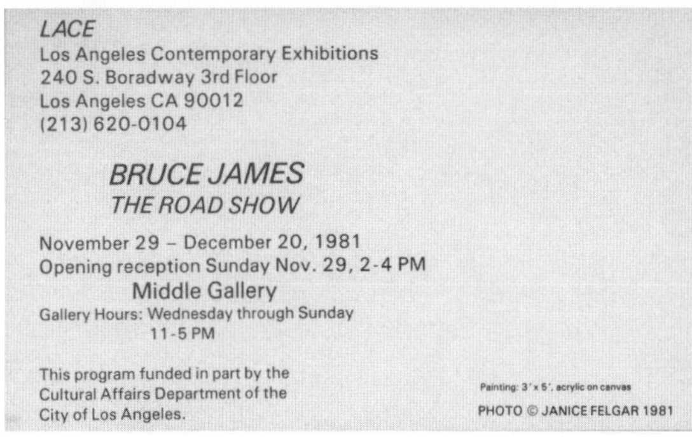

1980.11 Saibra Vickland, Expanding the
         Tonal, Poster
1981.02 Louie Lunetta, Chinese Room,
         Postcard

1981.03 B. Wurtz and Lynne Henckel, Postcard
1981.04 Bruce James, The Road Show, Postcard

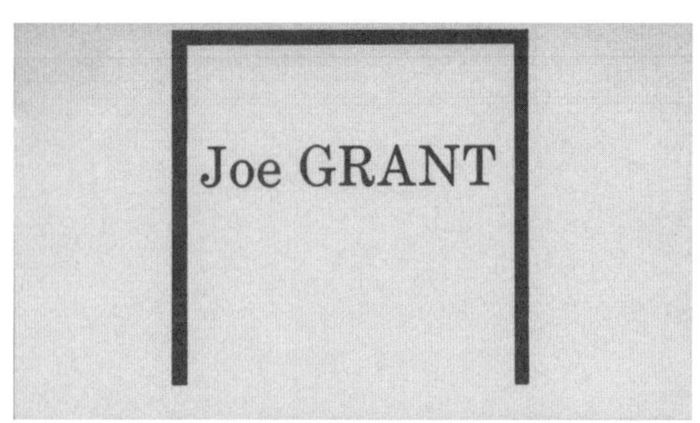

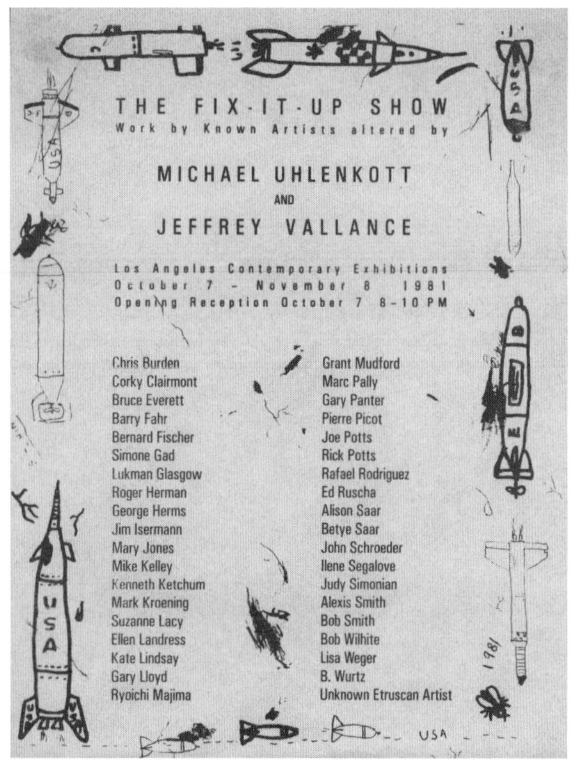

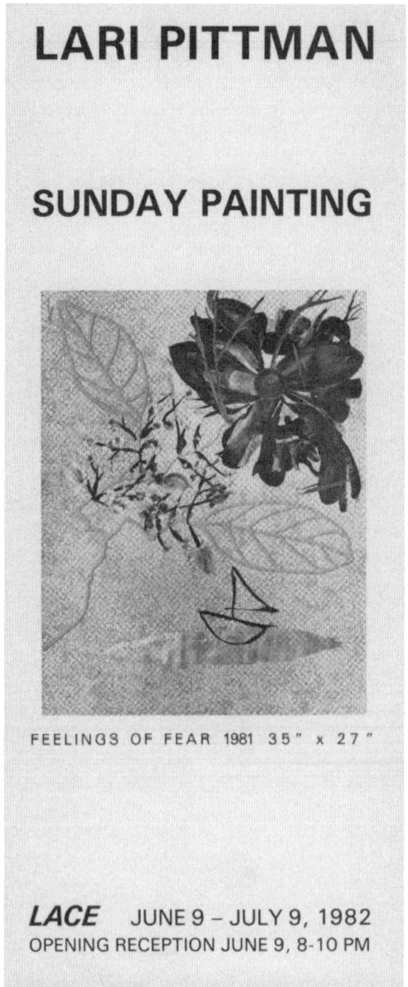

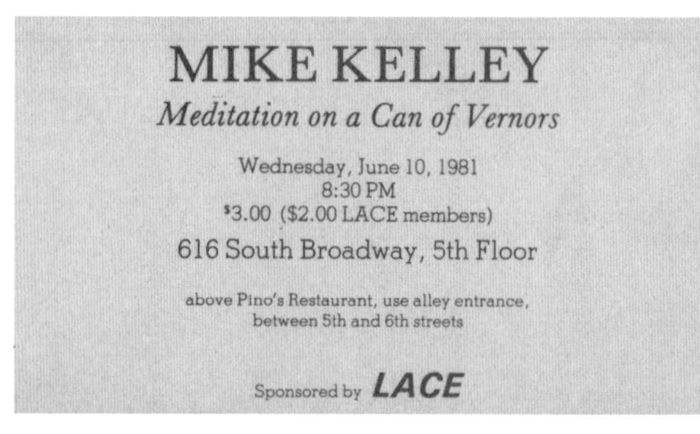

1981.05 Joe Grant, Postcard
1981.06 The Fix-It-Up Show, Works by Known Artists Altered by Michael Uhlenkott and Jeffrey Vallance, Flyer

1982.02 Lari Pittman, Sunday Painting, Postcard
1981.07 Mike Kelley, Meditation on a Can of Vernors, Postcard

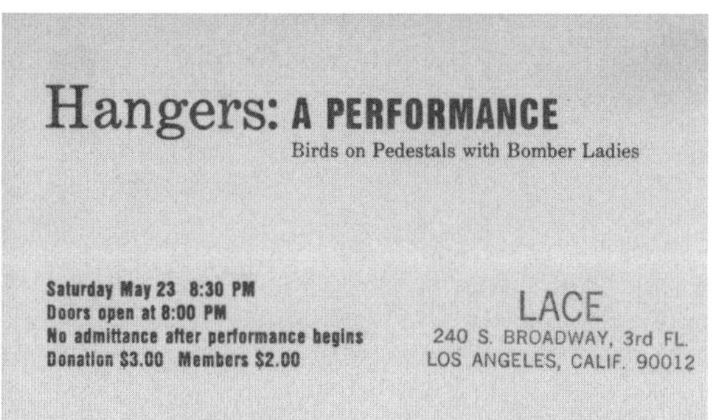
THE CANE MAN
Lee Leonard

Middle Gallery
Los Angeles Contemporary Exhibitions
October 7 – November 8, 1981
Opening Reception October 7, 8-10 PM

Hangers: A PERFORMANCE
Birds on Pedestals with Bomber Ladies

Saturday May 23 8:30 PM
Doors open at 8:00 PM
No admittance after performance begins
Donation $3.00 Members $2.00

LACE
240 S. BROADWAY, 3rd FL.
LOS ANGELES, CALIF. 90012

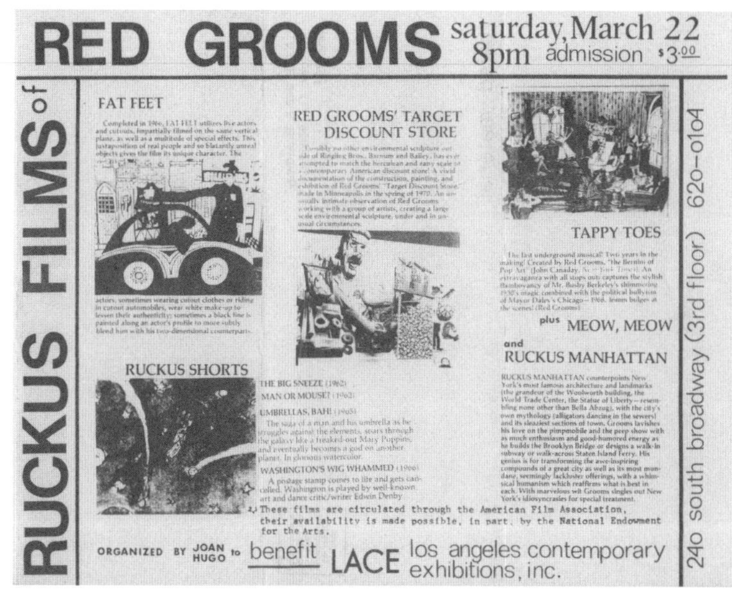
RED GROOMS
saturday, March 22
8pm admission $3.00

RUCKUS FILMS of

FAT FEET

RED GROOMS' TARGET
DISCOUNT STORE

TAPPY TOES

plus MEOW, MEOW
and
RUCKUS MANHATTAN

RUCKUS SHORTS

THE BIG SNEEZE (1962)
MAN OR MOUSE (1962)
UMBRELLAS, BAH! (1963)
WASHINGTON'S WIG WHAMMED (1966)

ORGANIZED BY JOAN HUGO to benefit LACE los angeles contemporary exhibitions, inc.

240 south broadway (3rd floor) 620-0104

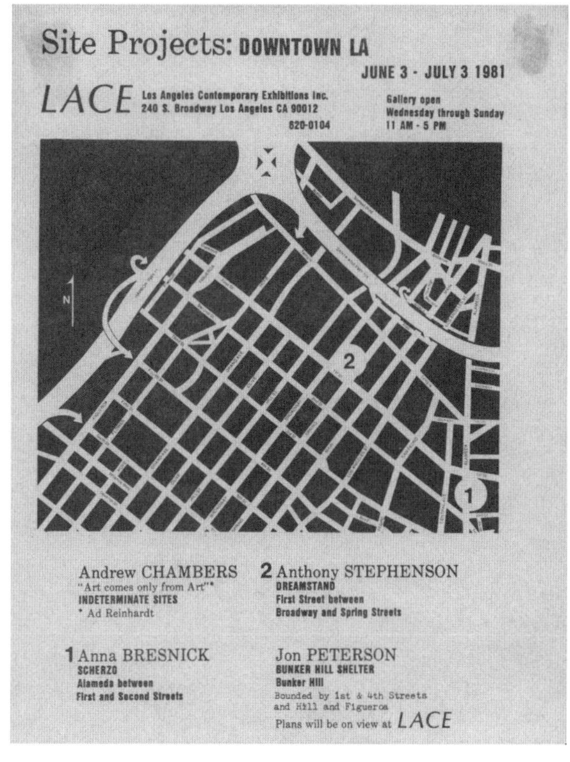
Site Projects: DOWNTOWN LA
JUNE 3 - JULY 3 1981

LACE Los Angeles Contemporary Exhibitions Inc.
240 S. Broadway Los Angeles CA 90012
620-0104

Gallery open
Wednesday through Sunday
11 AM - 5 PM

N

2

1

Andrew CHAMBERS
"Art comes only from Art"*
INDETERMINATE SITES
* Ad Reinhardt

2 Anthony STEPHENSON
DREAMSTAND
First Street between
Broadway and Spring Streets

1 Anna BRESNICK
SCHERZO
Alameda between
First and Second Streets

Jon PETERSON
BUNKER HILL SHELTER
Bunker Hill
Bounded by 1st & 4th Streets
and Hill and Figueroa

Plans will be on view at LACE

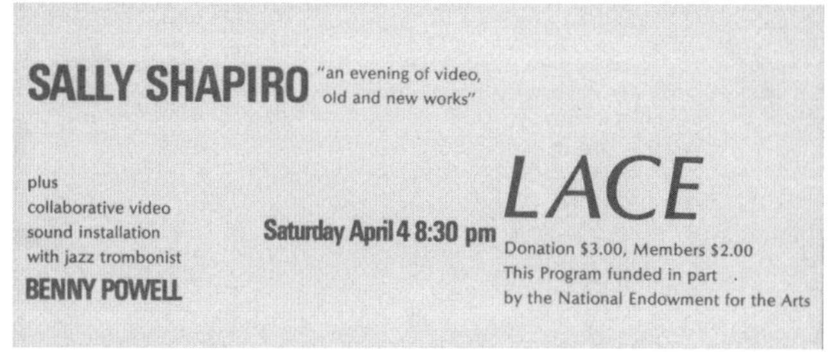
SALLY SHAPIRO "an evening of video,
old and new works"

plus
collaborative video
sound installation
with jazz trombonist

BENNY POWELL

Saturday April 4 8:30 pm

LACE

Donation $3.00, Members $2.00
This Program funded in part .
by the National Endowment for the Arts

TONY LABAT
a performance

Sunday September 13, 2 PM

Los Angeles Contemporary Exhibitions
240 S. Broadway 3rd Floor
LA CA 90012 620-0104

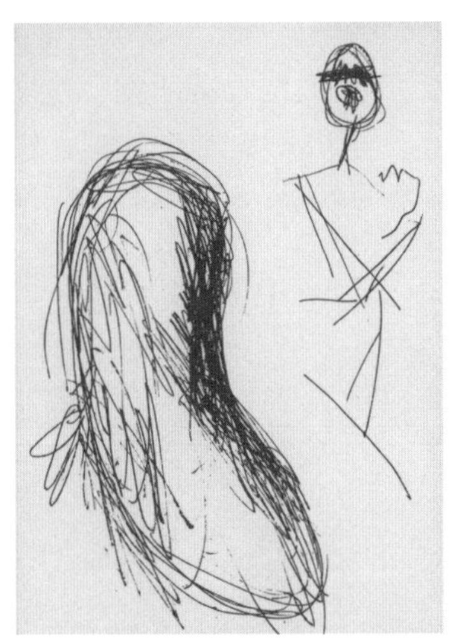

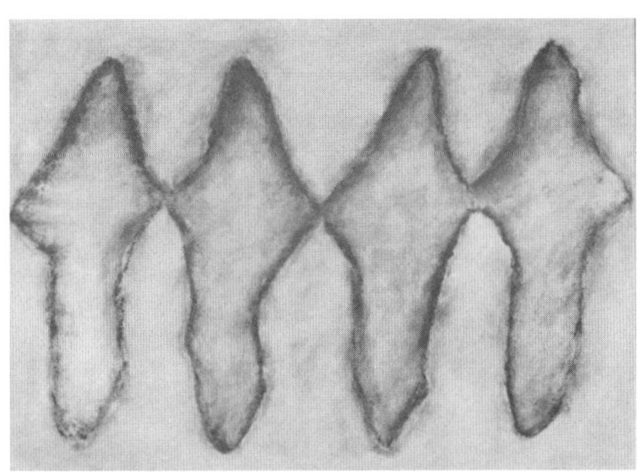

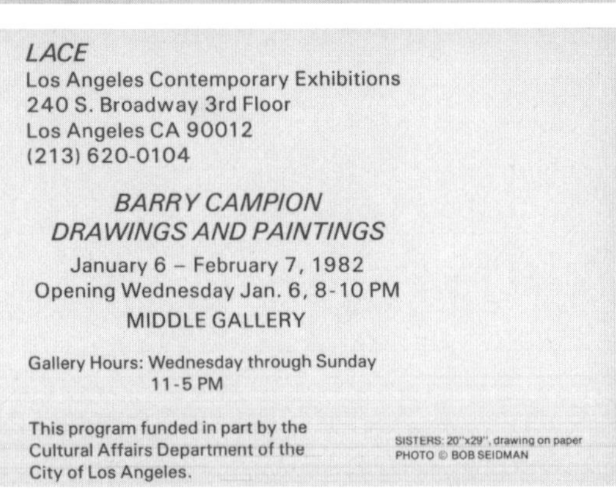

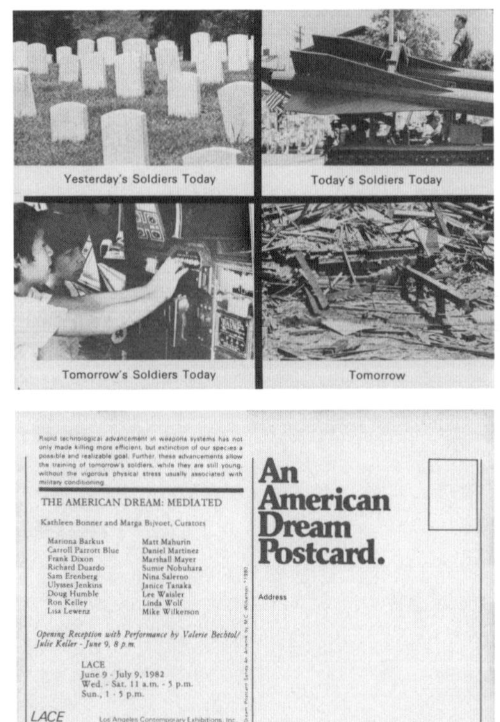

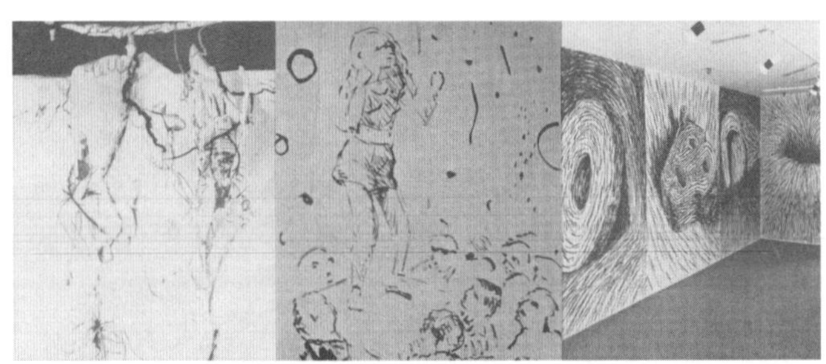

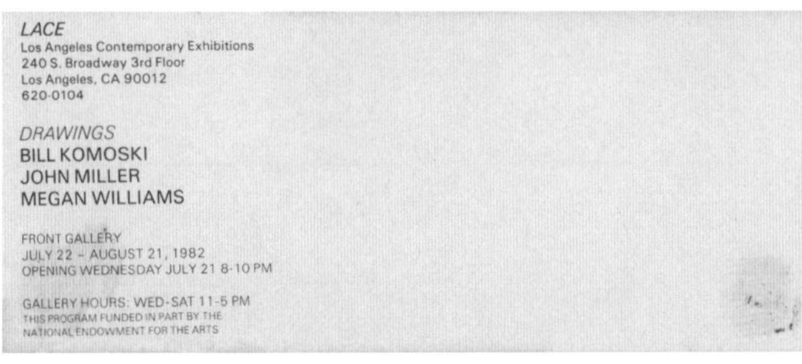

1982.03 Paul McCarthy, Humanoid, Postcard
1982.04 The American Dream: Mediated,
Postcard

1982.05 Barry Campion, Drawings
and Paintings, Postcard
1982.06 Drawings, Postcard

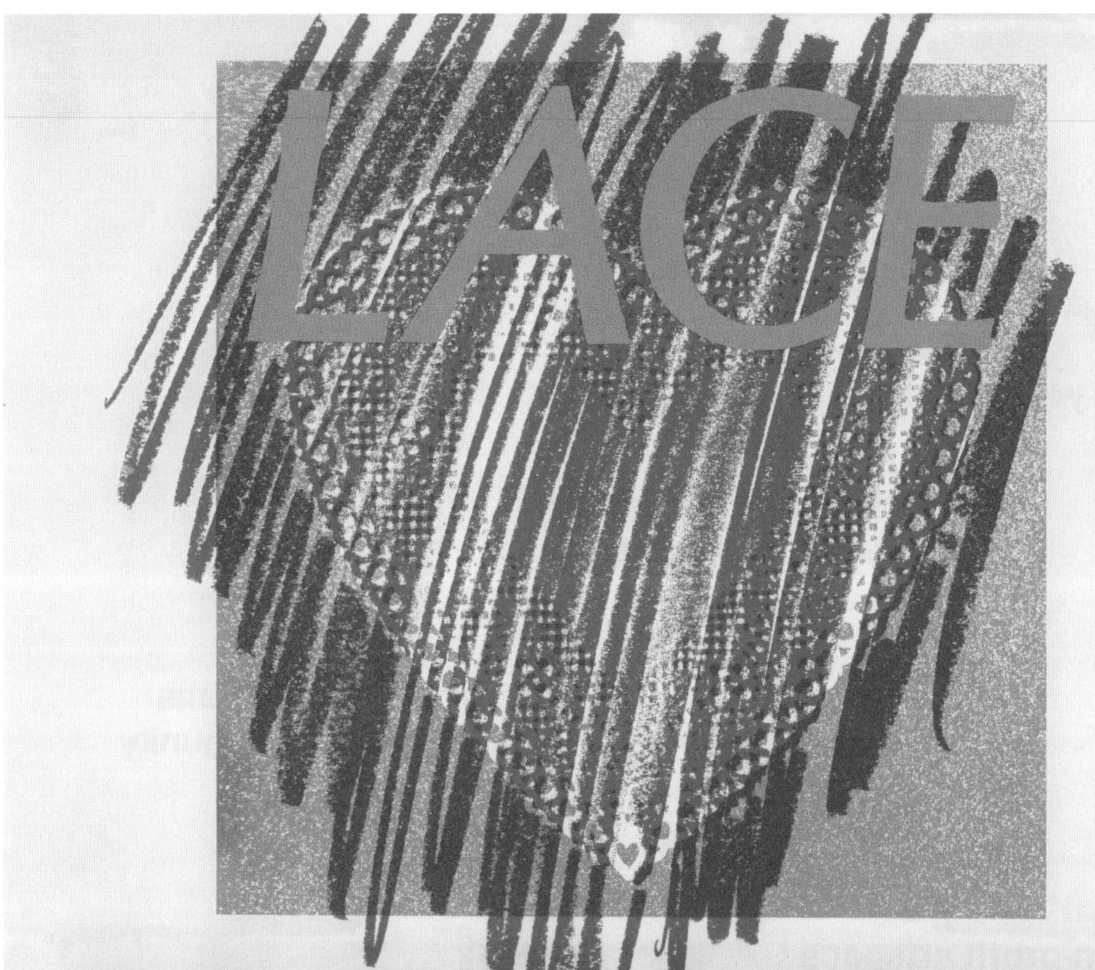

1981.13 <u>Eat Your Heart Out</u>, Poster

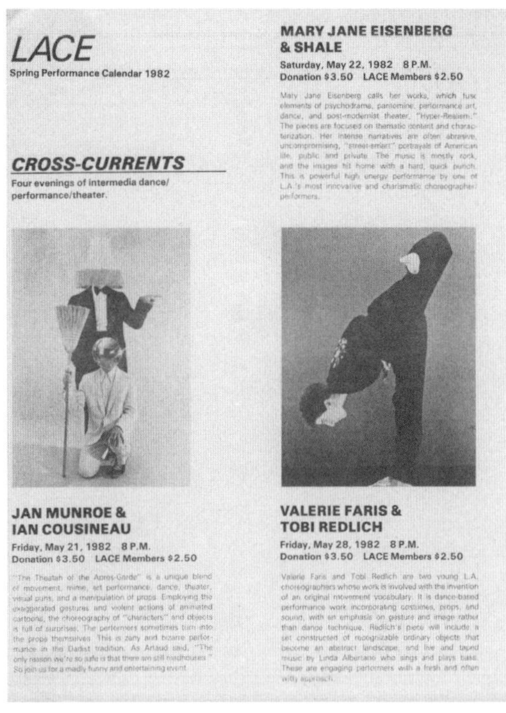

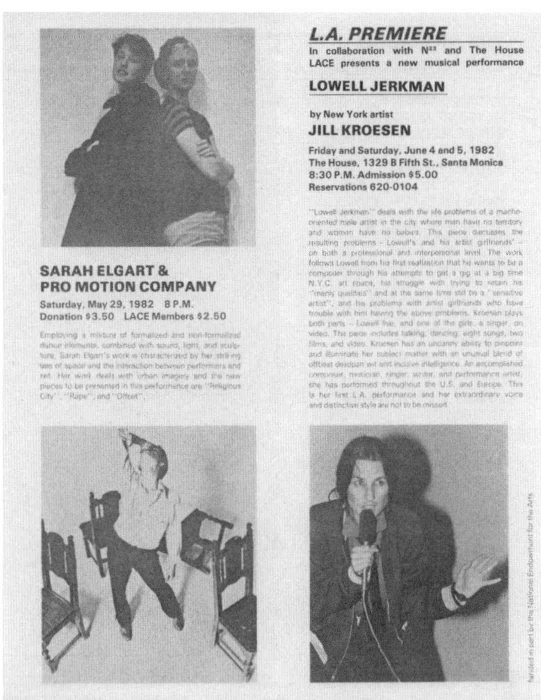

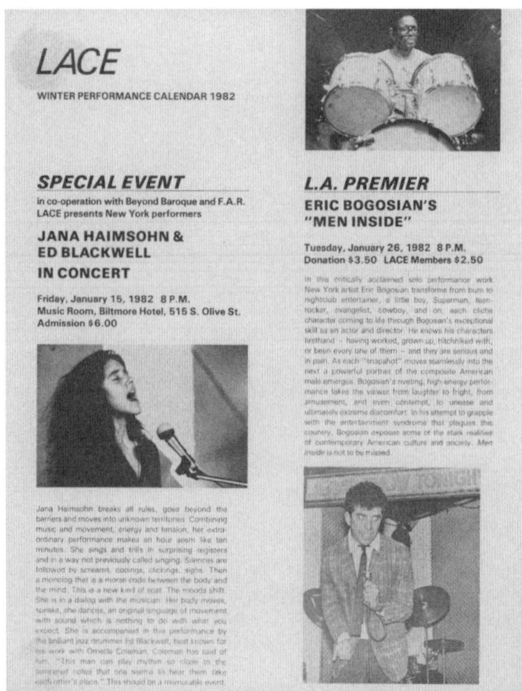

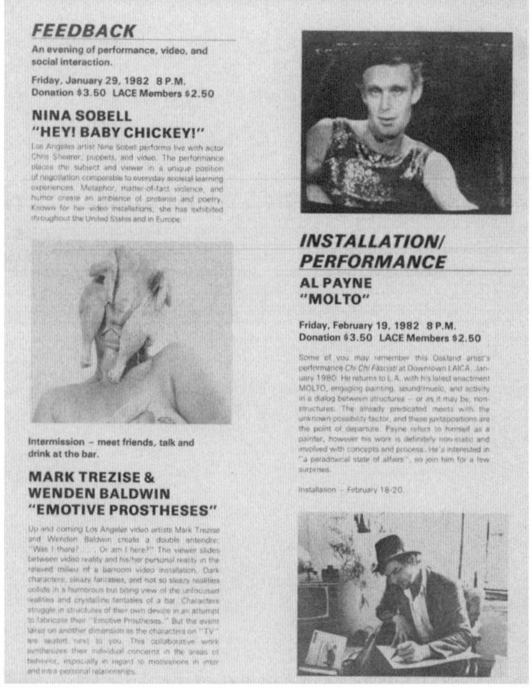

1982.07 <u>LACE Spring Performance Calendar,</u>
Calendar

1982.08 <u>LACE Winter Performance Calendar,</u>
Calendar

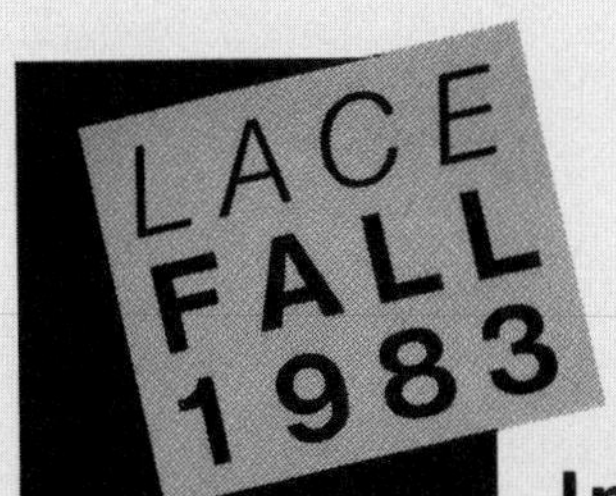

LACE FALL 1983

Intermedia Events

PERFORMANCE / VIDEO / FILM

OCT

Marcel Odenbach
Tuesday, October 18, 1983
8:00 p.m.
Donation $5.00
LACE Members $3.00
One of West Germany's most innovative intermedia artists working in video installation and performance, Marcel Odenbach broke all the rules in an international exhibition combining mythic and nationalistic elements with commercial functionalistic ones. Much of his work deals with the conflict between the burden of a heritage of traditions and the desperate attempt to escape from it. "I live with history which I . . . constantly experience in a new way." This is Odenbach's premier presentation in Los Angeles and a rare opportunity to view the work of a dynamic and controversial European artist. Co-sponsored with the Long Beach Museum of Art and Goethe Institute, Los Angeles.

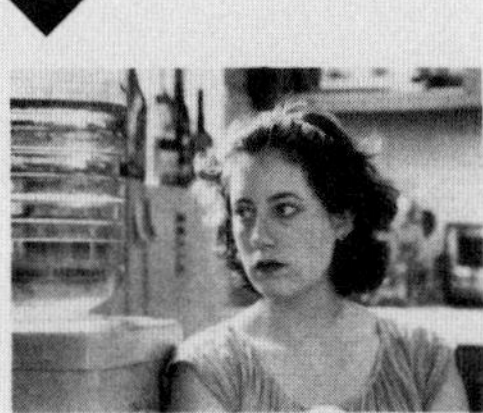

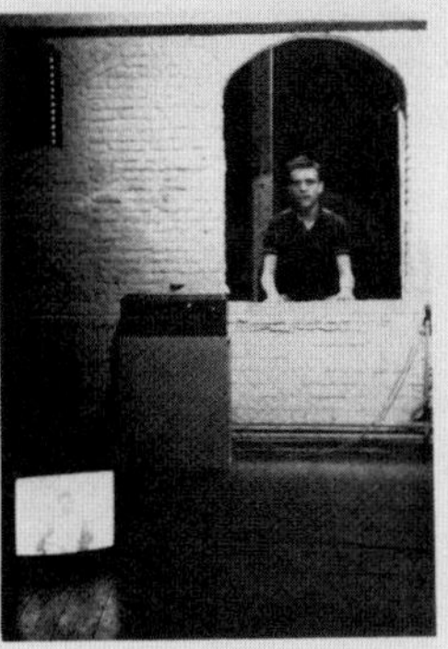

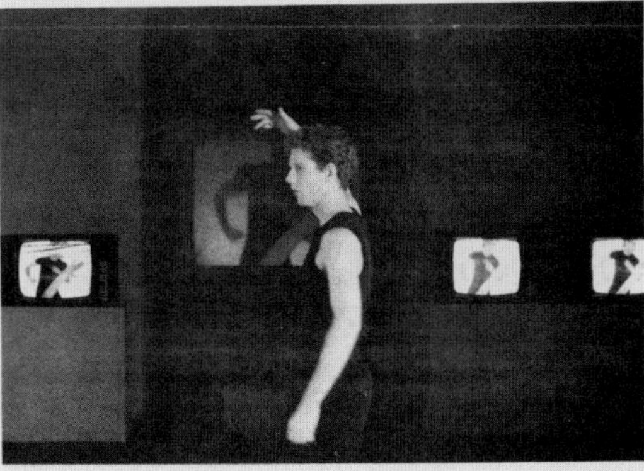

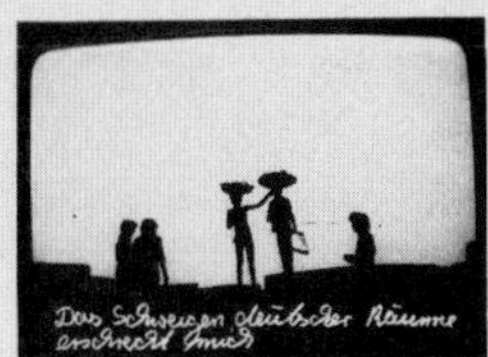

Jeff McMahon
Thursday, October 20, 1983
8:00 p.m.
Donation $5.00
LACE Member $3.00
Jeff McMahon grew up in Los Angeles and went to New York to do performance. Last year he returned to present his solo video performance "Rate of Exchange" at Beyond Baroque, after successful performances at Franklin Furnace and P.S. 122, New York. LACE will present his newest work "Believe You Me"—a video/dance work performed by McMahon and created in collaboration with Lucy Hemmendinger. McMahon's work focuses on the moving body—the interaction between live and recorded images and spoken texts. The power of McMahon's work is in the tension between the elements, the controlled clarity of action and the terseness of the dialogues. Jeff McMahon is an exciting new artist whose work is both intelligent and skillfully executed.

Liza Bear
Tuesday, October 25, 1983
8:00 p.m.
Donation $5.00
LACE Members $3.00
Since the late 1960's, writer, critic, video artist and filmmaker, Liza Bear has been a controversial and forceful figure in the New York art world. Co-founder and editor of the legendary magazine *Avalanche* in the early 70's, she began making video tapes and films in 1975 and working with new technologies and cable TV. Liza Bear was born in Casablanca and grew up in England and

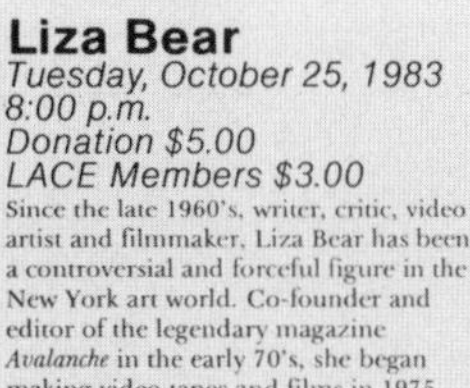

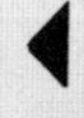

France. Her latest work, "Oued Nefifik: A Foreign Movie," draws upon her own experiences and background. It is an experimental narrative that incorporates a real political situation, having been shot in the immediate aftermath of a violent upheaval in Casablanca, June 1981. It is in French with English subtitles. Super 8 on Video, 28 minutes.

The artist will be present and will discuss her work after the screening.

**Molly Cleator &
Anita Rosenberg**
Friday, October 28, 1983
8:00 p.m.
Donation $5.00
LACE Members $3.00
Anita Rosenberg presents her newest film "Bachelorette Pad," starring Patti Astor as a swinging single bachelorette. Rosenberg thought the concept for "Bachelorette Pad" would make a great TV sitcom and so proceeded in that direction. Universal TV has optioned the project and ABC bought the project for the creation of a pilot episode, to air as a midseason replacement for a primetime network series. 16mm, 14 minutes.

Molly Cleator is one of the outstanding young performers in Los Angeles' new breed of emerging performance artists of the 1980's—whose autobiographically based works are highly charged theatrical monologues. Cleator uses personal experiences as metaphors for political and social issues. Her tone is intimate and vulnerable. She builds her characters slowly to an unexpectedly high tension pitch. A talented actress, Cleator's performances were memorable in Lin Hixson's "Swayback" (1982) and "Flatlands" (1983)—like a character in a Robert Altman movie.,"Private Molly, Public Molly," Cleator's newest work, to be premiered at LACE, is conceived, written and performed by Molly Cleator and directed by Lin Hixson.

NOV

Constance De Jong
Friday, November 11, 1983
8:00 p.m.
Beyond Baroque
681 Venice Blvd., Venice
Donation $2.00
A leading figure in the New York avant-garde literary scene, Constance De Jong will do a reading/performance from her recently published book *I.T.I.L.O.E. Top Stories #15* and brand new work. In addition to her published fiction, *The Lucy Amarillo Stories and Modern Love,* she was the collaborating librettist for Philip Glass' opera *Satyagraha.* She has performed extensively throughout the United States and Canada. Presented in collaboration with Beyond Baroque.

**An Evening with
Alan Lande**
Wednesday, November 16, 1983
8:00 p.m.
High Performance
240 South Broadway, 5th Floor
Donation $5.00
LACE Members $3.00

All events will take place at LACE unless otherwise indicated.

1983.01 <u>LACE Fall 1983 Intermedia Events,</u>
Calendar

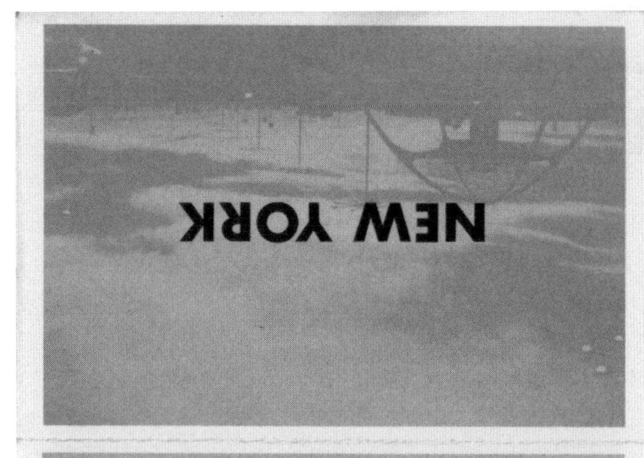

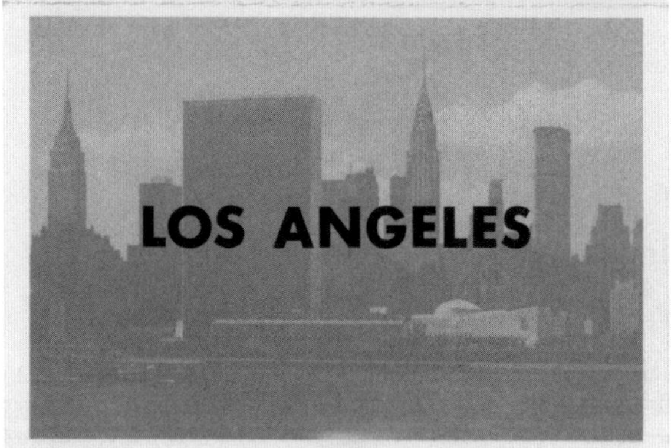

ARTISTS SPACE
May 21 - July 2, 1983
Opening: Saturday, May 21, 5-7pm

LOS ANGELES   NEW YORK EXCHANGE

JILL GIEGERICH
VICTOR HENDERSON
KIM HUBBARD
LARI PITTMAN
MITCHELL SYROP
MEGAN WILLIAMS

Artists Space
105 Hudson Street, New York, NY 10013

LACE
June 8 - July 16, 1983
Opening: Wednesday, June 8, 8-10pm

LOS ANGELES   NEW YORK EXCHANGE

CHARLES CLOUGH
REBECCA HOWLAND
JEFF KOONS
NACHUME MILLER
CHRISTY RUPP
REESE WILLIAMS

Los Angeles Contemporary Exhibitions
240 S. Broadway, Los Angeles, CA 90012

These exhibitions have been made possible, in part, by the support of the National Endowment for the Arts, Warner Communications, and the Atlantic Richfield Foundation

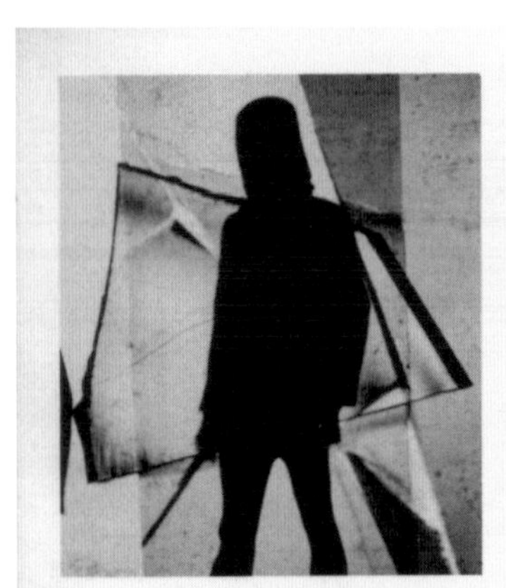

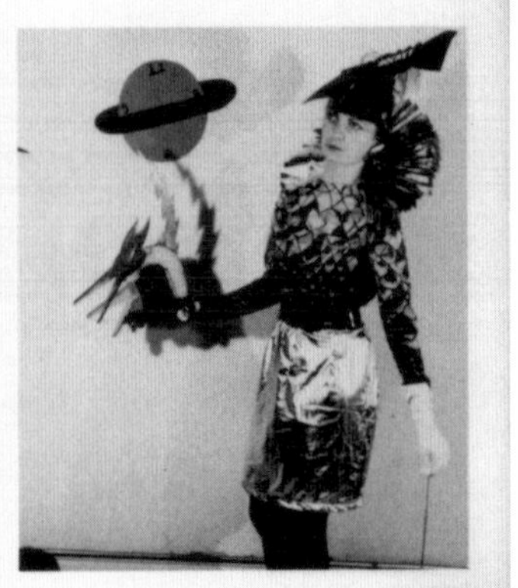

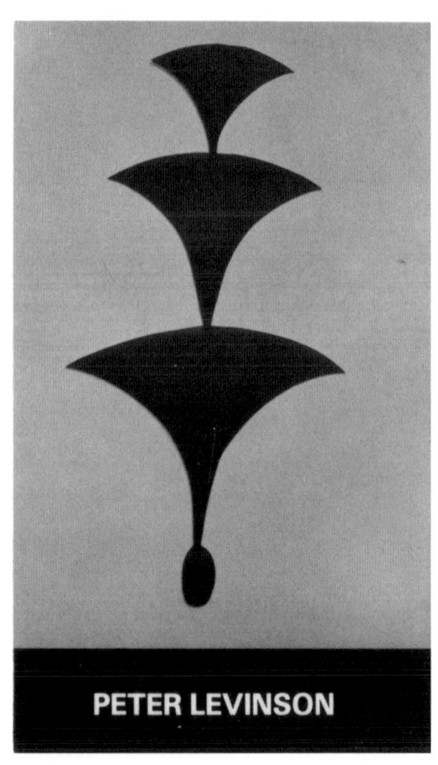

1983.03 Jim Pomeroy, Polarized Projections
         /Special Effects/Remote Control
         and Yura Adams, Orbit on the Hour,
         Postcard

1983.02 Los Angeles New York Exchange,
         Postcard
1983.04 Peter Levinson, Painted Reliefs,
         Postcard

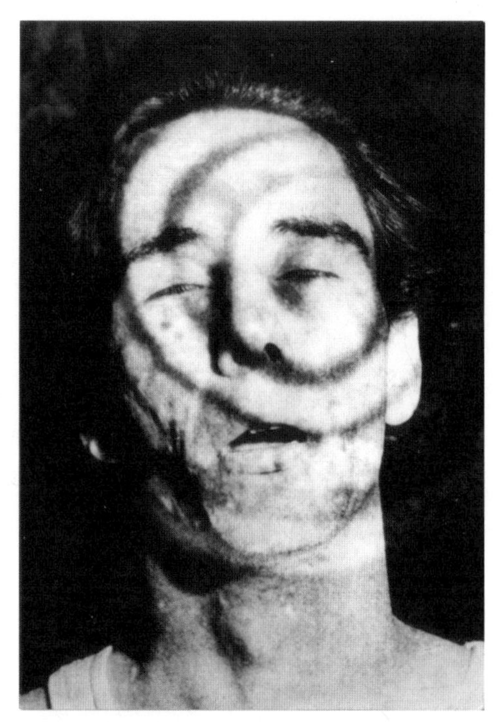

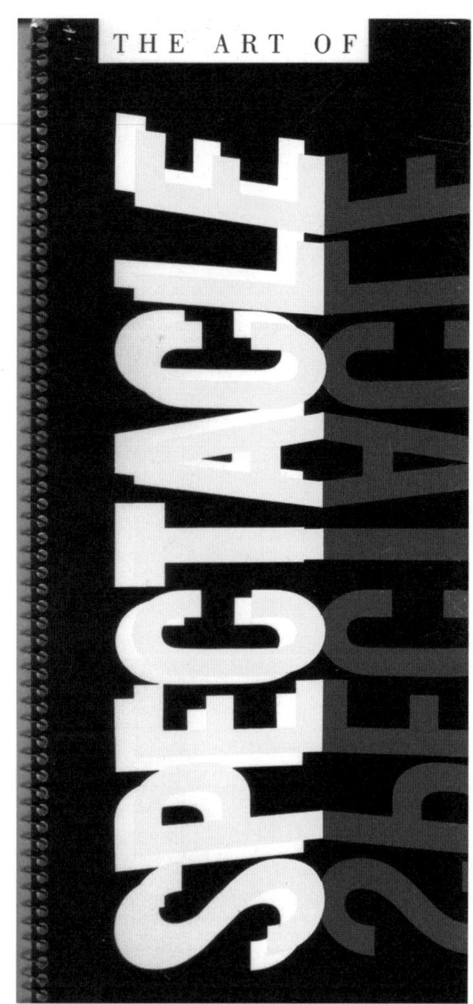

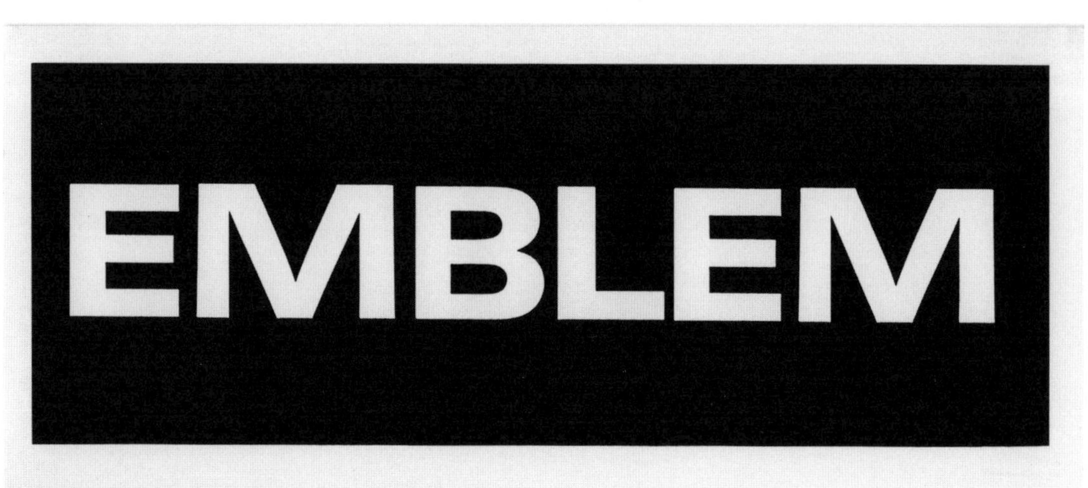

1983.05 Mike Kelley, Confusion: A Play
in Seven Sets, Each Set More
Spectacular Than the Last,
Postcard

1984.01 The Art of Spectacle, Catalog
1984.02 Emblem, Postcard

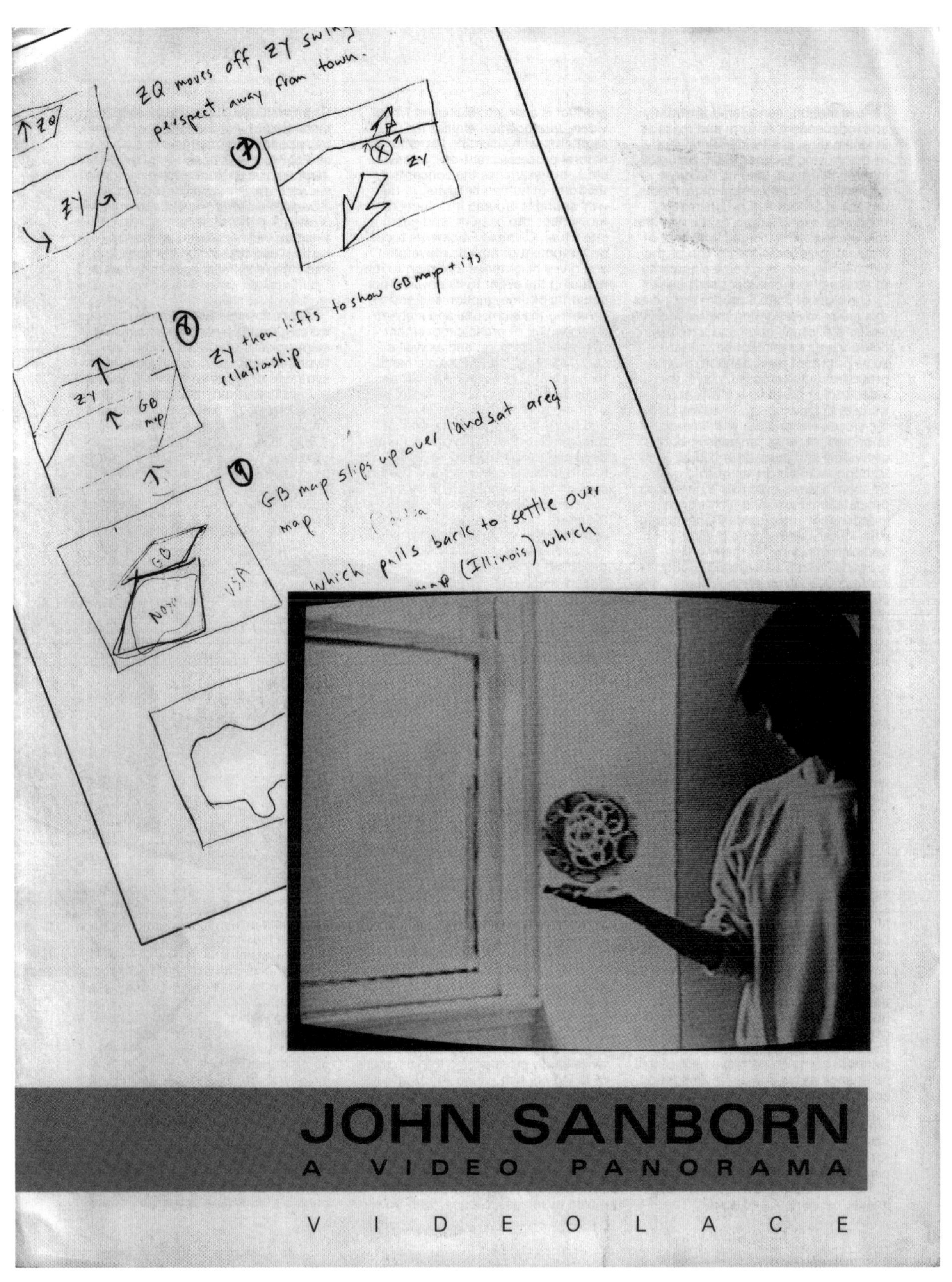

1984.03 John Sanborn, A Video Panorama,
         Brochure

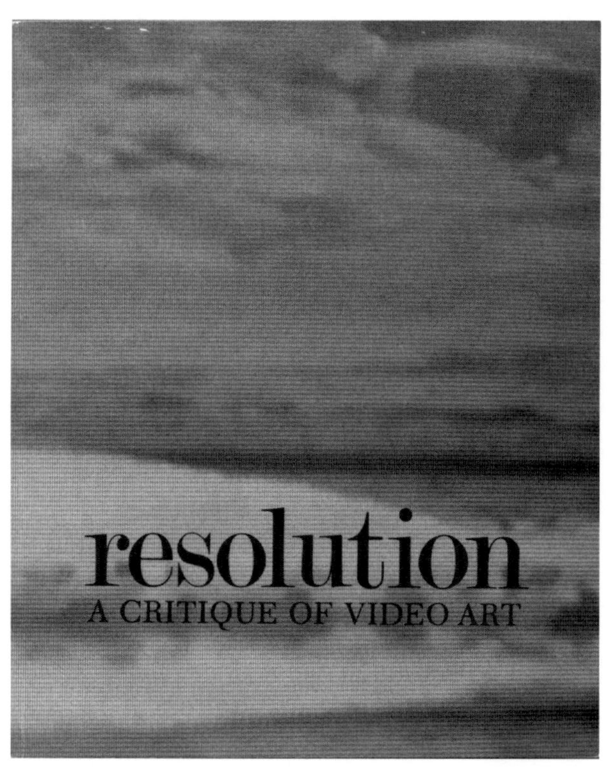

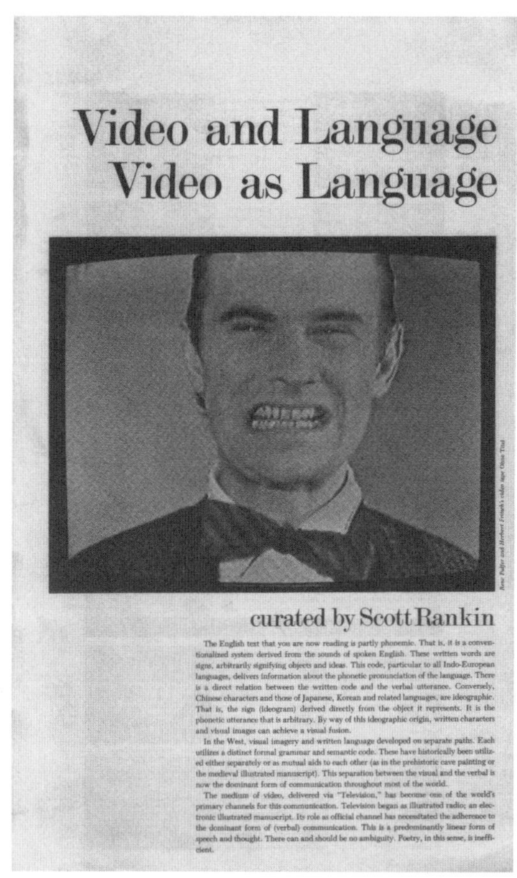

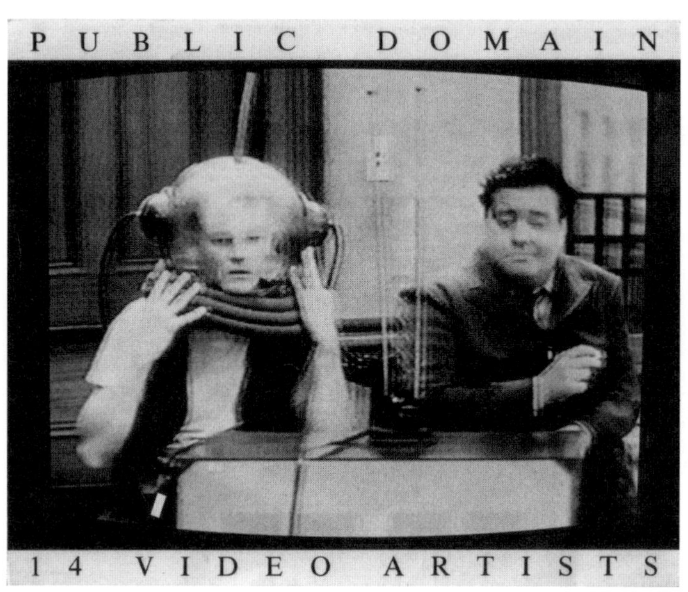

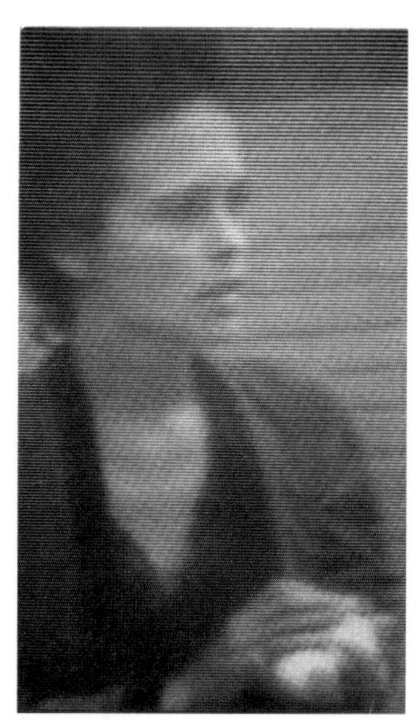

1986.01 <u>Resolution: A Critique of Video Art</u>, Catalog

1985.01 <u>Public Domain: 14 Video Artists</u>, Flyer

1986.02 <u>Video and Language, Video as Language</u>, Brochure

1983.06 <u>Jac Mote/Foehn</u>, Postcard

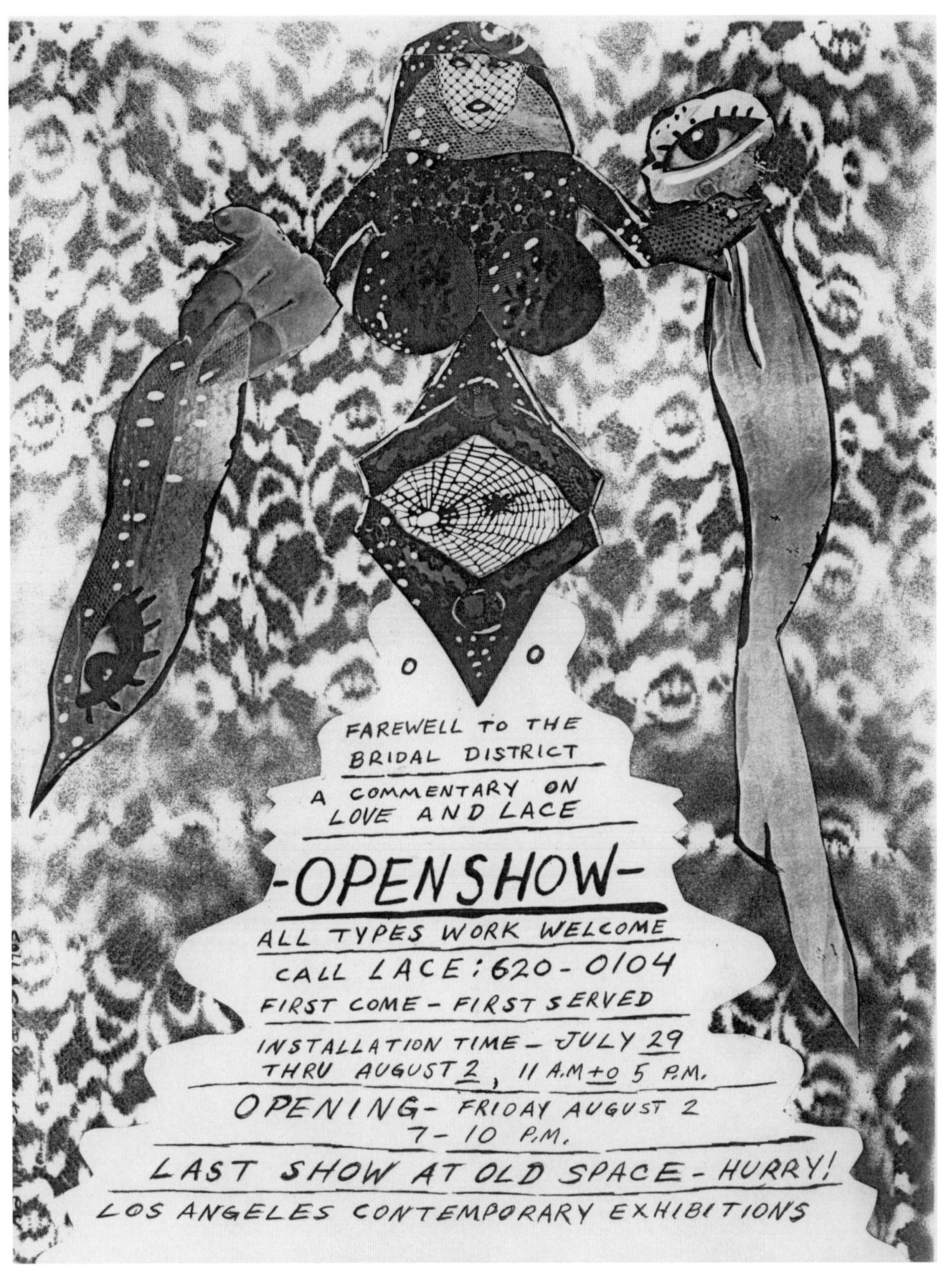

1985.02 <u>Open Show</u>, Flyer

<u>Weba Garretson</u>
LACE Performance Coordinator 1984-1989

In 1984, when I interviewed for the job as Performance Coordinator at LACE, I was so broke that all I had was the $2.00 to pay for the parking on Broadway and 3rd. I prayed that my interview didn't last for more than an hour. Director Joy Silverman took me to a McDonalds down the street. Being worried about my car and knowing absolutely nothing about Performance or Video Art, I don't think that I made much of an impression. I was just a cabaret singer with a background in avant-garde theater. Joy hired Deborah Oliver. I went back to being broke.

Two weeks later Joy called. Deborah didn't want the job. "Would you consider another interview?" she asked. This time we met at Cucina on Melrose. Maybe someone had told her that despite my ignorance I was a good performer. And I was in love and ready to build a life with the man that would become my husband. I wanted this job.

The first month at 240 South Broadway I spent taking out the garbage—dozens of fifty gallon, plastic bags that lined the walls of the office I shared with Jim Isermann, Exhibitions Coordinator. I remember sitting at a desk, incredibly bored, and aching to do my own work. But I also remember being enthralled. Each week a new artist would arrive with a new vision. All I had to do was listen, make phone calls, and write checks. Then this artist would blow the minds of a rapt audience. LACE was an education.

At the new building on Industrial Street, we had $125,000 every year for presenting New Music, Dance and Performance. (The NEA had not yet been gutted by Senator Jesse Helms.) I was a drunken Santa Claus, intoxicated by the power to give artists what they wanted—a space, technical support, an audience and recognition.

I say "I" but I mean LACE, the people who ran the place, led by Joy Silverman who had the vision to combine advocacy for the arts with hipness and a genuine concern for the public. We were her back up group: Judith Teitelman, the grant writing wizard who sold nail jewelry on the weekends; Anne Bray, who actually understood Video Art; Jeff Mann who was willing to transform the gallery for each show; Nancy Barton who created the best bookstore in Los Angeles; and Martin Kersels, the gentle giant who managed the building and kept our unruly "art boat" steady.

Our staff meetings were tireless exercises in shifting funds, borrowing from one account to pay for another. We lived on garlicky salads, kept track of our "comp" time as we logged 80 hour weeks, dreamed of vacations as we locked up the building at 3am and then returned at 8am the next morning to find Joy sleeping on her desk. None of us, even though we were hired because we were artists, had another life. For five years, LACE was the center of my universe.

"It was fantastic, beyond belief."*

*from *HAPPY END*, *Bilbao Song*
 by Bertolt Brecht and Kurt Weill

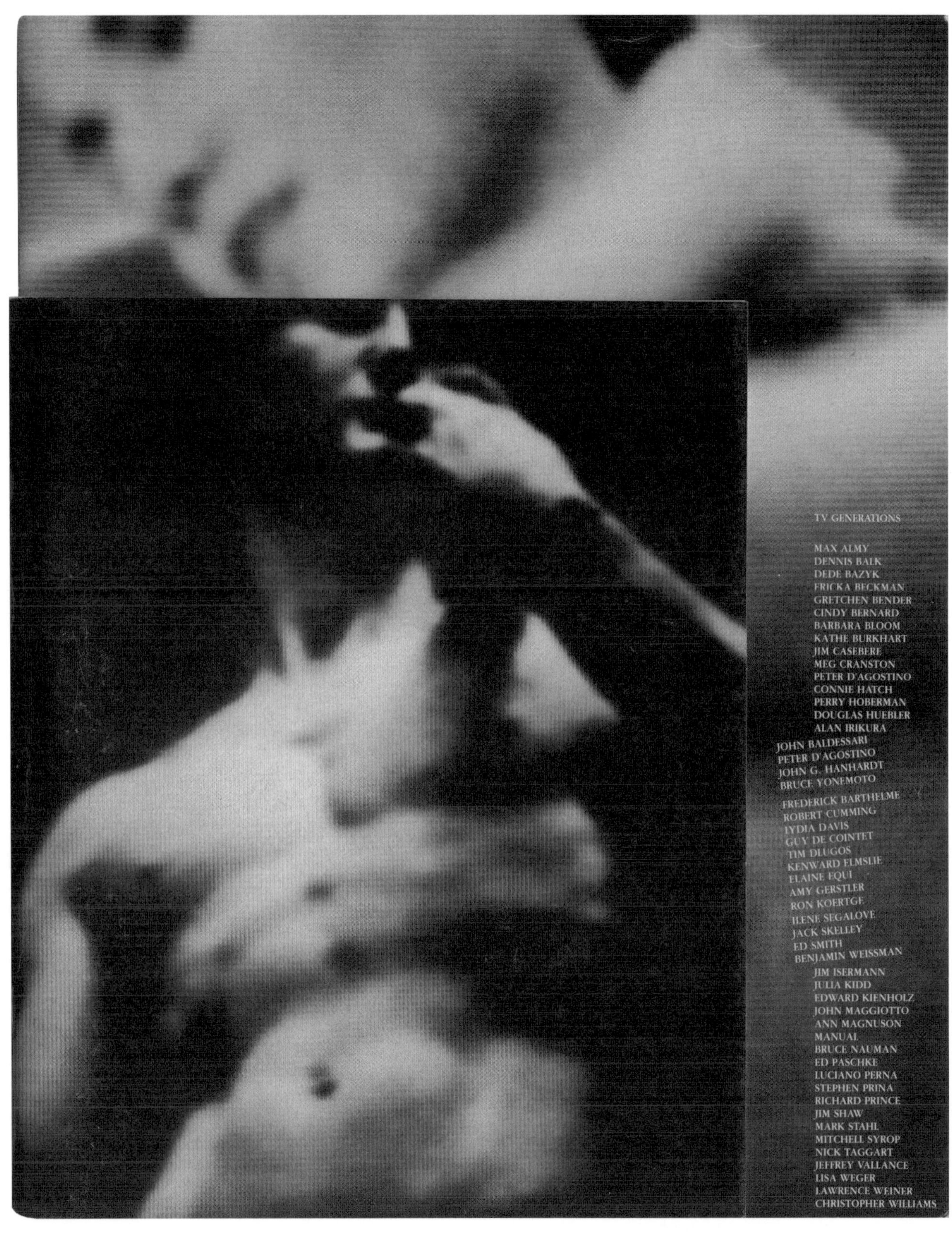

1986.03 <u>TV Generations</u>, Catalog
(front cover)

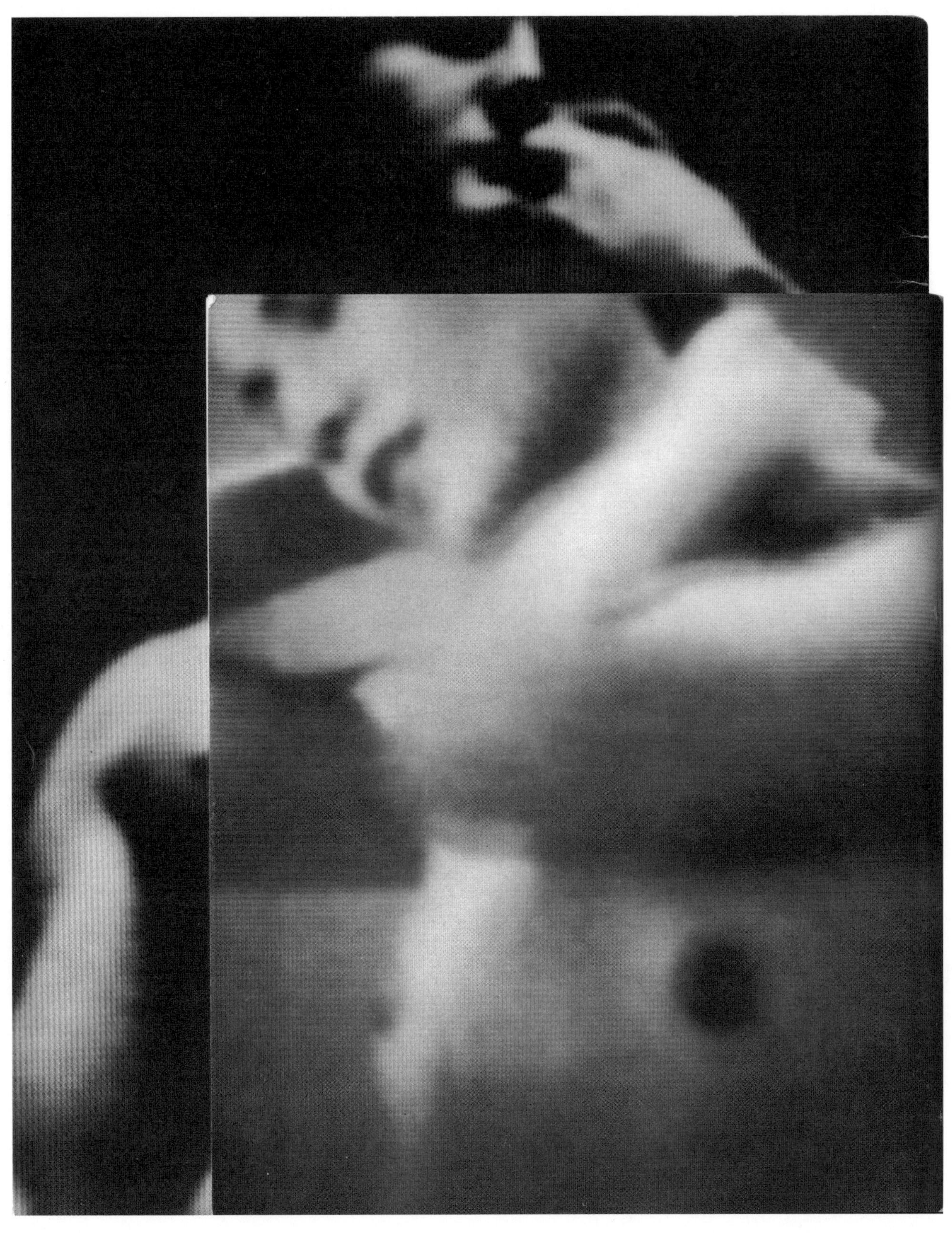

1986.03 <u>TV Generations</u>, Catalog
  (back cover)

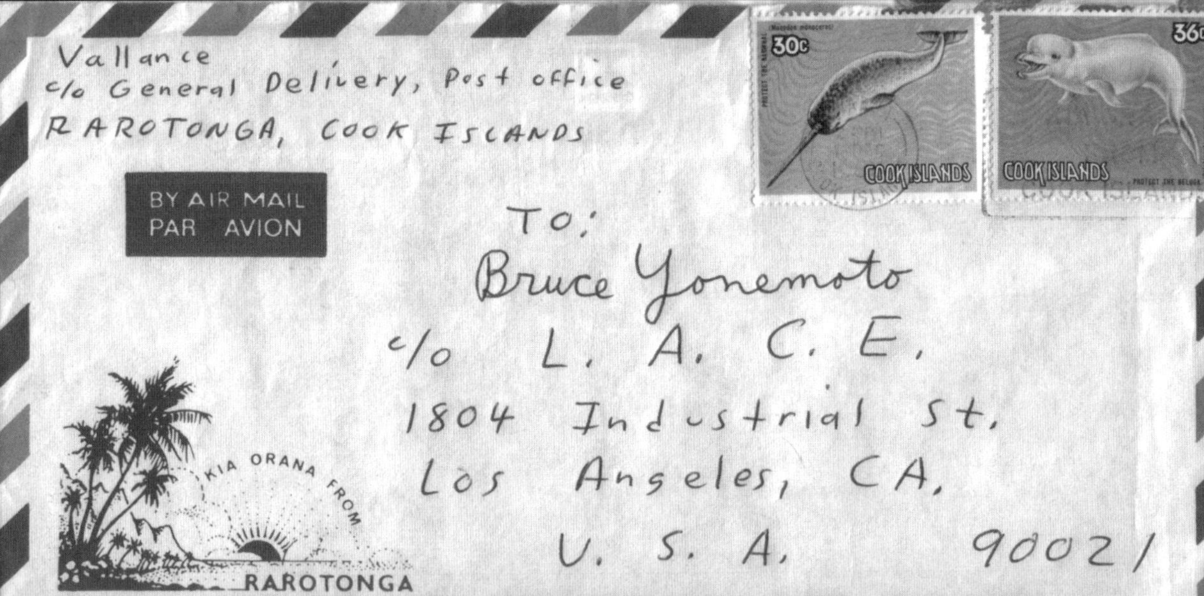

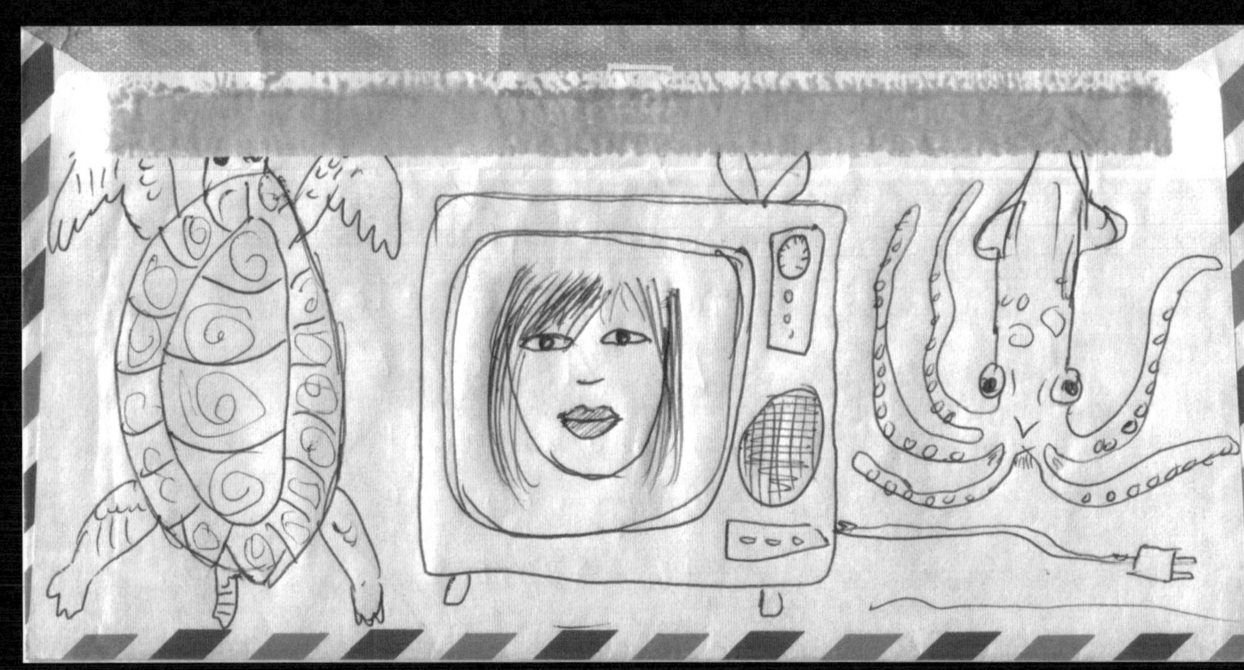

1986.04 <u>TV Generations</u>, Letter from
Jeffrey Vallance to Bruce Yonemoto,
December 17, 1985

Dec 17 85

Dear Bruce,   Here is a little
story about TV in Polynesia.
If you want you can post
"as is" = (please correct spelling).
or you can Type set it.
I'm having an amazing
time, and getting some
work done, The King is
a swell guy. What am
I missing in L.A.?
I'm living in a little house
on the beach.

                    Jeffry

DECEMBER 17, 1985

Dear L.A.C.E. :

In the South Pacific TV has taken some interesting turns. In Auckland, New Zealand there are only two TV stations. When I stayed at the Y.M.C.A. of Auckland, guests were not allowed to change the station. The building had two TV rooms one for each channel. So if one wanted to see a different program, one would just have to change rooms. The first show I saw there was HAPPY DAYS. That show must be popular, because, downtown, there is a snack bar bearing the same name. The most interesting programs are in the MAORI language. (Polynesian people indigenous to N.Z.)
The Kingdom of TONGA does not have a T.V. station. The Tongans have jumped from the stone age into: VIDEO. On November 22, 1985 I had a personal audience with His Majesty TAUFA'AHAU TAPOU IV King of Tonga. The King was recently in the U.S.A. He met with TRINITY BROADCASTING NETWORK. The christian television firm plans to set up the Kingdom's national TV service.
American SAMOA gets all the mainland shows blasted at them. Western Samoa picks up the same broadcasts. In W. Samoa, I saw more video movies in a week than I have ever seen in a similar period of time.

TV Continued

Polynesians Love films on the subjects of: KUNG-FU, VIET NAM-WAR and BLOOD-AND-GUTS. Many new born baby boys are being named "RAMBO" this season I personally met one of them.
The Cook Islands does not have a Television system yet. Video has swept the WORLD.

Connie Chung where are you now?

Sincerely,

Jeffrey Vallance
c/o General Delivery
RAROTONGA
COOK ISLANDS
(till Jan. 20, 1986)

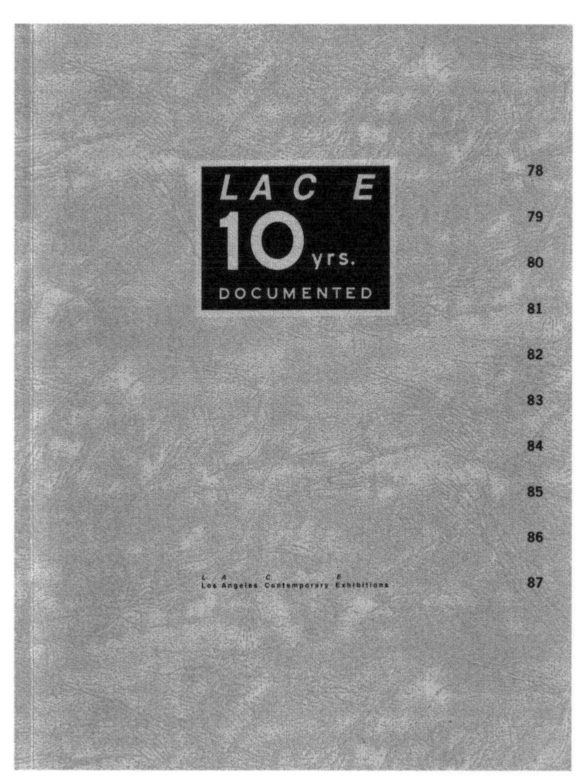

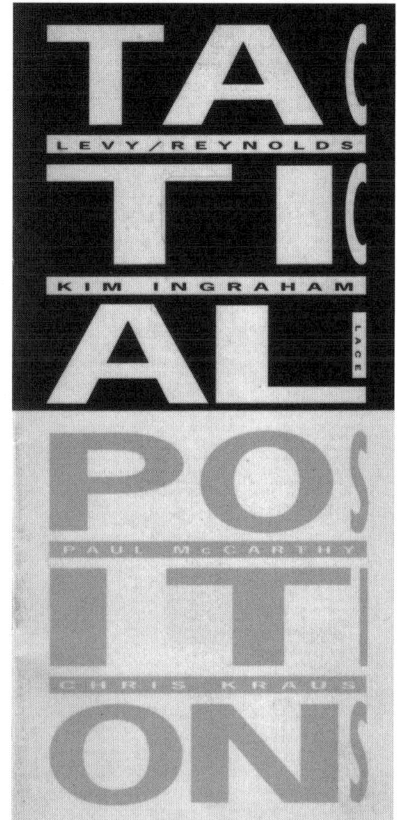

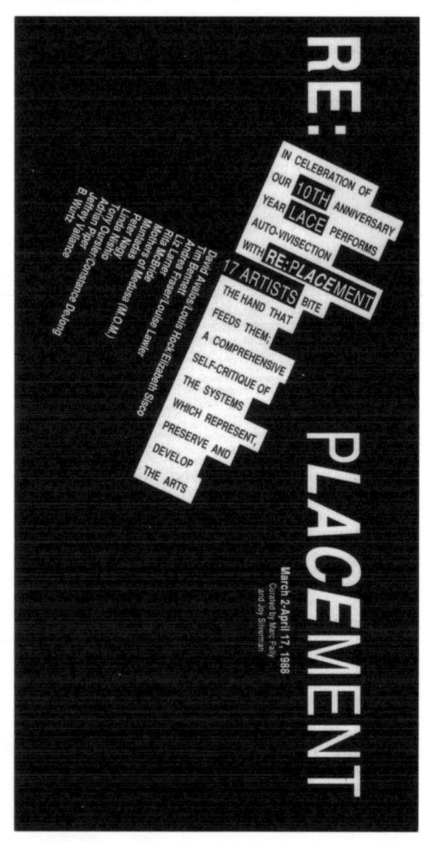

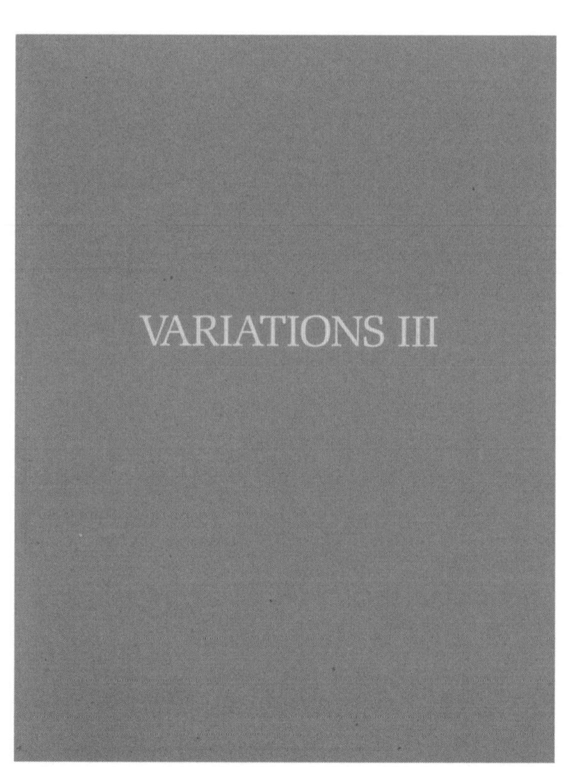

1987.01 <u>LACE 10 yrs. Documented</u>,
       Publication
1988.01 <u>Re:Placement</u>, Brochure

1988.02 <u>Tactical Positions</u>, Catalog
1987.02 <u>Variations III</u>, Catalog

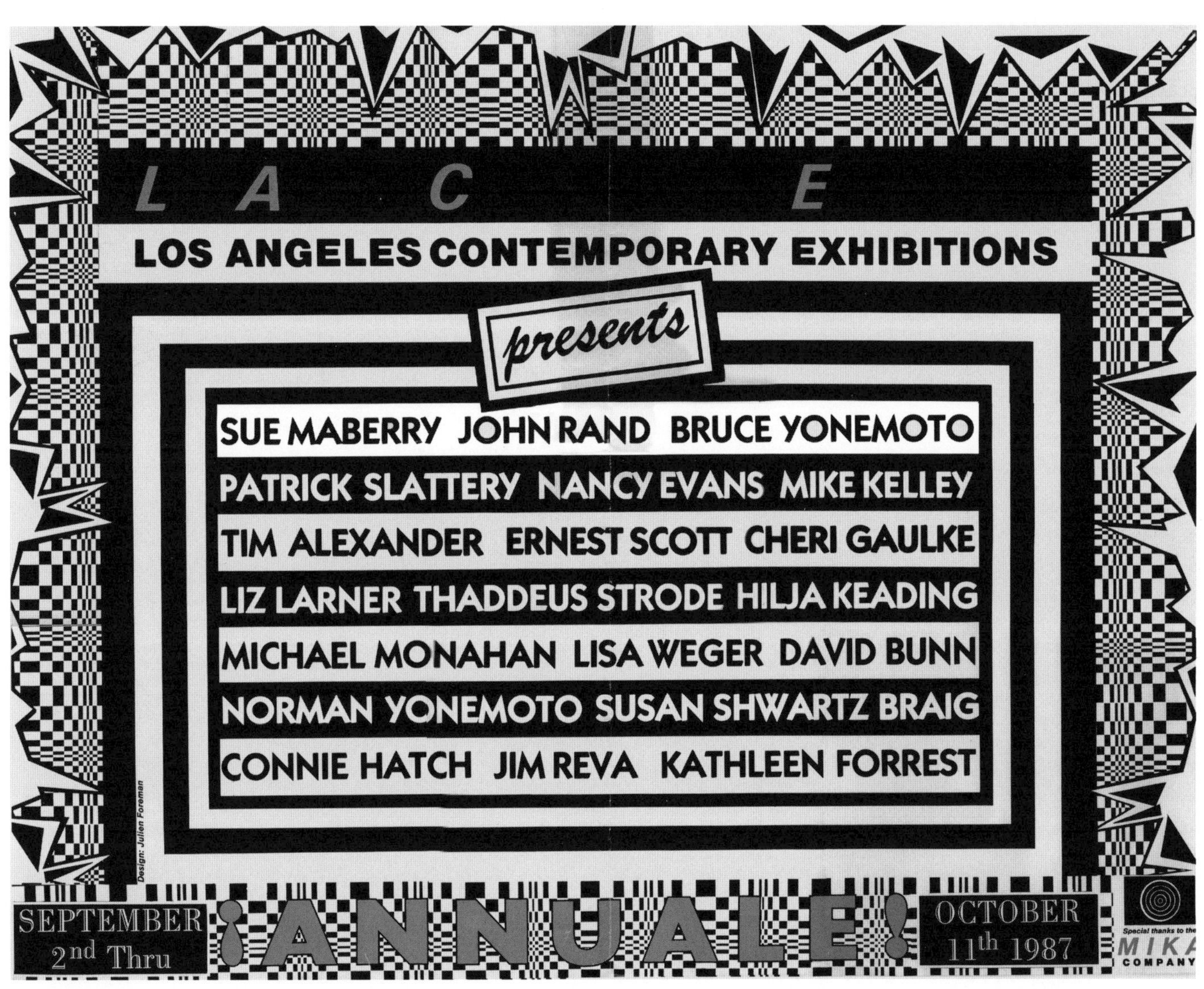

1987.03 <u>LACE Annuale 1987</u>, Poster

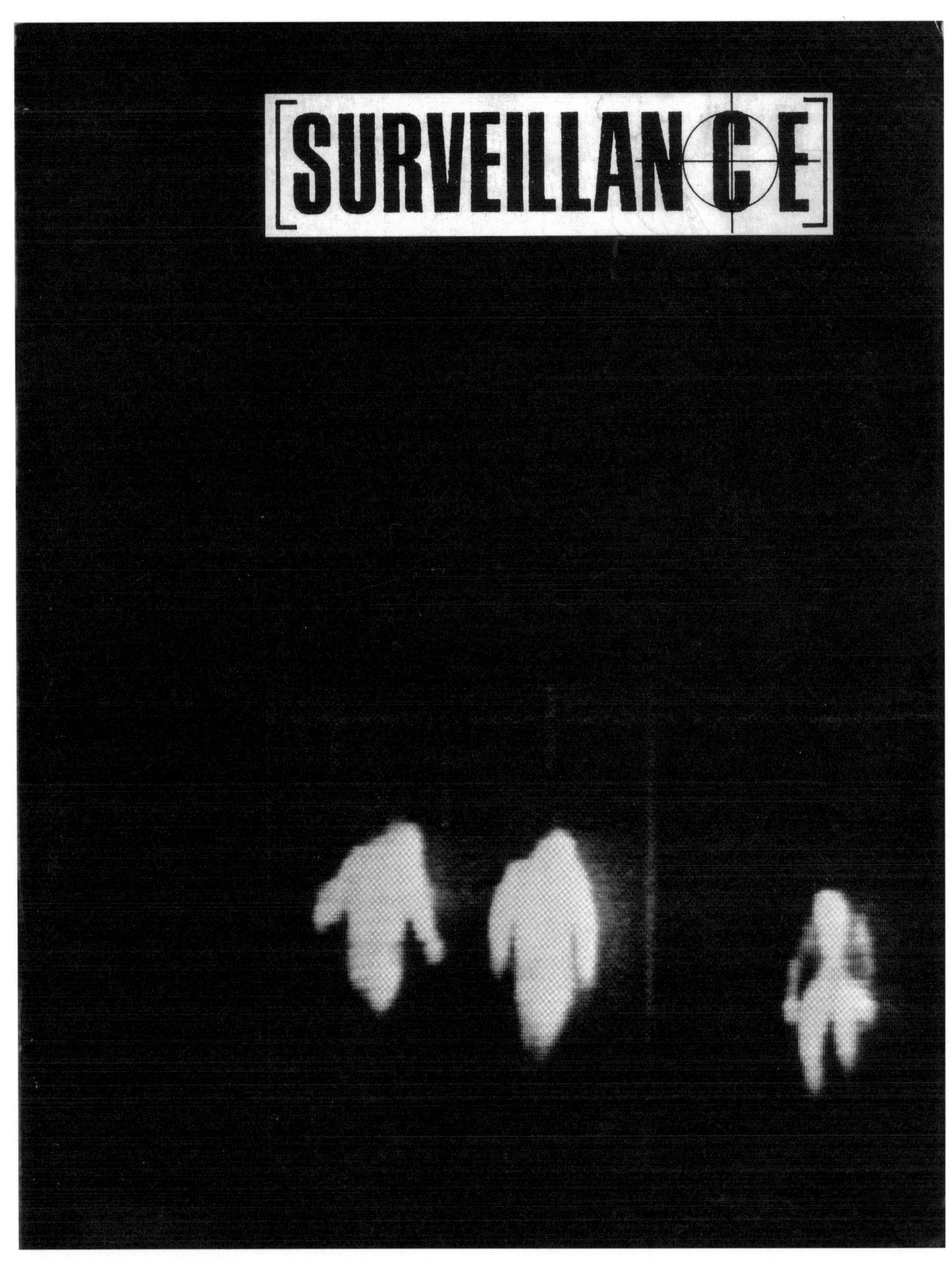

1987.04 <u>Surveillance</u>, Catalog

THE ART OF INVASION

by Branda Miller

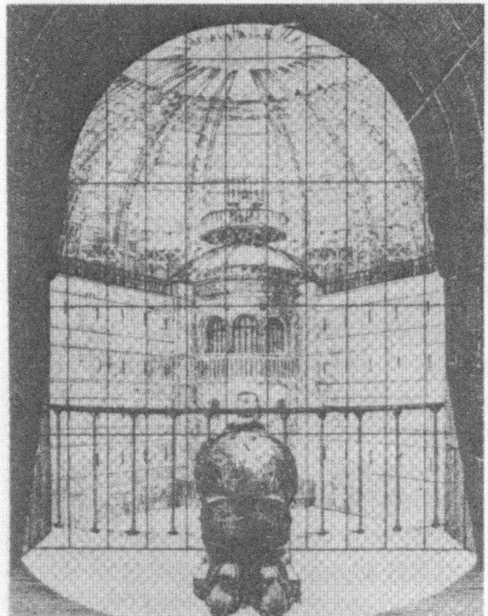

Modeled after J. Bentham's plan of the Panopticon. N. Harou-Romain, Plan for a Penitentiary, *1840*

In the 18th century Jeremy Bentham conceived of the Panopticon, envisioning a prison space with a central tower, where one gaze reaches out, continuously monitoring individual activities for discipline and control.

In "Discipline and Punish," Michel Foucault applies the Panoptic mechanism to examine the exercise of power in society, writing:

> It [the Panopticon] is an important mechanism, for it automatizes and disindividualizes power . . . in order to be exercised, this power had to be given the instrument of permanent, exhaustive, omnipresent surveillance, capable of making all visible, as long as it could itself remain invisible. It had to be like a faceless gaze that transformed the whole social body into a field of perception: thousands of eyes posted everywhere, mobile attentions ever on the alert, a long hierarchized network . . . [1]

In 1980, I lived in Skid Row in Los Angeles, across the street from the downtown Los Angeles Police Control Facilities and Motor Transport Division, known as "The Bunker." I spent hours gazing out of the window with a feeling of disbelief as I watched with horror the spectacle of the police apparatus combatting displaced people, "to clean up the area" for urban development. I was fascinated by the secretive aspects of my center of observation.

The idea of curating an exhibition about surveillance began here, with my own latent voyeurism—hidden from view in my window, using a zoom lens and a video camera, I shot L.A. NICKEL, which premiered at LACE in 1983. Setting a continuous monitoring system of the street corner from my downtown loft window, and hiding radio mics on "audio agents" who ventured onto the street to gather sound, I attempted to capture information without disrupting the daily activities of the area.

I again employed surveillance techniques during the shooting of UNSET BLVD. from MEDIA HOSTAGES, yet changed the methods of operating the technology, passing the control of the surveillance tools to the subject of the tape. Sherry Davis, contestant of the Living Billboard Contest, *self*-activated the equipment (a continuously panning camera mounted on top of the billboard where she lived), therefore taking control of her own monitoring process.

Being at once inside and outside of the Panopticon's central tower, led me to question the consequences of power relationships that result from having access to sophisticated technology, how those tools are used and in whose hands. How had other artists worked with the surveillance process? What value systems did they apply to their own investigations? What alternative applications of the technology had they produced?

Examining the benefits as well as the dangers posed by our information-age gluttony, particularly as it reduces our perception of self and de-limits the boundaries of community, was a primary concern in my selection of the works exhibited.

This show underscores various processes of surveillance and the effects that its institutionalization has wreaked on everyday life. Here, artist/activists such as Michael Klier, Dieter Froese and Elsa Cayo use the weapons of surveillance—35mm cameras, TV cameras, monitors and tape recorders—to deconstruct the industry while others appropriate its techniques. Margia Kramer, for example, has used the Freedom of Information Act—a fissure in the Agency's protective seal—to gain access to Jean Seberg's government files;

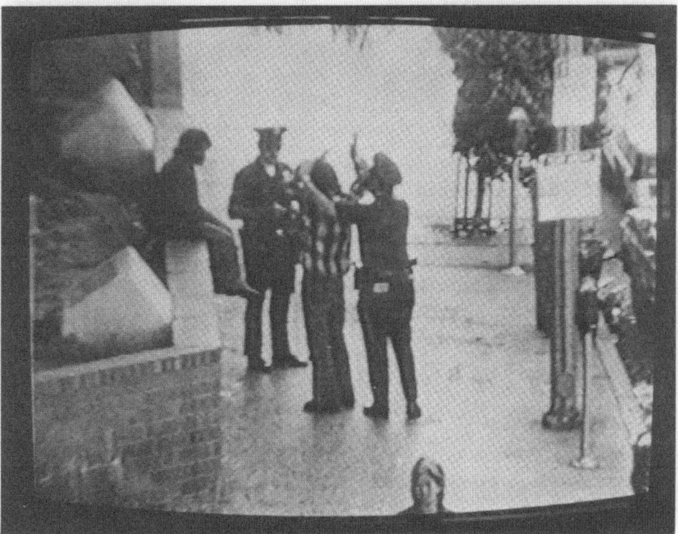

L.A. NICKEL, *1983, Branda Miller.*

while Ann Mari Buitrago's book ARE YOU NOW OR HAVE YOU EVER BEEN IN THE FBI FILES[2] is a how-to guide for those who want to secure and interpret their FBI files.

The subject of surveillance offers an excellent opportunity to examine the relationship between different artistic mediums, stimulating the viewer to look beyond the fetishistic examination of the technology itself in favor of the multi-faceted information gathering process's greater implications. Although personally interested in video and installations, I consider the historical evolution of the still photograph as relevant, and invited Deborah Irmas to curate a photography section for the exhibition. Her overview adds a historical context, and brings an added dimension through the exhibition of video with its predecessor, photography.

Related mediums not incorporated within the dimension of this show include film, television, music, theatre and performance. Government Cold War vintage films like THE BATTLE OF THE UNITED STATES OF AMERICA (narrated by J. Edgar Hoover) and THE CASE OF COMRADE X look back on never before publicized activities of G-men versus Nazi spies and saboteurs, employing hidden clips of camera footage recorded for their lurky trade. More recent feature films, from Hitchcock's REAR WINDOW (1954) to Powell's British classic PEEPING TOM (1959) to Copolla's THE CONVERSATION (1974), have applied surveillance techniques significant in the films' construction. Godard, in the TV tapes SIX FOIS DEUX/SUR ET SOUS LA COMMUN-ICATION (1976), experimented with a camera hidden during interview sequences. La Paluche (slang for 'the hand") camera was created in the early '70s especially for Godard by Jean Pierre Beauviala; it could be strapped to a leg or attached to the body, enabling the camera to be used in an inconspicuous experimental way.

Early television's CANDID CAMERA, first broadcast in 1948, attempted through humor to incorporate living with surveillance into the social body, while today's Geraldo Rivera employs surveillance techniques to sensationalize drug busts and boost ratings, both tapping on the audience's voycuristic delights.

In VARIATIONS IV (1963), John Cage used surveillance as an element for a musical performance, playing to a mix

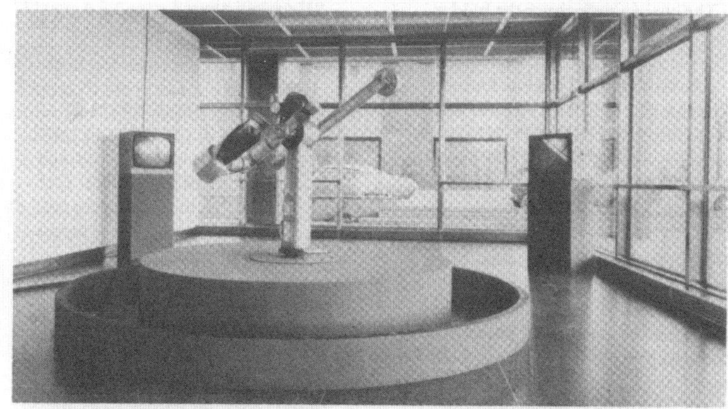

Michael Snow, DE LA, *video installation, The National Gallery of Canada, 1971.*

of pre-recorded sound and live audio tracks fed from the exterior and interior of a Los Angeles gallery. Squat Theatre combined a live and played-back video feed from the street with theatre performance in ANDY WARHOL'S LAST LOVE (1978). Bill Beirne's video installation and performance RUMOR AND INNUENDO (1979), was designed specifically for the architectural space of the Whitney Museum. Delineating surveillance areas in the non-exhibition spaces of the museum (curator's office, lobby, restaurant, etc.), intermittent unannounced performances by 20 actors behaving like the public allowed an exploration of the modification of behavior to adapt to those monitored situations. These examples from other mediums offer a broader scope of artists working conceptually with surveillance, and are noteworthy when examining the LACE exhibition.

The individual spectator's perception and the viewer's awareness as subject can be identified as primary concerns by artists who first explored video as an art form. There was a new sense of the medium affecting the entire environment, and as the spectator increasingly entered the physical situations, the result would be an aspect of self-confrontation. This seems to parallel the reinforcement and circulation of the surveillance apparatus distributed throughout the social network, present everywhere, exercising an invasive power over the individual.

For example, in Bruce Nauman's VIDEO SURVEILLANCE (1970), viewer becomes subject by means of camera and video monitor. As the spectators move through long corridors in a realm of perceptual technology, they must keep up with a certain game to remain in view with the camera and thereby their images on the monitor. Michael Snow's mechanical sculpture

DE LA (1969-1972), incorporates electronic controls, television camera and four monitors, its rotating arc transforming real time and actual space into fleeting images on the TV screen. In Frank Gillette and Ira Schneider's WIPE CYCLE (1969), nine monitors repeat a cycle of live surveillance, with delayed feedback and broadcast television; the mediated access of time-and-space-lag enhance a sense of "information overload." Dan Graham's TWO VIEWING ROOMS (1980), leads the viewer into a closed circuit of video and mirror images; as spectators assume the role of voyeur, they observe their projection of "self." Other installations serve as an early warning of technology's invasive power to penetrate even the seemingly private space of the mind. The interaction of people's real brainwaves are recorded on video in Nina Sobel's ELECTRO-ENCEPHALOGRAPHIC VIDEO DRAWINGS (1973-1983). These are just a few examples of pioneering video works that altered visual and spatial perceptions as spectators were confronted with their own mediated images. These fundamental investigations with perceptual technology significantly overlap much of the video works and installations presented in this exhibition.

LACE UNDER SURVEILLANCE

SURVEILLANCE places the entire gallery under surveillance by artists' installations, thus the viewer becomes part of the spectacle. The gallery-goer trips invisibly projected infra-red beams at the entrance's exterior, setting off an alarm and flashing lights in targets of human torsos imbedded in P.R.A. (Personal Reception Area), the painted banner of Julia Scher.

The chain continues as the hidden microphones in Gary Lloyd's THE HEART OF LOS ANGELES sculpture and RADIO PAINTING pick up the screeching of the alarm's buzzer as well as passing comments of those unknowing gallery-goers/targets entering the space.

Simultaneously, within the closed circuit of NOT FOR BIG BROTHER'S SPY CYCLE, by Dieter Froese, three real cameras pan along with three dummy cardbord cameras, recording the spectators as they move through the photographs and installations. Nine real monitors and nine dummy cardboard monitors also loop throughout the gallery space, encapsulating real-time surveillance mixed with pre-recorded "fake" surveillance and interrogations, transforming the viewer into suspect, caught in the absurd trap of the ever-watching cycle. The threatening voice of the interrogator on the screen demands:

> "Do you plan to overthrow the
> system?"

> "Have you abused your NEA grant?"
> "Do you engage in art politics?"
> "Who are your informants?"

While the viewer experiences the fabricated impositions of the surveyed space, Margia Kramer's video installation JEAN SEBERG/THE FBI/THE MEDIA offers an important reminder of a real life and death story of harassment and surveillance. Watching a monitor through phototext panels of selected documents from declassified F.B.I. files, one learns of Jean Seberg, target of the U.S. government's Counterintelligence Program.

In the LACE bookstore, roles reverse again as suspect becomes agent. Rick Prelinger's audio scanning installation, LISTENING POST, enables the gallery-goer to become a communications professional, eavesdropping on the airwaves throughout the Los Angeles area. One hundred frequencies can be scanned with the turn of a dial, including those of the police, federal agents, emergency medical and fire, disaster units, sanita-

tion, media and the film industry, museums and educational institutions, and "private" conversations from car telephones, providing an opportunity to hear actual surveillance and investigative operations as they happen.

But the agent is not the only one activating the surveillance in this picture—watching eyes scan silently from the high corners as the cameras deployed in Louis Hock's installation FOR YOUR OWN PROTECTION record both bookstore and behind-the-scene staff offices. Taking the technological control away from the viewer, the monitoring process is installed in a separate location of the gallery. There, the viewer/victim is reduced to tiny image fragments within twenty seven 1" monitors, the feed from each camera forming the separate letters of the word DON'T, beckoning/warning the spectator about to enter the Video Screening Room.

Within the Screening Room, fifteen single channel videotapes divided into six programs redefine the representation of surveillance for the viewing audience.

PROGRAM 1– PRIVATE SPACE/PUBLIC SPACE

Whether in the home or in the subway, one can no longer escape anonymity.

An excerpt from Michael Smith's, IT STARTS AT HOME (1982, 25:00) begins the program with a humorous note. Unaware that he is being broadcast, Mike realizes the technicians who visited his home have done more than connect his Cable TV. Mike is now plugged into a continuously monitoring system, his own TV set reflecting as a mirror his every move. In the bars, living rooms and media producer's offices around the country, the public follows on their TV monitors in fascination, as all watch Mike in the routine setting of his private home.

Carol Rainey and Steven Feldman employ the narrative format for another view into the home, with MOMMA GETS HER READY (1985, 12:00). Taking a cue from child psychiatrist B.F. Skinner, "good parenting" means continuously surveying one's own child from a home "central control room."

Chip Lord, in ABSCAM (FRAMED) (1981, 10:30), re-frames a publicly shared TV news event, where deceptive uses of

video surveillance sufficiently convicted the defendants. Playing a whispering newsman returning to the scene of the crime, Lord mixes original surveillance footage with "fake" artists' surveillance, re-enacting the "evidence."

West German artist Heiner Mühlenbrock's BILDERMASCHINEN (1982, 15:00) reconstructs footage from the surveillance cameras at the International Congress Center in West Berlin, editing onto its soundtrack the scores from old crime movies. Transforming the banal comings and goings of businessmen/women into suspect actions, the routine public setting becomes a scenario of suspicion and intrigue.

Two monitors fill the screen like the piercing eyes of the unseen specialized agent in Peter D'Agostino's PARIS METRO: comings and goings (1977, 5:00). The sped-up, stop-framed imagery shakily monitors the undifferentiated mass in the routine of the Paris Metro, as a voice-over presents the etymology of the word "metro":

> "Metro: measures (verse) madness
>   for measures . . .
> metro: uterus . .
> poly: many . . .
> poly: sell . .
> metropolis . . .

> metro: mother . . .
> pol: city . . .
> mother city . . .
> altogether, a source of confusion"

This "source of confusion" is felt by the individual as one's body, time and every day activities are subjected to the institutionalized mechanisms of control. This seemingly unlimited access "starts at home," spreads through the "metropolis," and extends beyond our planet, as spectator becomes an object of representation.

PROGRAM 2– CONFRONTATION

In Program 2– CONFRONTATION, artists challenge the institutionalization of surveillance, through surveillance tactics, deconstruction and parody.

Video pioneers Paul Ryan and Michael Shamberg's SUPERMARKET (1969, 14:30) documents the highly visible early surveillance systems of a Safeway Supermarket, using ½" reel-to-reel B&W unedited imagery. As they record the large signs hanging from the ceiling, stating, "Smile You Are On

Photo-Scan T.V.", the manager demands they turn off their camera, insisting it is illegal to shoot any images in the store. Arguing, "You're taking pictures of us on TV, so why can't we take pictures of you?", this early video confrontation questions the rights of an individual in a public environment.

In QUI VOLE UN OEUF VOLE UN OEUF — HE WHO STEALS AN EGG STEALS AN EGG (1982, 15:00), Peruvian born artist Elsa Cayo plugs her video recorder into a Parisian supermarket's surveillance circuit, made possible by the complicity of the supervisor of the security monitoring console. Cayo plays an adversarial game of recording images of herself shoplifting, changing her role as involuntary target into artist/provocateur. She transforms a routine setting of surveillance for deterrence to her own performance stage.

Paper Tiger TV Collective looks inward with a mock self-incriminating surveillance scene in NOLAN BOWIE READS ARTICLES ABOUT PRIVACY (1985, 28:00). As Nolan Bowie, former director of Citizens Communication Center in Washington, D.C., reads articles about the government's surveillance activities, the Collective superimposes their own fictitious "classified" FBI records over B&W monitoring of the live studio set.

Aron Ranen's TELEVISION BELIEVERS (1986, 26:00) serves as a revealing expose of Peter Popoff, a self-proclaimed faith healer who uses sophisticated audio technology to "perform his miracles." While the artist records the on-the-surface reality of the location, psychic debunker the Amazing Randy, with the help of specialized agent Alec Jason, record the inner-reality of the event: the preacher is fed information about the audience by his wife on a hidden audio channel.

(Wife of Popoff, during an audio test):
"Hello, Petie. I love you. Can you hear me? If you can't, you're in trouble."

The combined data produces an exceptional alliance of artist and specialized agent using surveillance technology to debunk myths perpetrated on the public.

PROGRAM 3– GOVERNMENT SPOOKS

Government operatives are referred to as "spooks." Many lives are touched by these ghosts, innocents turned into targets. Few share the surveillance tools to fight back.

In an excerpt from Louis Hock's THE MEXICAN TAPES (1985, 3:50), dark running figures glow green on La Migra's (Border Patrol) monitor, as the helicopters, bright lights and infra-red cameras transform people into criminals. Transcending the traditional privacy afforded by darkness, the advanced surveillance technology leaves the illegal immigrants nowhere to hide.

RED SQUAD (1971, 45:00) by Pacific Street Films, documents an alliance between the FBI and the NYPD called the Red Squad, who were (and are) engaged in illicit surveillance activities of American citizens since 1912. In direct confrontation with the government's illegal use of power, the filmmakers engage in a battle of the cameras, following the Red Squad and openly recording their activities. Who uses surveillance and why, and citizens' rights within a democratic society to fight back with the same technology, are issues effectively brought up in this documentary.

PROGRAM 4– VIEWER/VOYEUR

Bruce Charlesworth's SURVEILLANCE (1984, 21:00) employs a single, fixed 21-minute shot, as two undercover detectives stake out a window, using binoculars to monitor the activities of an unknown suspect across a lake. The boredom and frustrations of their routine give way to paranoia and shock at the realization that they are being watched as well. Roles of agent and target become intertwined, as the audience discovers they too are participants in the monitoring process.

In Martha Rosler's VITAL STATISTICS OF A CITIZEN SIMPLY OBTAINED (1977, 38:00), a woman is measured, and statistics are accumulated and analyzed — "standard, above standard, below standard." The viewer becomes participant in the external vision of the self, surveying the woman's body, which is being monitored from the outside as if divorced from itself. Continuous measurement and control, through extraneous data, applied categorically and revealed inferentially,

intrudes into privacy, probing further into the body and deeper into the social landscape.

(Rosler's Voice-over):
"This is a tape about perception of self, meaning of truth, definition of fact, this is a work about being done to . . . about scrutiny on a mass level."

PROGRAM 5– DER RIESE—THE GIANT

Berlin filmmaker Michael Klier's DER RIESE (1982-1983, 82:00) is a classic essay comprised of real surveillance images displaying our society under the constant watch of our ubiquitous surveillance cameras.

Where and what the images were taken from:
1. Airport surveillance, Berlin-Tegel.
2. Private property surveillance (house and garden), Hamburg.
3. Department store surveillance (shoplifter, store detective), Berlin.
4. Bank teller and money transporting surveillance, Furth.
5. Gas station surveillance, Berlin.
6. Peep-show surveillance, Berlin.
7. Traffic surveillance, pedestrian zone, Hamburg.
8. Surveillance of the annual Parade of the Allies (excluding the Soviet Union), on the street, the 17th of June, West Berlin.
9. Police investigation image generator, Dusseldorf.
10. B-level surveillance, Hamburg.
11. Monitoring of a conversation between a doctor and a patient in a psychiatric hospital, Berlin.
12. Driving a simulator for tank drivers, Ulm.

PROGRAM SIX– LOVE HOTEL (xxx)

LOVE HOTEL (1986, 30:00) was presented by an anonymous donor to Japanese artist Noriaki Nakagawa. In a high-tech Love Hotel in Japan, clientele enter hotel rooms rigged with surveillance equipment. Voluntarily activating the monitoring of their own sex acts, they satisfy their personal desires for voyeurism. While the camera's presence alters their behavior, the mysterious video burglar steals a permanent record, passing it on to Nakagawa, who digitizes the faces and genitalia into mosaic patterns to protect the identities in this real-life encounter. (X-rated)

CONCLUSION

Surveillance has become omnipresent in our society, an essential element to maintaining the political and economic status quo. Its future manifestations, however, promise to extend the power beyond simply surveying, categorizing, and analyzing. Surveillance of the future could be "coming next fall" from your favorite network, reaching through your television screen to effect physical changes in your home.

From THE HOLLYWOOD REPORTER, Friday, January 16, 1987:

> ACT angry over new interactive TV shows:
>
> . . . "the next trend" in kidvid . . . "Moto Monsters and the Tech Force" and "Captain Power" . . . Both shows emit inaudible signals that allow viewers to participate by responding to on-screen "targets" with the toy . . . applied for and received FCC approval to broadcast the hidden signals . . . a new chapter in children's television. "There won't be a show without an inaudible beep". . . Calling petitions to the FCC a "waste of time" under the Reagan administration, ACT President Charren said ACT will ask congress to pass legislation compelling the FCC to re-evaluate children's programming policy, including consideration of the impact of new technologies.

Obviously this mechanism could be easily perverted. In today's technological vortex, mythology becomes reality, science fiction fact. The artists in SURVEILLANCE were selected to provocatively deconstruct the myth of surveillance in the real world of recording and processing. A response to the fragmentation and isolation resulting from the accelerated development and distribution of information could be the desire for anonymity, a wish for invisibility. Yet with the burden of anxiety comes the opportunity for awareness, growth and political action.

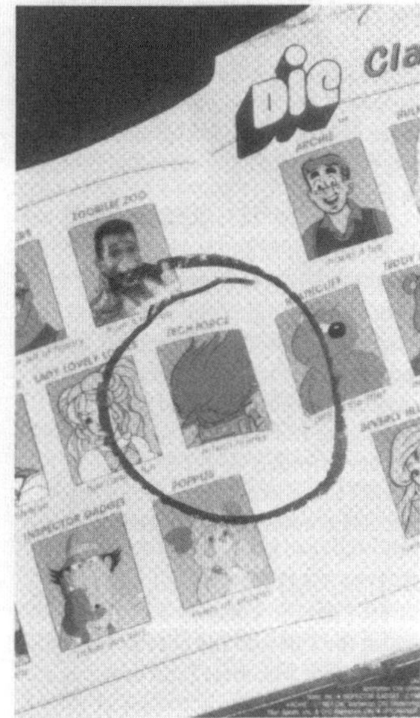

From the cover of ANIMATION SPECIAL REPORT, The Hollywood Reporter, *Jan. 22, 1987.*

Notes

[1]Michel Foucault, *Discipline and Punish, The Birth of the Prison,* Vintage Books, a division of Random House, New York. © 1977 by Alan Sheridan

[2]Ann Mari Buitrago and Leon Andrew Immerman, *Are you Now or Have You Ever Been in the FBI Files, How to Secure and Interpret Your FBI Files,* Grove Press, 196 West Houston Street, New York, N.Y. 10014. © 1981 by Fund for Open Information and Accountability, Inc.

AIN'T IT THE GOD'S TRUTH?

by Deborah Irmas

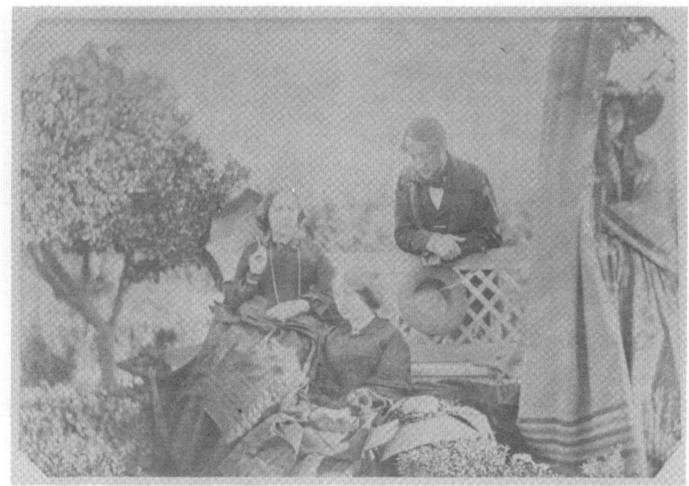

George Fenwick, 1856, salt print (Courtesy, Stephen White Gallery of Photography, Beverly Hills)

"You slew him with that tomahawk; and as you stood over his body with the letter in your hand, you thought that no witness saw the deed, that no eye was on you— but there was, Jacob M'Closkey, there was. The eye of the Eternal was on you—the blessed sun in heaven, that, looking down, struck upon this plate of the image of the deed. Here you are in the very attitude of your crime!" [1]

Now we know that photography can easily lie. But the truth addicts of the nineteenth century strongly believed that it didn't and couldn't so that they could use it as evidence. Photography was a science that replicated nature . . . and nature was god—while science was truth. How fitting to use this medium to point the finger at suspicious behavior. They hoped that photography—the god's truth— would change society, and thus make everyone behave accordingly. Years before the medium developed to the stage where it was even feasible to put this notion into practice, men yearned to use it for the purpose of exposing secrets that they imagined must be exposed.

These envisioned capabilities of early photography, described in plays and short stories, magically followed performers of evil deeds, or young lovers and *watched over* them. The word "surveillance" is from the words "watch" and "over." Like the writers who imagined what truth the photograph might reveal, surveillance photographers surmised beforehand what could be uncovered. They knew the punchline before telling the joke. An impetuous private act revealed forever in black and white, or the extended construction of a visual dossier would only be actuated if a healthy possibility of finding an unknown truth existed.

This element of "deduction," or the self-fulfilling prophecy is a critical component in surveillance work. A surveillance photographer monitoring a subject asks beforehand, what sort of acts photograph best? Where would they most likely occur and most importantly what kind of person will most likely perform them? Finally the question of where the photographer situates himself in relation to the deed is considered . . . in the open but with a concealed camera? Secreted from public view? Or miles away from the action itself?

A portrait from 1856 clearly reveals how little was understood about the nature of having one's picture taken. An unsuspecting young woman standing beside a group about to be photographed is, herself, an integral part of the image. Purposely incorporating her, the photographer establishes his position of authority and the image defines a gap between the surveillor and the subject, setting up a baseline for the discussion of surveillance photography. Eventually subjects become more aware; cameras became smaller and photographers learned to invent subversive means in order to acquire evidence without the collaboration of a subject. By the end of the century, the public's level of awareness and understanding of the camera had increased to the point that they understood the relationship between their stance and the camera's gaze.

Paul Strand's famous series of portraits of 1916 taken on the streets of New York underscore this point. Made with the assist of a fake lens mounted to the side of his lunchbox-sized Graflex, Strand circumvented the expected responses and attitudes people assume when a camera is pointed at them. Although these photographs are considered monuments of modernism, they must also be considered within the realm of surveillance methodology—the artist employed deceitful means to acquire an image. These extra precautions taken to insure that he would not be discovered before or after securing the pictures places them squarely within this discussion.

By the end of the 1920s, the development of the miniature camera—coupled with the advancement of fast lenses— enabled indoor shooting without the use of blinding flash. Erich Salomon's photographs of meetings of heads of state have the appearance of surveillance photography—grainy, contrasty, prints with subjects completely oblivious to the photographer. But even to have entered into the room required permission, and his Ermanox camera still required the use of every visible tri-pod. The spirit of cooperation (although not evident) is an element that separates surveillance photography from other kinds of documents.

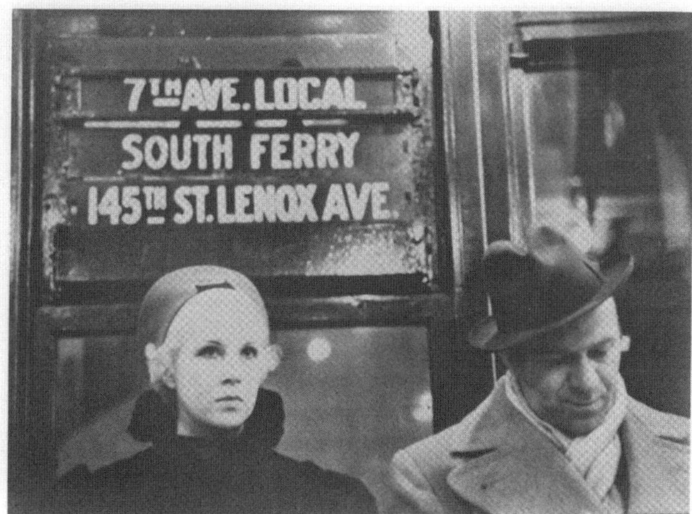

Walker Evans, © 1940 (Courtesy, Fraenkel Gallery, San Francisco)

In 1938 and 1941 Walker Evans strapped a LEICA around his neck and attempted a series of "unposed portraits" in the New York subways. Purposely concealing it underneath his jacket he positioned himself in front of his subjects and much like a detective released the shutter intermittently, without looking directly at the subject. In an unpublished draft of a text written to accompany these portraits he says:

> *"The portraits on these pages were caught by a hidden camera, in the hands of a penitent spy and an apologetic voyeur . . ."* [2]

Evans perceives this method of working as ultimately pure because the photographer takes no care to "pre-visualize" the image. Rather, the happenstance release of the shutter either secured an image or it didn't. Morally Evans finds this secretive gathering of visual information pure because he is able to side-step the usual issues of vanity that arise when subjects engage with the photographer in the making of a picture. The young woman standing to the side of the group posing for the portrait in the 1850s would now be subconsciously primping for the camera. For Evans this false gesture would interfere with his 20th century concept of "truth" in a photograph as much as the photographer's own hand/eye maneuvering. And yet he encourages the kind of observation that is considered socially discourteous (for research?):

> *"Stare. It is the way to educate your eye and more. Stare, pry, listen, eavesdrop. Die knowing something. You are not here long."* [3]

Curiously he raises the issue of privacy but defends his actions by arguing that he has waited twenty years before showing the portraits or publishing them.

> *" . . . the rude and impudent invasion involved has been carefully softened and partially mitigated by a planned passage of time."* [4]

Weegee, however, was not the least concerned with the issues of privacy and was known to photograph people in any public situation that would make an interesting picture and then publish them as soon as a newspaper or magazine would buy them. Infrared film allowed him the opportunity to photograph in a darkened theater where the audience believed their physical responses were undetected. In the 1940s he photographed Frank Sinatra's young audience at the Paramount Theater. Their stolen frenzied expressions captured in his camera are thought to be documents of popular American culture as well as indicative of his boisterous individual photojournalistic style. Considered within the realm of surveillance photography these photographs further demonstrate the radical technical means photographers would take in order to acquire what they believed to be a "good shot" without any cooperation or interaction with their subject.

These photographers set the stage for a wide range of contemporary photographic work. Artists today have co-opted the latest high-technology, or conceptually seized the procedures that their predecessors took to acquire images. But whereas Strand, Evans and Weegee quested after an image saturated with a declaration of pictorial modern reality, contemporary artists reject the belief of an imaged truth and employ or subvert these procedures in order to illustrate the lunacy of the concept of truth itself. Before, the means justified the end; now, in the post-modern era, the inverted version carries more weight. The means themselves have not only become the end, but they also perform as questions to a society that has forgotten the morality of chosen means.

In *Borrowed Time,* Jake Seniuk for instance, follows Paul Strand's tactic of remaining in full view while secretly photographing. Strand's New York side-walk however, is now the Seattle freeway. Situated above an overpass, Seniuk peers into the private retreats of contemporary man that travel at (freeway) speeds of 50 miles per hour. Piercing the windshield with his gaze, we see the same blank generic expressions that Strand recorded. Seniuk's account however is not only to picture the unpicturable but also to declare the insidious presence of the unseen camera in our urban culture . . . even if it is his own.

This excessive hunger for chronicling information—even worthless information—and the ongoing paranoia that necessitates the research and development of highly sensitive and grossly expensive recording tools are the stimulus for Richard Lowenberg's body of work. His performance, installation, and video work co-opts the state-of-the-art technology employed by the government and private enterprise surveillance industry. As in his other work, the night photographs of military installations circumvent the entire system of information gathering and the corporate vow of secrecy. To the artist, these secrets are not worth keeping. High-powered equipment loaned by individuals who work inside the "military-industrial complex" are used to photograph radar sites, and activity and installations in restricted areas. His work is as much about this "collaboration" as it is about what he photographs.

Lewis Stein, too, looks the ever-present surveillance instruments straight in the eye. His bold blurry square pictures of scanning devices used in banks and public buildings are instructive reminders of the rampant imaging of normal day to day public activities. Stein's work raises the question: does the presence of these monitoring devices subconsciously alter our behavior in public?

Sam Samore's *Suspect* appropriates the methodology of a private detective, hiring an "investigator photographer" and instructing him to photograph suspicious looking people or people doing suspicious looking things. The resulting images come straight from B-movie iconography. Racial stereotypes surface, confirming the notion that surveillance activity requires not only a vivid imagination but also a deter-mination to capture something useful, even if it isn't true. These mural-sized images lit with red light predict a kind of headquarters interrogation between the authorities and the suspect. His work heeds the warning that our own fears coupled with a predisposition to believe the veracity of the photograph sets in motion the possibilities of corruption and disruption of innocent people's lives.

Sophie Calle, a French artist, has used surveillance strategy in her work since 1980. In *Suite venitienne,* 1983, the published version of this piece, she followed a man picked randomly from a crowd to Venice, Italy, documenting with photos and notes his location and the time of each record. In a more recent piece, *L'hotel,* 1984, Calle engages even more with the operation of securing private photographic information. Gaining employment as a chambermaid she photographs each unmade room and records detailed information about the personal articles she observes. Her accounting injects an imaginary horror. Any of us could be violated in similar circumstances.

"Wednesday, the 18th, 10:20 a.m. She wears green pajamas, they're layed out on the pillow. On the table, 'Kleenex' and a book, Terapia 80. *She took a bath. The room is always neat and empty. I douse myself with her perfume and use her cosmetics. I clean the room and leave."* [5]

Security, a wall installation by Nancy Buchanan, deals with the very real effects of exaggerated surveillance activity in human terms. Her father, a brilliant outspoken scientist was monitored throughout his life by the F.B.I., which was documented in his excessive file. Layering copies of his file with photographs and personal mementos, she builds a complex portrait of a man and the chilling consequences this activity may have had on his shortened life.

John Baldessari's 1976 piece *David: One Day—Sixty Shots Named and Alphabetized,* reminds us of the gargan-tuan disconnected surveillance industry—the hunting, gathering and deciphering of visual data. Baldessari removes his direct involvement in the acquisition of the information when he assigns the 24 hour photographic monitoring of his subject to one person. A second person collects the data and codes the dossier, interrupting any notion of sequential ordering. Finally this mechanistic arrangement is presented with an osten-sible structure of ultimate reason and logic. What becomes clear, however, is that there is only an arbitrary logic. Baldessari's conceptual organization reaffirms Barbara Kruger's dictum "Surveillance is your busywork."

Notes

1 Dion Boucicault, *The Octoroon,* reprinted in *Representative American Plays,* edited with an introduction and notes by Arthur Hobson Quinn (New York: The Century Company, 1917), p. 442. Quoted in Richard Rudisill, *The Mirror Image, the Influence of the Daguerreotype on American Society,* (Albuquerque: University of New Mexico Press), p. 222.

2 Walker Evans, *Walker Evans at Work,* (New York: Harper & Row), 1982, p.160.

3 Ibid, p. 161.

4 Ibid, p. 60.

5 Sophie Calle, *L'hotel,* 1983, Paris: Editions de' l'Etoile, p. 33. Unfortunately, we were unable to exhibit Calle's work in the LACE exhibition.

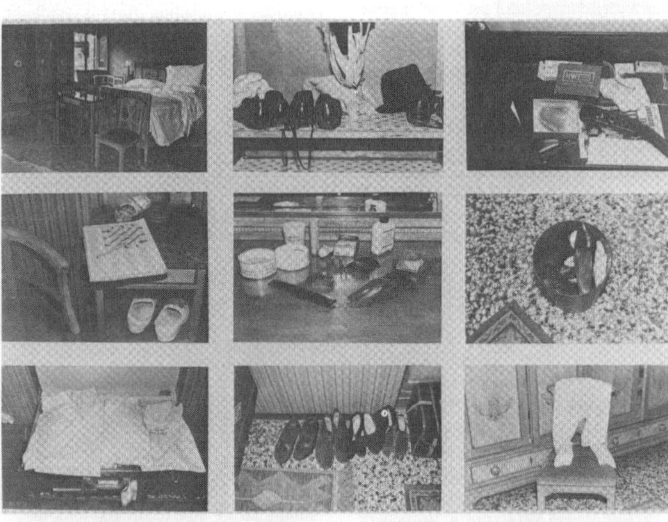

Sophie Calle, 1983, from L'HOTEL *(Courtesy Galerie Crousel-Hussenot, Paris)*

13

The Scope of the Early Warning System

locations of eight radar stations and the range of their surveillance.

NORAD Air Warning Sites and Interceptor Bases

U.S. ICBM Warning Sites
(Except Satellites)

U.S. SLBM Warning Sites
(Except Satellites)

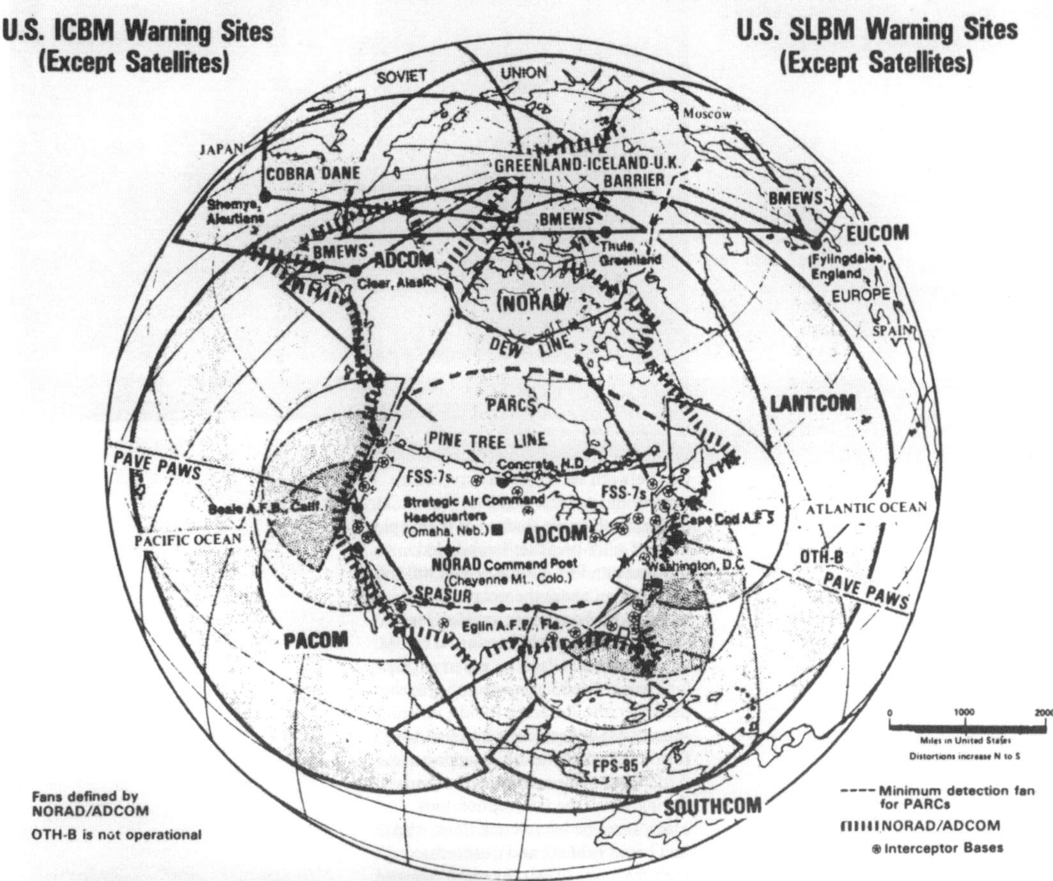

U.S. UNIFIED AND SPECIFIED COMMANDS

NOTES: Whether or not there is a boundary between EUCOM and PACOM through the Soviet Union is classified information. Readers can presume that if such a line could be identified, it would in some way join the two water boundaries between those commands.

No unified or specified command has overall responsibility for CONUS in the way that EUCOM, LANTCOM, PACOM, and SOUTHCOM are charged with geographic areas. ADCOM is a component of NORAD, a combined U.S./Canadian command that covers all of North America.

Several areas, such as Mexico and Africa south of the Sahara, lie outside the jurisdiction of any U.S. unified or specified command.

the cost of control of global reach is fascination with the (game of the)(exploding)(historical) hollow leg.

I

imagine a mound. tumulus. a burrow under the earth. you watch the depths of the air, water, sky, space; from under the earth you look above, looking for fire. burrow under to look above. you make all your senses one: *sight*. you put your eyes everywhere. you hide to be safe.

What would you need to protect yourself from the sky, the ocean, air, wind, space. how to protect yourself from protecting yourself from birds, blips, atmospheric disturbances, storms, stars, shooting stars, asteroids, planets, galaxies. from drugs, fear, craziness, paranoia; neurosis, loss of vigilance, loss of interest, sabotage. from loners, spies, assassins, inventions, terrorism. how to wait, how to stay in place, how to keep place.

II

In your mother's body your senses are touch, sound, taste, smell, skin sense. your world is your network is you. what is the price of separation, of separation as rejection? you create an Other. you erect dualisms wherever you go. make all your senses give place to sight. you create the world as *picture*. invent linear perspective. the objectification of the world. the objectification of the Other (of the Mother?). what is the cost of control as domination? extend yourself over oceans. set up a network of control over lives, labor, places, materials. subjugate earth and people. the cost of control is the armed eye. (fratricide, decapitation, hardened silos, racecourse basing, dense pack.) launch on warning. launch under attack.

MARTHA ROSLER

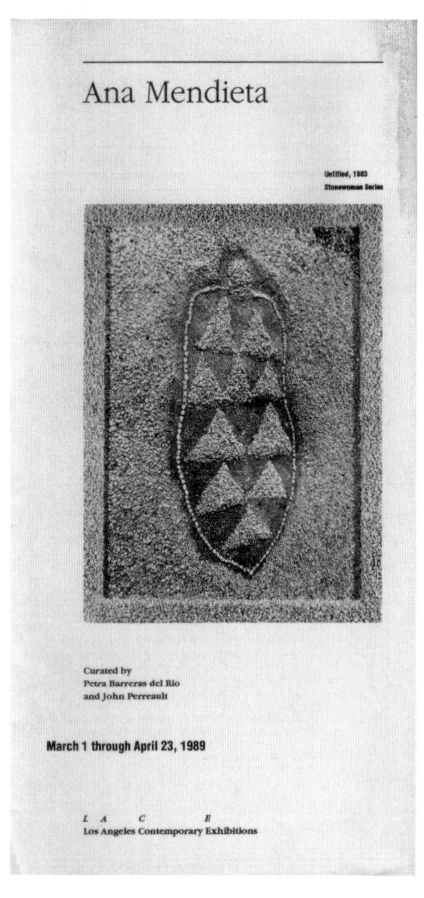

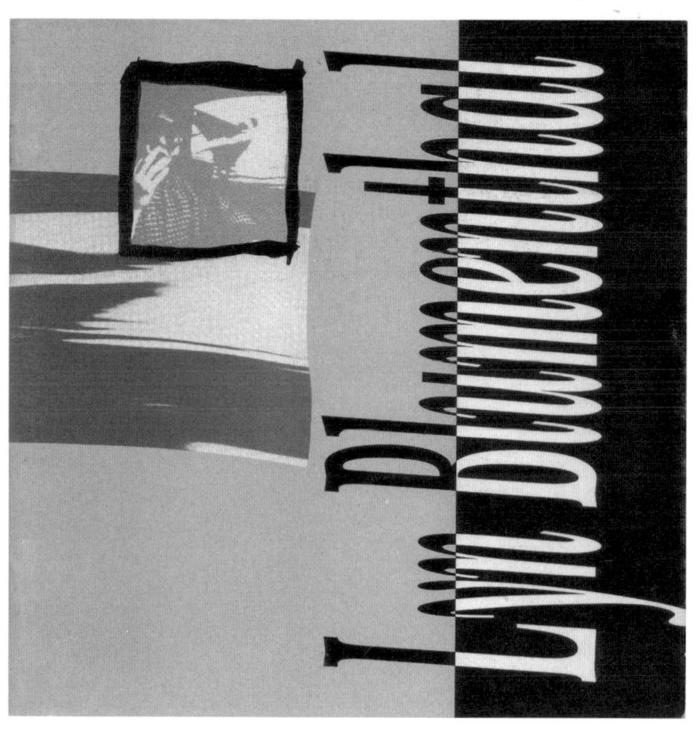

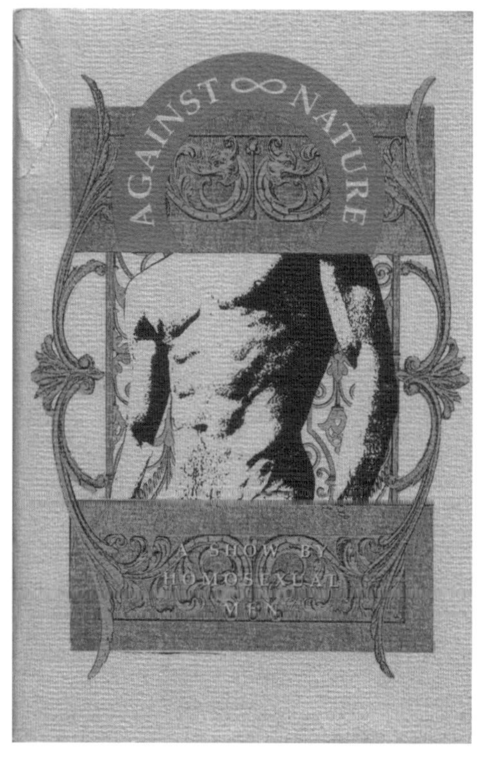

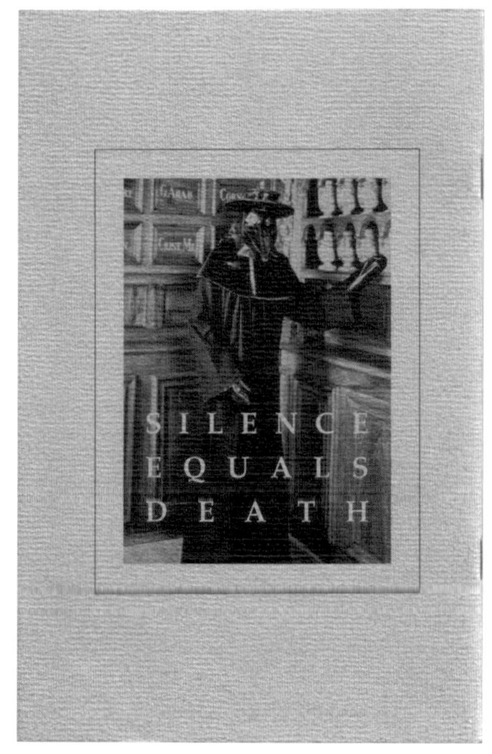

1989.01 <u>Ana Mendieta, A Retrospective</u>, Catalog

1989.02 <u>Lyn Blumenthal, Force of Vision</u>, Brochure

1988.03 <u>Against Nature: A Show By Homosexual Men</u>, Catalog

self·evidence

1989.03 <u>Self-Evidence</u>, Catalog

1987.05 Victor Burgin, Office At Night, Brochure

1987.06 Allan Sekula, Geography Lesson: Canadian Notes, Brochure

1988.04 Mary Kelly, Interim – Part I: Corpus, Brochure

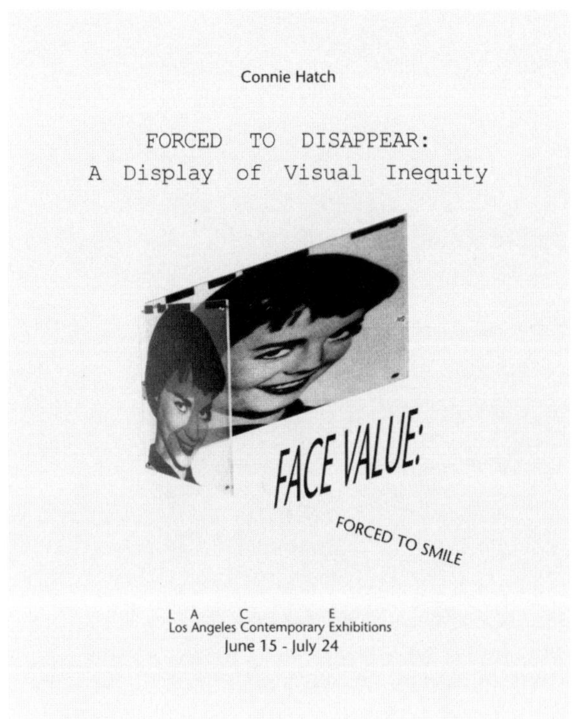

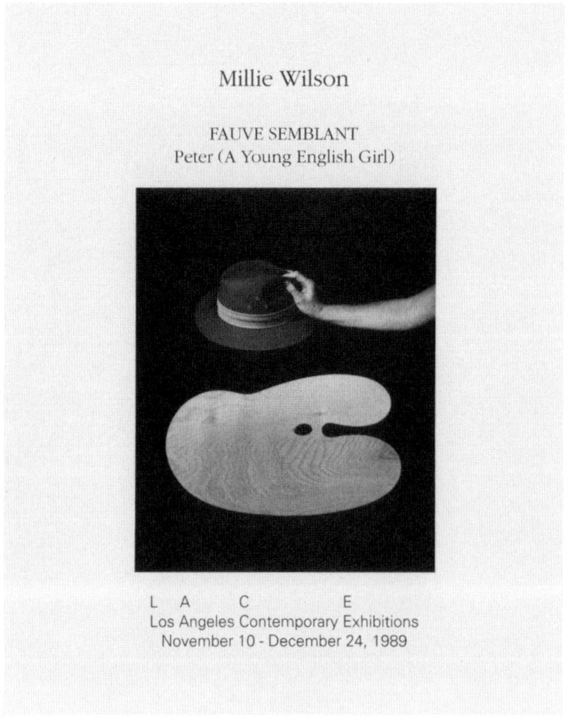

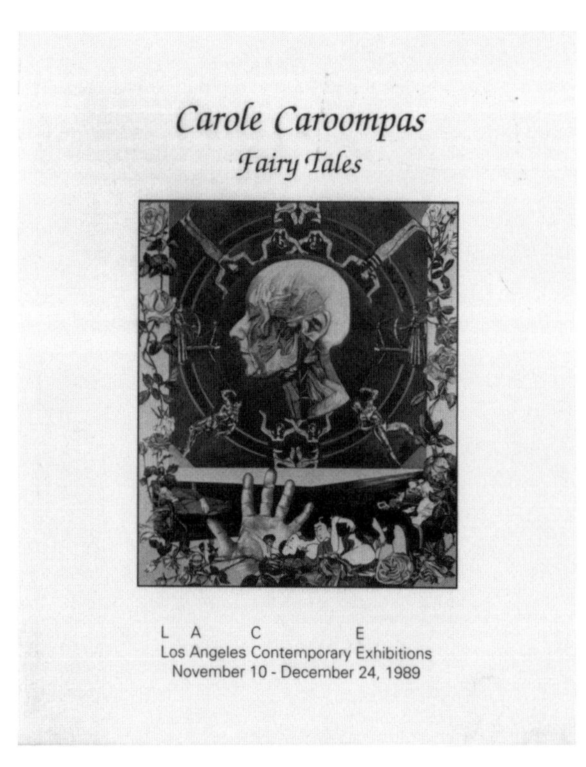

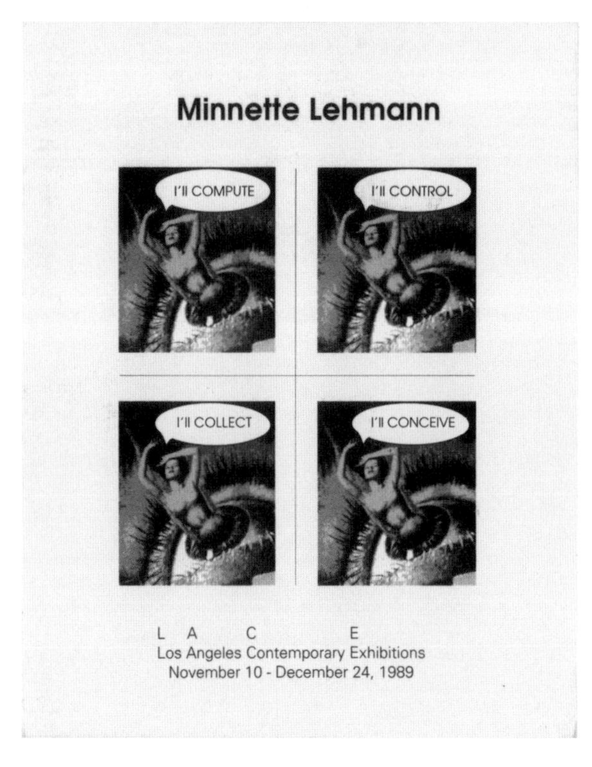

1988.05 Connie Hatch, FORCED TO DISAPPEAR
and FACE VALUE, Brochure
1988.06 Carole Caroompas, Fairy Tales,
Brochure

1988.07 Millie Wilson, FAUVE SEMBLANT,
Peter (A Young English Girl),
Brochure
1988.08 Minnette Lehmann, Brochure

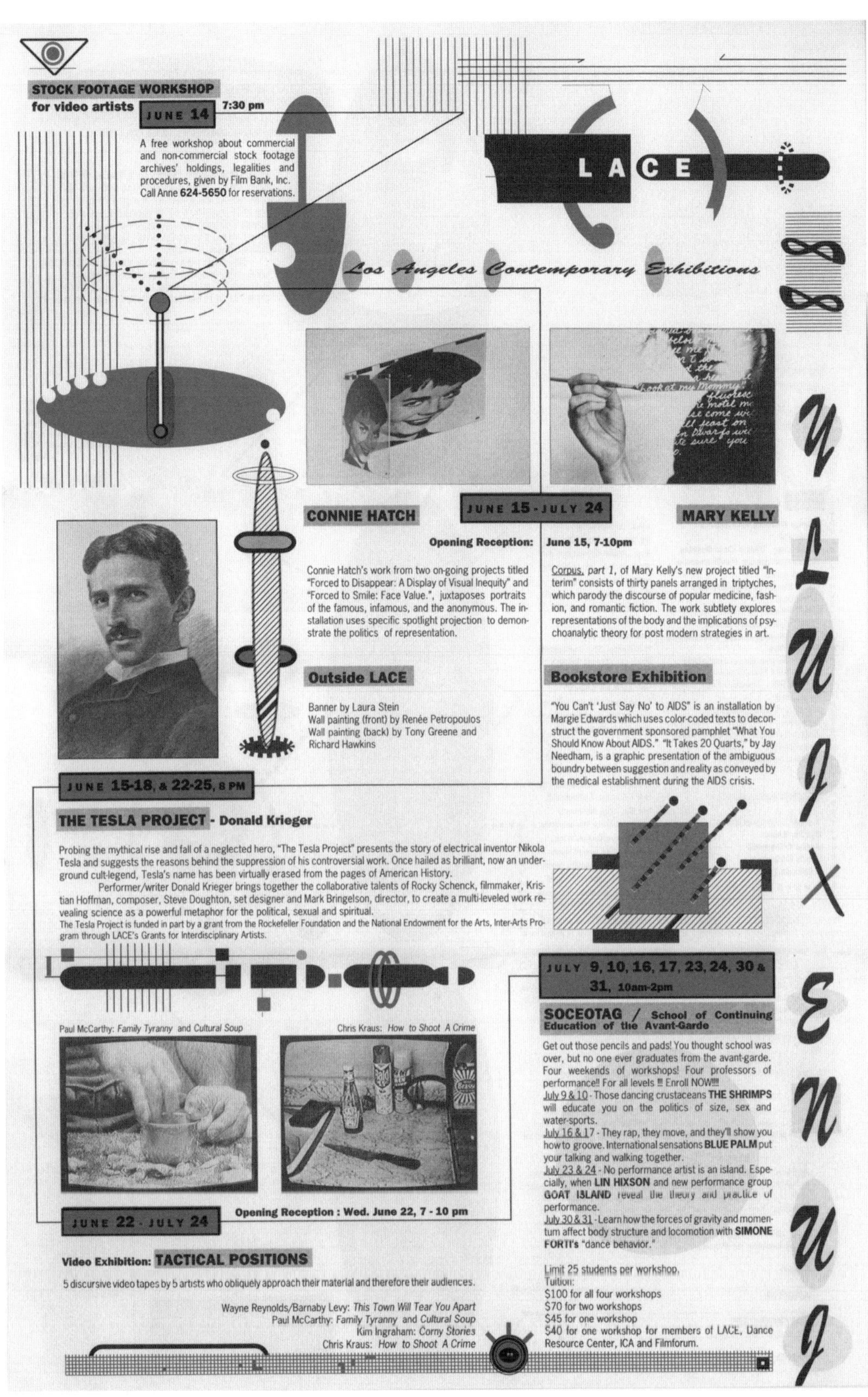

STOCK FOOTAGE WORKSHOP
for video artists   JUNE 14   7:30 pm

A free workshop about commercial and non-commercial stock footage archives' holdings, legalities and procedures, given by Film Bank, Inc. Call Anne 624-5650 for reservations.

L A C E

Los Angeles Contemporary Exhibitions

CONNIE HATCH   JUNE 15 - JULY 24   MARY KELLY

Opening Reception: June 15, 7-10pm

Connie Hatch's work from two on-going projects titled "Forced to Disappear: A Display of Visual Inequity" and "Forced to Smile: Face Value.", juxtaposes portraits of the famous, infamous, and the anonymous. The installation uses specific spotlight projection to demonstrate the politics of representation.

Corpus, part 1, of Mary Kelly's new project titled "Interim" consists of thirty panels arranged in triptyches, which parody the discourse of popular medicine, fashion, and romantic fiction. The work subtlety explores representations of the body and the implications of psychoanalytic theory for post modern strategies in art.

Outside LACE

Banner by Laura Stein
Wall painting (front) by Renée Petropoulos
Wall painting (back) by Tony Greene and Richard Hawkins

Bookstore Exhibition

"You Can't 'Just Say No' to AIDS" is an installation by Margie Edwards which uses color-coded texts to deconstruct the government sponsored pamphlet "What You Should Know About AIDS." "It Takes 20 Quarts," by Jay Needham, is a graphic presentation of the ambiguous boundry between suggestion and reality as conveyed by the medical establishment during the AIDS crisis.

JUNE 15-18, & 22-25, 8 PM

THE TESLA PROJECT - Donald Krieger

Probing the mythical rise and fall of a neglected hero, "The Tesla Project" presents the story of electrical inventor Nikola Tesla and suggests the reasons behind the suppression of his controversial work. Once hailed as brilliant, now an underground cult-legend, Tesla's name has been virtually erased from the pages of American History.
Performer/writer Donald Krieger brings together the collaborative talents of Rocky Schenck, filmmaker, Kristian Hoffman, composer, Steve Doughton, set designer and Mark Bringelson, director, to create a multi-leveled work revealing science as a powerful metaphor for the political, sexual and spiritual.
The Tesla Project is funded in part by a grant from the Rockefeller Foundation and the National Endowment for the Arts, Inter-Arts Program through LACE's Grants for Interdisciplinary Artists.

Paul McCarthy: Family Tyranny and Cultural Soup

Chris Kraus: How to Shoot A Crime

JULY 9, 10, 16, 17, 23, 24, 30 & 31, 10am-2pm

SOCEOTAG / School of Continuing Education of the Avant-Garde

Get out those pencils and pads! You thought school was over, but no one ever graduates from the avant-garde. Four weekends of workshops! Four professors of performance!! For all levels !!! Enroll NOW!!!
July 9 & 10 - Those dancing crustaceans THE SHRIMPS will educate you on the politics of size, sex and water-sports.
July 16 & 17 - They rap, they move, and they'll show you how to groove. International sensations BLUE PALM put your talking and walking together.
July 23 & 24 - No performance artist is an island. Especially, when LIN HIXSON and new performance group GOAT ISLAND reveal the theory and practice of performance.
July 30 & 31 - Learn how the forces of gravity and momentum affect body structure and locomotion with SIMONE FORTI's "dance behavior."

Limit 25 students per workshop.
Tuition:
$100 for all four workshops
$70 for two workshops
$45 for one workshop
$40 for one workshop for members of LACE, Dance Resource Center, ICA and Filmforum.

Opening Reception : Wed. June 22, 7 - 10 pm

JUNE 22 - JULY 24

Video Exhibition: TACTICAL POSITIONS

5 discursive video tapes by 5 artists who obliquely approach their material and therefore their audiences.

Wayne Reynolds/Barnaby Levy: This Town Will Tear You Apart
Paul McCarthy: Family Tyranny and Cultural Soup
Kim Ingraham: Corny Stories
Chris Kraus: How to Shoot A Crime

As a graphic designer working for a non-profit arts organization like LACE it was a great opportunity to do more than just grease the wheels of Capitalism. Over a three-year period I designed membership pleas, exhibition brochures and the LACE 10yrs. Documented book, all with painfully small budgets and overly ambitious goals. But the project that I enjoyed the most was the design for the bi-monthly calendar of events.

The LACE calendars were a self-mailer with all the performances and exhibitions for the next two months listed on the front, all the less important boilerplate information like address, postal permit, staff, and membership on the back. And that is the territory I claimed for my own design experiments using new typefaces and a deconstructive approach to typography. Since it was the early days of computer graphics, printers were not yet able to work with digital files so I made paste-ups, or mechanicals, frequently using hand made and collaged elements, because in spite of using a computer, the calendars were still essentially hand made art. I thought the LACE audience would appreciate experimental typography more than a generic layout, but I was wrong.

Fortunately for me, Joy Silverman, the director of LACE, thought that the mandate to champion the free expression of emerging artists should include designers as well. Her commitment to that idea was regularly put to the test in the following three years because she got a lot of grief for the weird, hard-to-read, no-two-alike designs. In the late '80s design was still expected to be "transparent" or at least subservient to the content, even in an alternative space. But not everyone hated them. The office and building manager, Martin Kersels, who helped get the calendars out, was always very supportive, as was the LACE staff, probably because they understood how much work was involved. But when Joy left in 1990 I knew my days were numbered at LACE.

By the late 1990s magazines like Ray Gun, Speak, and Plazm made expressive typography and graphic design pyrotechnics fashionable. The strange new typeface I used in the calendars (Keedy Sans) was made available to the general public and started to appear in national advertising campaigns. The LACE calendars themselves appeared in design books and magazines, while ugly, anti-aesthetic, eccentric graphics became a fashionable signifier of the hip and cool. Today, it is hard to imagine what the problem was, but at the time it was disappointing to see how provincial the alternative art crowd could be.

As with most commercial products, design for art is used to create an environment of credibility, importance and exclusivity. Most graphic designers seem content to do minor variations on the old, Helvetica and white space minimal style, but I wanted the calendars to be an ephemeral graphic free-for-all that would convey the spirit of the place. The LACE calendars were true experiments in that they were in a small way like the artwork, allowed to risk failure in the pursuit of new possibilities. Looking back I'm grateful for having had the opportunity to collaborate, experiment, and most importantly, have fun with design for art's sake.

LACE

WOODWORKS

By Jan Munroe — **APRIL 8, 9, 10 & 15, 16, 17 AT 8 PM**
A MOVEMENT-BASED PIECE WITH IMAGES AND TEXT DERIVED FROM HIS EXPERIENCE AS A CARPENTER. PERFORMED BY A COMPANY OF ACTORS AND DANCERS WITH ORIGINAL MUSIC BY STEVE MOSHIER. TICKETS: $10/$8 LACE MEMBERS.
WOODWORKS IS PRESENTED IN ASSOCIATION WITH THE MODERN ARTISTS COMPANY AND NATIONAL/STATE/COUNTY PARTNERSHIP.

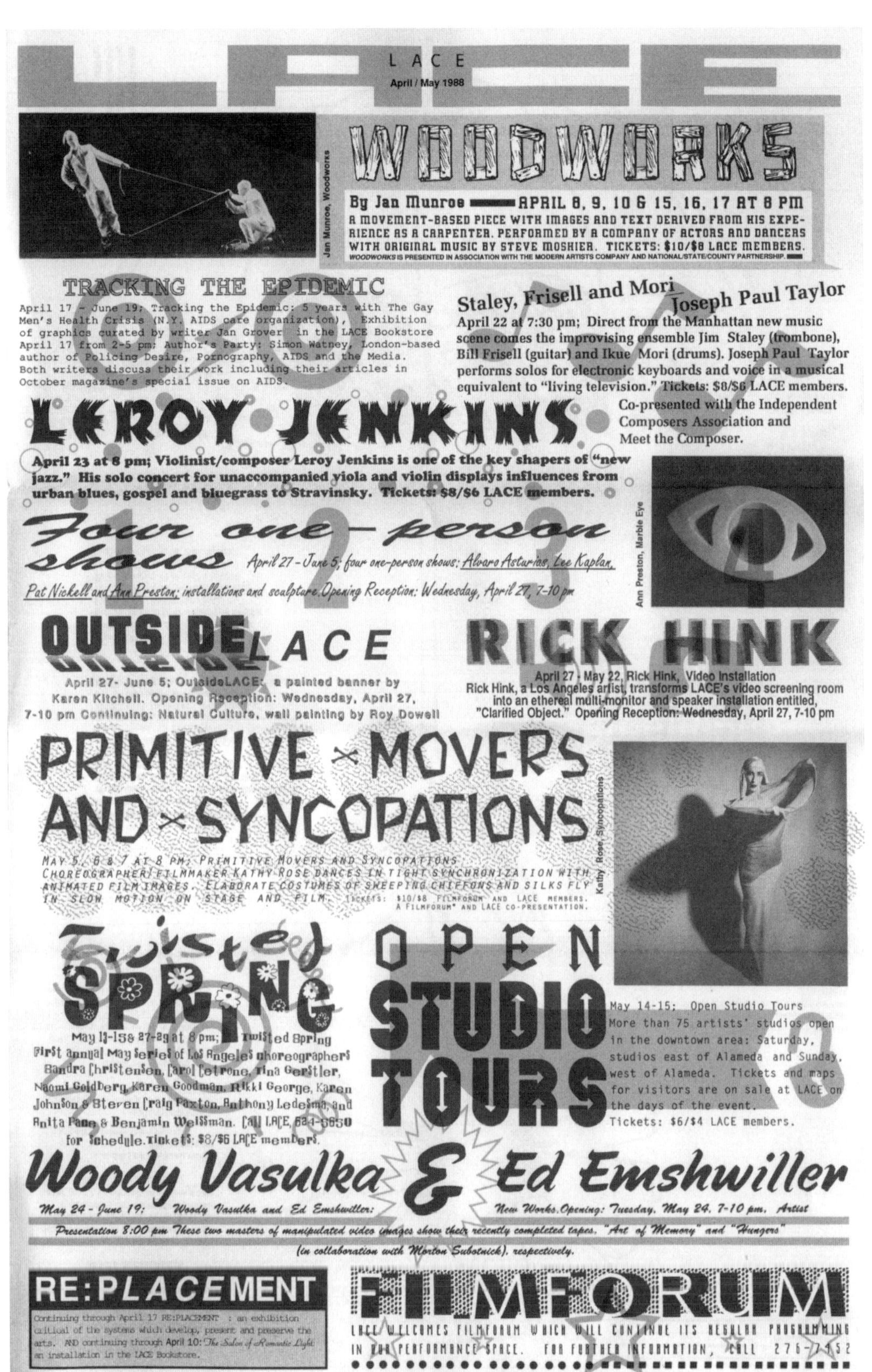

Jan Munroe, Woodworks

TRACKING THE EPIDEMIC

April 17 – June 19: Tracking the Epidemic: 5 years with The Gay Men's Health Crisis (N.Y. AIDS care organization), Exhibition of graphics curated by writer Jan Grover in the LACE Bookstore April 17 from 2-5 pm: Author's Party: Simon Watney, London-based author of Policing Desire, Pornography, AIDS and the Media. Both writers discuss their work including their articles in October magazine's special issue on AIDS.

Staley, Frisell and Mori

Joseph Paul Taylor

April 22 at 7:30 pm: Direct from the Manhattan new music scene comes the improvising ensemble Jim Staley (trombone), Bill Frisell (guitar) and Ikue Mori (drums). Joseph Paul Taylor performs solos for electronic keyboards and voice in a musical equivalent to "living television." Tickets: $8/$6 LACE members.

Co-presented with the Independent Composers Association and Meet the Composer.

LEROY JENKINS

April 23 at 8 pm: Violinist/composer Leroy Jenkins is one of the key shapers of "new jazz." His solo concert for unaccompanied viola and violin displays influences from urban blues, gospel and bluegrass to Stravinsky. Tickets: $8/$6 LACE members.

Four one-person shows

April 27 - June 5: four one-person shows: Alvaro Asturias, Lee Kaplan, Pat Nickell and Ann Preston: installations and sculpture. Opening Reception: Wednesday, April 27, 7-10 pm

Ann Preston, Marble Eye

OUTSIDE LACE

April 27 - June 5: OutsideLACE: a painted banner by Karen Kitchell. Opening Reception: Wednesday, April 27, 7-10 pm Continuing: Natural Culture, wall painting by Roy Dowell

RICK HINK

April 27 - May 22, Rick Hink, Video Installation
Rick Hink, a Los Angeles artist, transforms LACE's video screening room into an ethereal multi-monitor and speaker installation entitled, "Clarified Object." Opening Reception: Wednesday, April 27, 7-10 pm

PRIMITIVE MOVERS AND SYNCOPATIONS

May 5, 6 & 7 AT 8 PM: Primitive Movers and Syncopations Choreographer/filmmaker Kathy Rose dances in tight synchronization with animated film images. Elaborate costumes of sweeping chiffons and silks fly in slow motion on stage and film. Tickets: $10/$8 Filmforum and LACE members. A Filmforum* and LACE co-presentation.

Kathy Rose, Syncopations

Twisted SPRING

May 14-15 & 27-28 at 8 pm: Twisted Spring First annual May series of Los Angeles choreographers Sandra Christensen, Carol Cetrone, Tina Gerstler, Naomi Goldberg, Karen Goodman, Rikki George, Karen Johnson & Steven Craig Paxton, Anthony Ledesma, and Anita Pace & Benjamin Weissman. Call LACE 624-5650 for schedule. Tickets: $8/$6 LACE members.

OPEN STUDIO TOURS

May 14-15: Open Studio Tours More than 75 artists' studios open in the downtown area: Saturday, studios east of Alameda and Sunday, west of Alameda. Tickets and maps for visitors are on sale at LACE on the days of the event. Tickets: $6/$4 LACE members.

Woody Vasulka & Ed Emshwiller

May 24 - June 19: Woody Vasulka and Ed Emshwiller: New Works. Opening: Tuesday, May 24, 7-10 pm. Artist Presentation 8:00 pm These two masters of manipulated video images show their recently completed tapes, "Art of Memory" and "Hungers" (in collaboration with Morton Subotnick), respectively.

RE:PLACEMENT

Continuing through April 17 RE:PLACEMENT : an exhibition critical of the systems which develop, present and preserve the arts. AND continuing through April 10: The Salon of Romantic Light, an installation in the LACE Bookstore.

FILMFORUM

LACE WELCOMES FILMFORUM WHICH WILL CONTINUE ITS REGULAR PROGRAMMING IN THE PERFORMANCE SPACE. FOR FURTHER INFORMATION, CALL 276-7452

1988.10 <u>LACE April/May Events</u>, Calendar

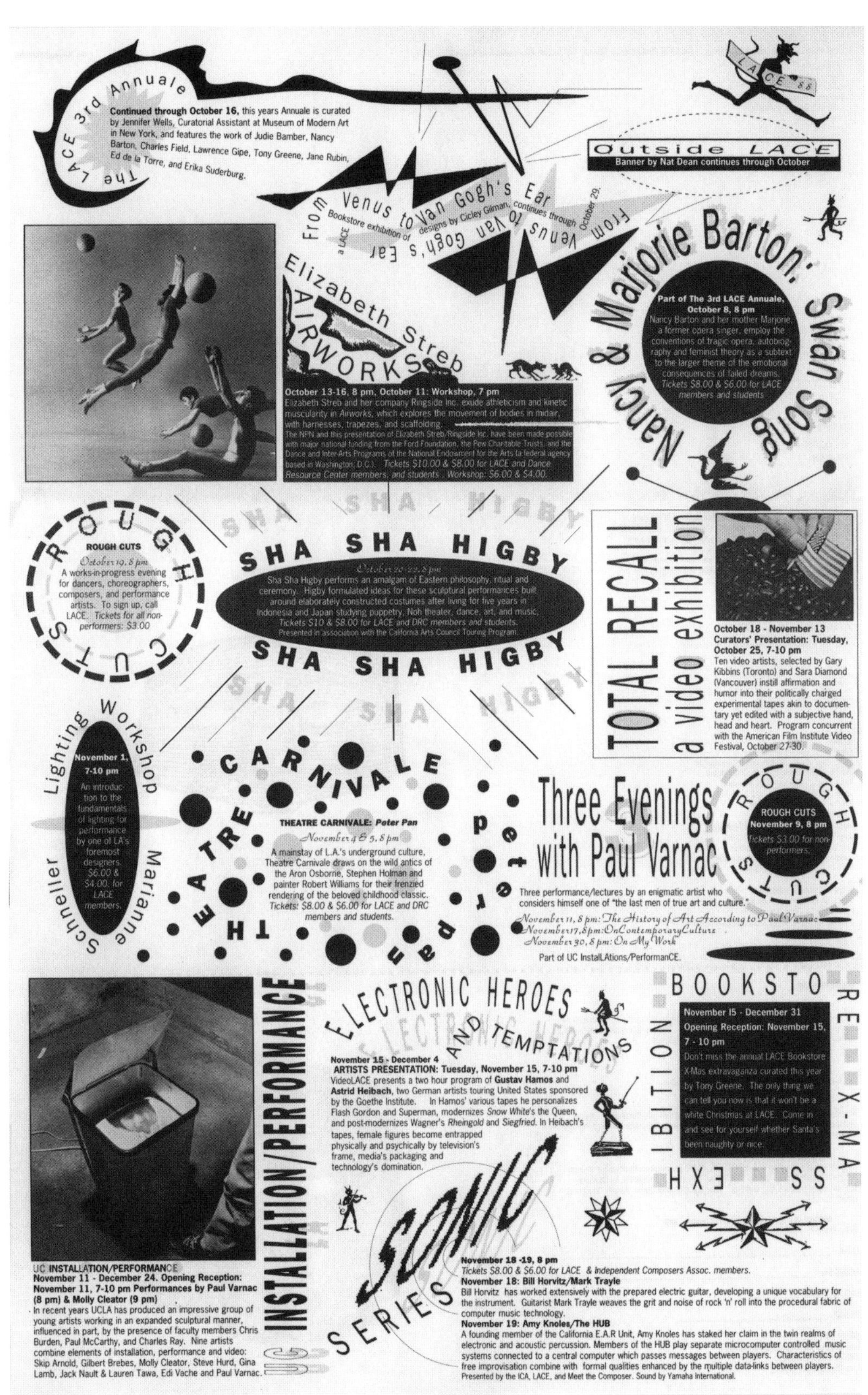

1988.11 <u>LACE</u> Oct./Nov. Events, Calendar

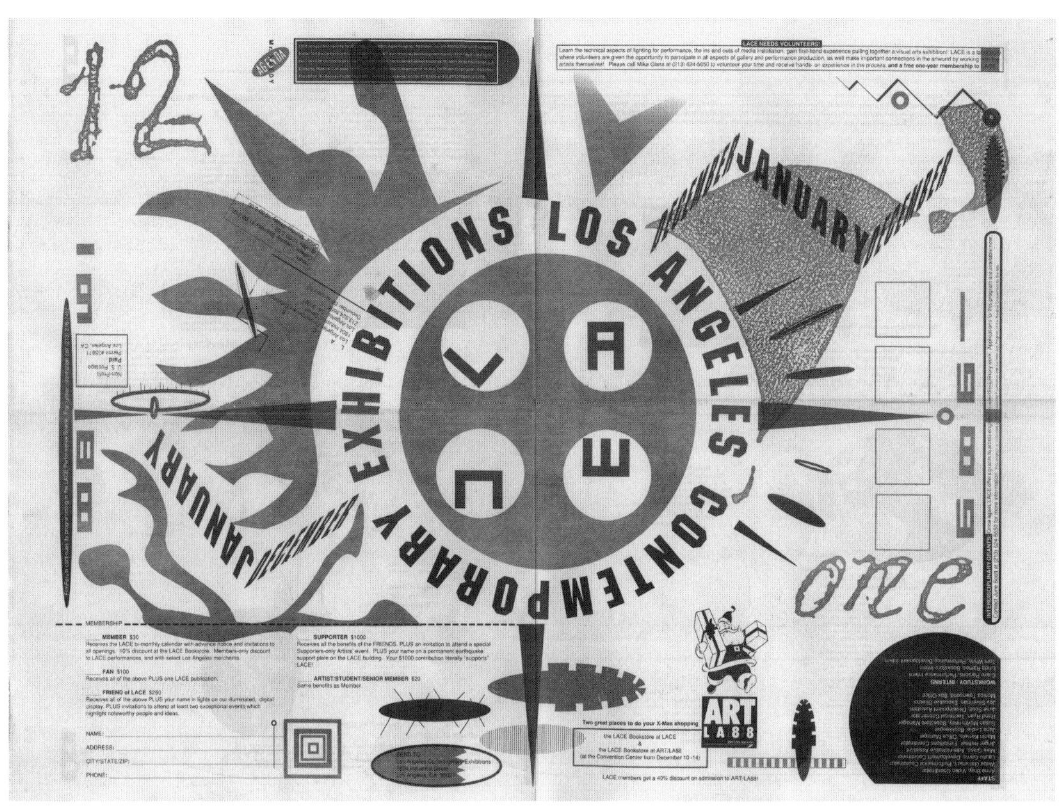

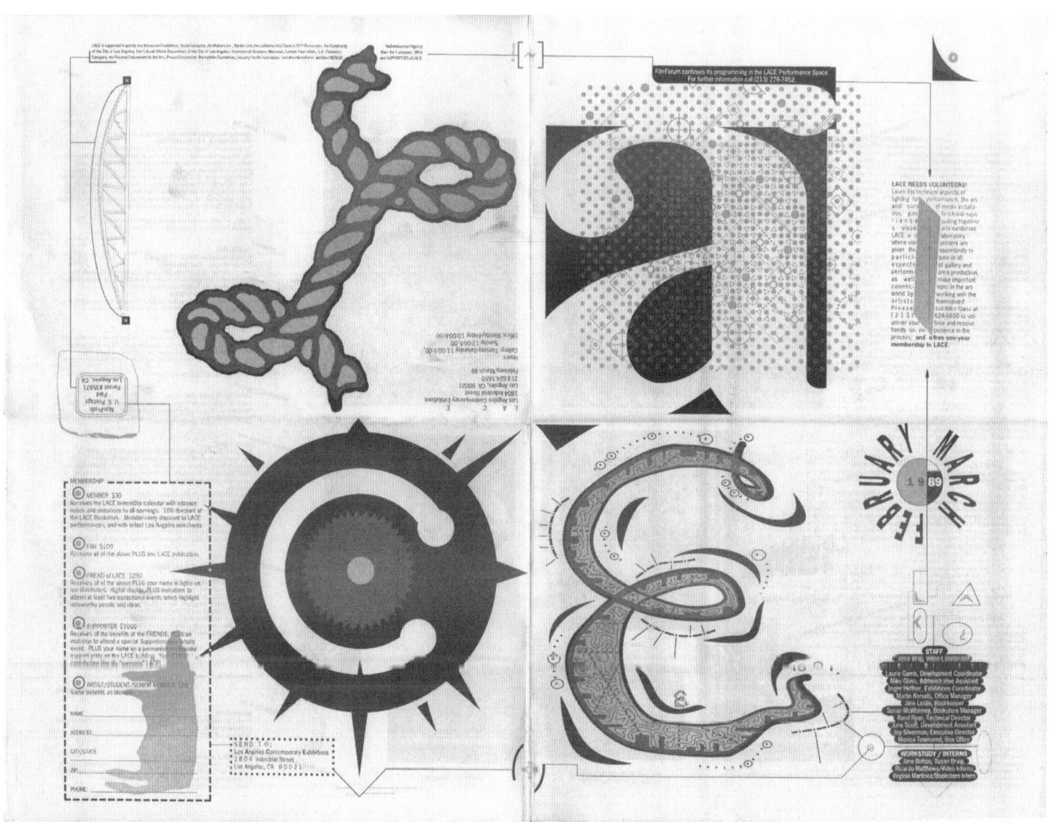

1988.12 <u>LACE Dec./Jan. Events</u>, Calendar
1989.04 <u>LACE Feb./March Events</u>, Calendar

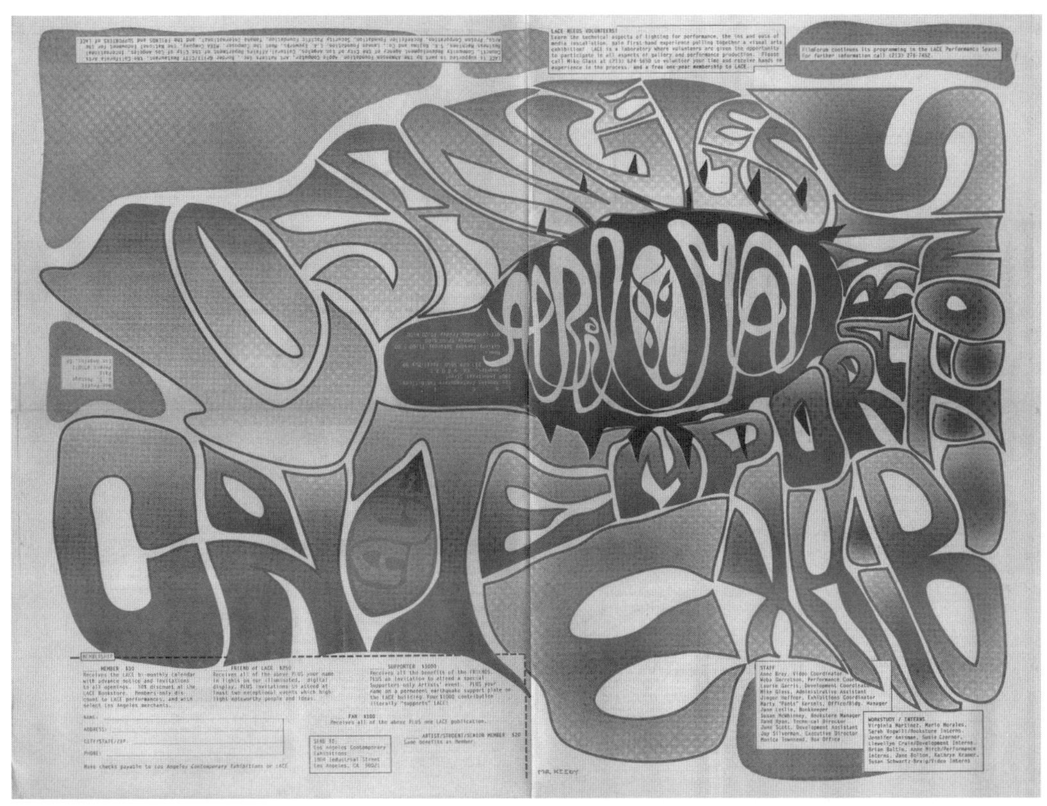

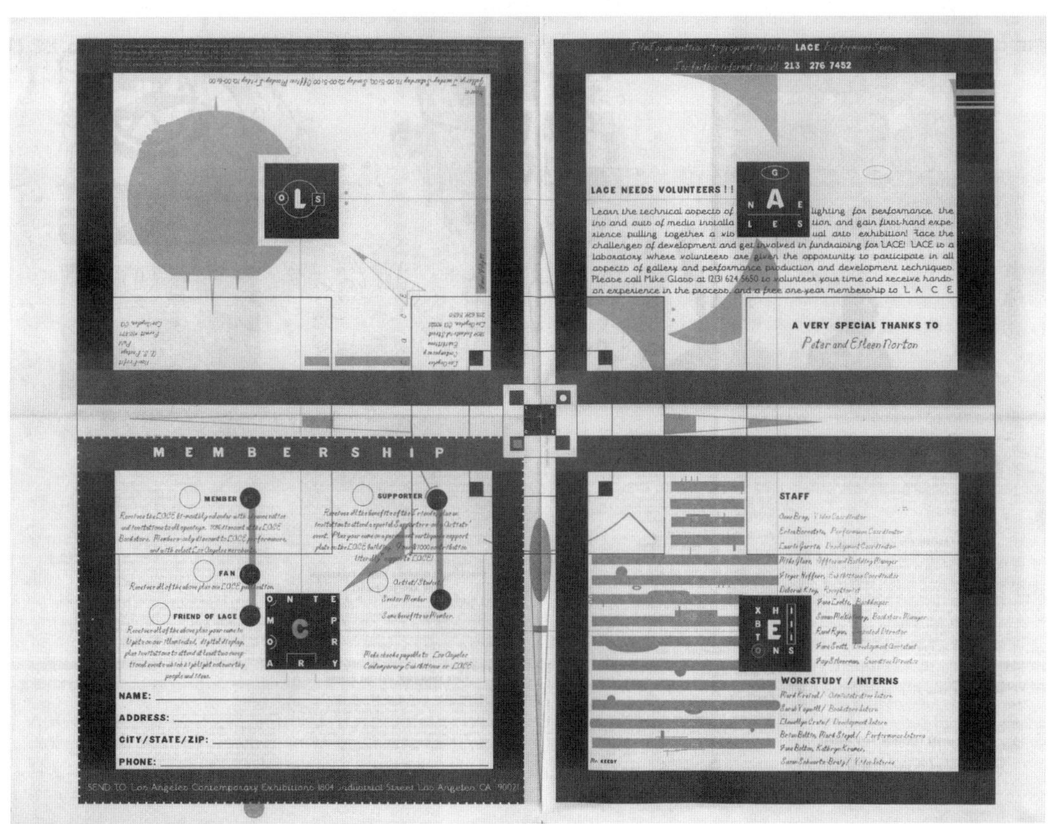

1989.05 <u>LACE</u> April/May Events, Calendar
1989.06 <u>LACE</u> June/July Events, Calendar

1990.01 <u>All But the Obvious: Writing,
Visual Art, Performance, Video
by Lesbians, Catalog</u>

(from) WORLD WITHOUT END

holly hughes

written and performed by Holly Hughes

SHE OPENS HER EYES BUT DOESN'T YET FOCUS ON ANYONE ELSE, HER FOCUS IS STILL INTERNAL. SHE TAKES A LONG DRINK FROM THE VASE AS THE LIGHTS SLOWLY CROSSFADE UP TO A MORE GENERAL, BRIGHTER LEVEL. AFTER THE LIGHTS COME UP, THE WOMAN TAKES A DRINK FROM THE VASE. LIGHTS FADE UP, BECOME MORE GENERAL. THERE IS A SENSE OF WAKING UP. OF COMING "TO." GEE, I HOPE THAT DOESN'T SOUND TOO HOKEY. I THINK IT WORKS.

TO THE AUDIENCE.

All I really wanted from my mother was her French.

THE WOMAN LEANS BACK IN THE CHAIR AND CLOSES HER EYES. REMEMBERING HER MOTHER'S IMMORTAL FRENCH. FROM OFFSTAGE LEFT COMES THE FAINT SOUNDS OF AN ACCORDION. I'D REALLY PREFER A SET OF BAGPIPES, BUT THE ACCORDION IS MORE REASONABLE. THE SONG IS SWEET, LIKE A REMEMBERED CHILDHOOD SONG, SOMETHING UPBEAT, POR FAVOR. THE WOMAN SMILES, THE SONG IS PART OF HER REVERIE. SUDDENLY, HER EYES OPEN. SHE REALIZES THE SONG IS NOT PART OF THE DREAM, BUT IS REALLY HAPPENING. A WOMAN ENTERS PLAYING THE ACCORDION. SHE IS TALL, WITH BROAD SHOULDERS AND GOOD BONES, ELEGANT AND ECCENTRIC. A MID-WESTERN MARLENE DIETRICH, LET'S SAY. SHE'S WEARING A SMOKING JACKET AND VERY LITTLE ELSE OTHER THAN THE ACCORDION. SHE REMINDS YOU OF THOSE SATURDAY MORNINGS WHEN YOUR DAD WOULD DRESS UP LIKE CLARK GABLE AND CHASE YOUR MOTHER AROUND THE BREAKFAST NOOK WITH HIS SEMI-ANNUAL HARD-ON.

AS THE SONG PROGRESSES, THE WOMAN IN THE CHAIR RELAXES AND DIVES BACK INTO HER DREAM. SHE SPEAKS AS THOUGH SHE'S DICTATING A LETTER INTO A FOREIGN LANGUAGE, ONE SHE BARELY KNOWS.

I'd say, "O Mama, I can't sleep at night. I smell the ocean. Not that far-off Atlantic, not the unbelievable Pacific. I'm talking about that old ocean, that blue blanket that used to cover this country, all of us, from the teenage anorexics to the Burger King

remains invisible or silent in mainstream culture. These doctors coax lesbians out of their "twilight world" and thus hope to establish the contours of the normal/abnormal divide. The isolation and identification of visible, recognizable characteristics plays an especially prominent part in this discourse. This attention to narrative descriptions of lesbian lives may seem at odds with the practical invisibility of lesbian subcultures and social attitudes that regard lesbianism as a stigma to be kept out of sight, but it is precisely the need to maintain the boundaries of sexual normality that demands the constant retelling of individual stories of sexual deviance while simultaneously denying lesbian social histories not premised on pathology.

CONTRA DICTIONS

This conflict between modes of representation is hardly abstract, in so far as it constitutes the struggle over definitions of lesbian

16

FIFTEEN

The Theoretical Closet

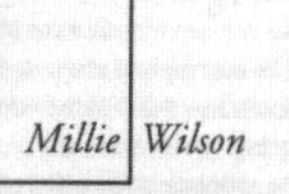

Millie Wilson

Due in part to the virtual absence of the lesbian in feminist and postmodern theory, I devised a retrospective exhibition for a fictitious lesbian artist and called it "Peter (A Young English Girl)." The reference is a portrait of the lesbian painter Gluck by the lesbian painter Romaine Brooks. The show included a deliberately aggrandizing photo blow-up of me, crossdressed as a turn-of-the-century artist/dandy. The show invoked Left Bank lesbians of early modernism, issues of cross-dressing, exoticism, the foibles of history and theory, and the intertwined pathologizing of sexual deviance and race. The following were comments in response to that work. Everyone quoted is more or less an avid reader of postmodernist discourse. Most are engaged with theories of feminism, though many straight feminist friends and colleagues whose practices are informed by gender made no comment at all.

Straight feminist art historian *Someone really should theorize the lesbian gaze.*

Straight feminist friend *You did it so tastefully. No one was offended.*

Lesbian feminist stranger *I was totally outraged and insulted by the title "A Young English Girl." She was clearly an adult woman.*

Closeted lesbian dealer *No one is as interested in this as you are. There are no collectors for this work. Isn't there something else in your life to make art about?*

Straight male critic *It was great. No, I didn't write about it.*

Straight male stranger *It was well done. There was no bitter aftertaste.*

Straight male artist *Last year I invented a lesbian artist and painted all her works for her.*

Straight feminist artist *When I first saw that photograph of you, I thought it was a mistake.*

Gay male editor *That's all very well, but what does your work have to offer gay men?*

Another straight feminist *I've been writing the story of an art historian nineteenth-century lesbian artist. You stole my idea.*

MILLIE WILSON IS CURRENTLY PRODUCING THE MUSEUM OF LESBIAN DREAMS. SHE LIVES IN LOS ANGELES AND DIRECTS THE PROGRAM IN ART AT CALARTS. © 1990, MILLIE WILSON.

evangelists, all of us sleeping with the dinosaurs, the black-capped chickadees, our heads full of fish, waiting to be born.

That's the ocean that floods my bed each night and what can I do about it, Mama?

I get up in the morning and the world is just flat and dry and there is no hint, in the parking lot, at the mall, at the 7-11, of why I am so full of ocean. Do you know what I saw?

I saw a boy grab a cat and sit on it and pee all over it. I saw a man hit his wife so hard the whole house cried, I swear. The big, blue colonial was weeping to see this woman down on her hands and knees, picking up the three bean salad, picking it up, bean by bean.

All I want to do is sleep, Mama. I'm just like everybody else.

But I'm sinking. I'm turning to stone because of what I saw that night: That woman's blood and tears on the dining room shag, snaking out of her, spelling out curses in a language NOT english. She was saying: "I'm sorry, I'm sorry," but her blood was singing another tune. It was singing....SHE PAUSES

16

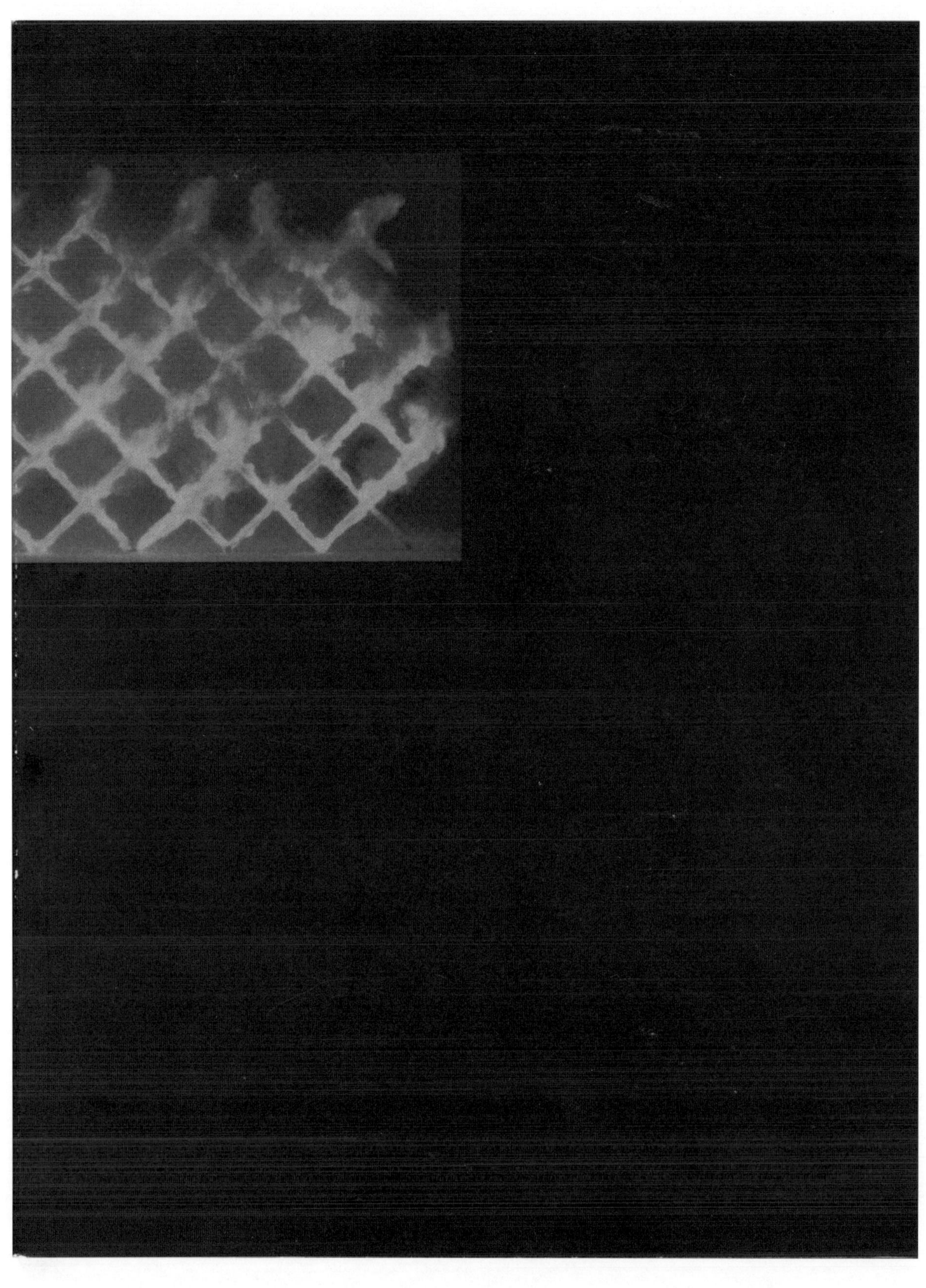

1991.01 <u>Destination L.A.</u>, Catalog

ARTES de MEXICO

FESTIVAL COMMITTEE

C/O USC CIVIC
AND COMMUNITY
RELATIONS
835 WEST 34TH STREET
SUITE 102
LOS ANGELES, CA
90089-0751
(213) 743-5480
FAX: (213) 747-9456

ARMANDO DURON, ESQ.
President

FRANK CRUZ
*Honorary Fundraising
Chairman*

MICHAEL E. ALEXANDER
*Metropolitan
Structures West*

ERWIN BINDER
Artist

EDUARDO DOMINGUEZ
KWHY-TV, Channel 22

JOHN ECHEVESTE
*Valencia, Maldonado
and Echeveste*

PATRICIA H. HAMM
*Mexican Cultural
Heritage Foundation*

SAMUEL MARK
*USC Civic and
Community Relations*

SYBIL ALICIA McNAIR
Gelman & Gray

RAUL MIJARES
*American Institute of
Printing and Graphic Arts*

JESUS PEREZ
Artist / Consultant

VIRGINIA G. RAFELSON
BASE

LORENZA RIO DE ICAZA
Consulate General of Mexico

BEATRIZ OLVERA STOTZER
KCET-TV, Channel 28

MARTHA L. TAPIAS
KMEX-TV, Channel 34

SAL M. VARELA
*Equitable Life
Assurance*

ELENA WELTE
*Luga Corporation
International*

February 15, 1991

Ms. Jinger Heftner
Exhibitions Coordinator
LACE
1804 Industrial Street
Los Angeles, CA 90021

Dear Ms. Heftner:

I am very pleased to inform you that the Review Committee has approved your participation in ARTES DE MEXICO with the project entitled --

"Destination L.A.: Departing from ´One Square Mile of Hell´"

During the coming months, please keep us informed of any new developments regarding your project. We will need all detailed, final information by Wednesday, May 1st, in order for your project to be listed in the ARTES DE MEXICO programs to be published by The Los Angeles Times "Nuestro Tiempo" and La Opinión.

Please include the ARTES DE MEXICO logo in your project´s printed and promotional materials so you can benefit from our planned publicity campaign.

During the summer we will send you an ARTES DE MEXICO poster for display at your project´s site.

Finally, please sign the enclosed participation form and mail it back to us in the envelope provided. Feel free to call me at (818) 985-6859, or Samuel Mark at (213) 740-5480, if you should have questions about your participation in ARTES DE MEXICO.

We look forward to a stimulating and unique project.

Sincerely,

Erwin Binder
Chair, Talent Committee

enclosures

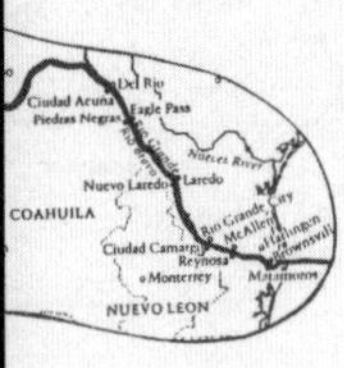

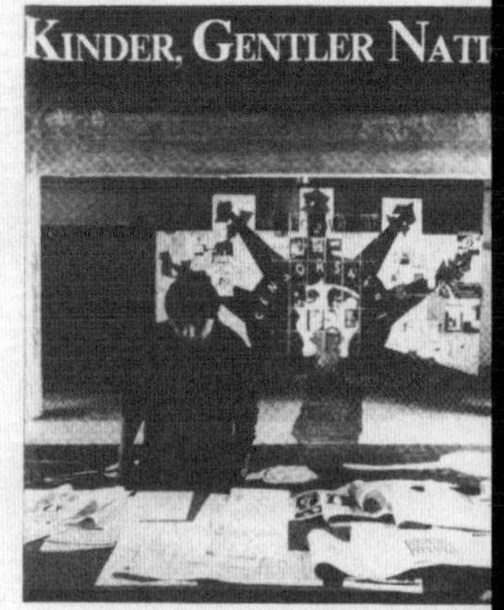

KINDER, GENTLER NATI

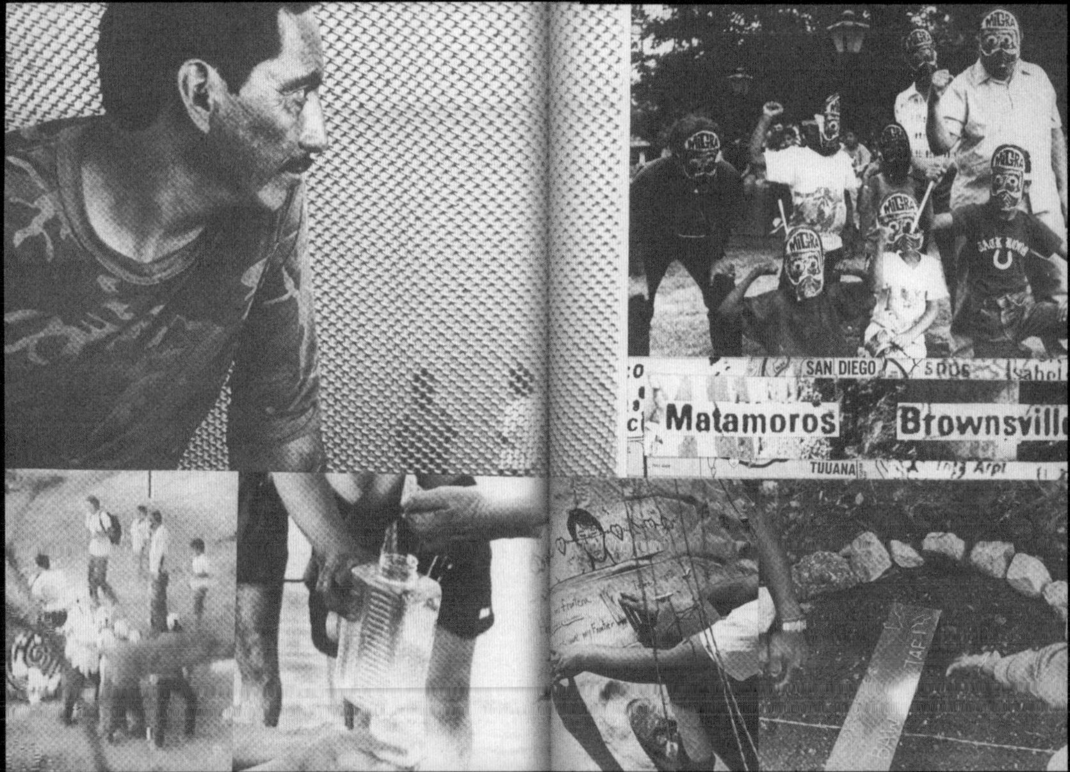

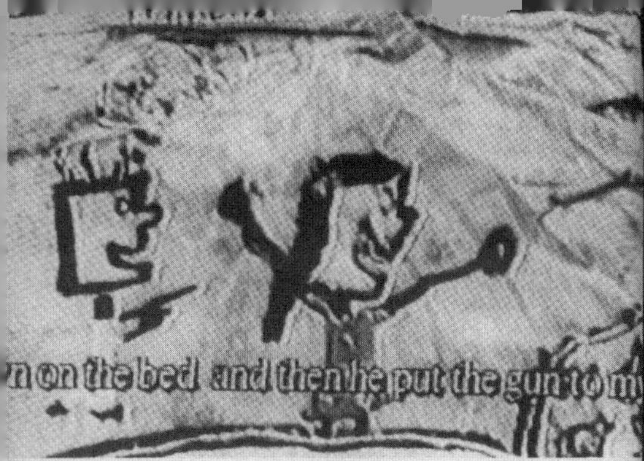

n on the bed and then he put the gun to m
People would give me more respect. I would also be looked up to not looked down on. 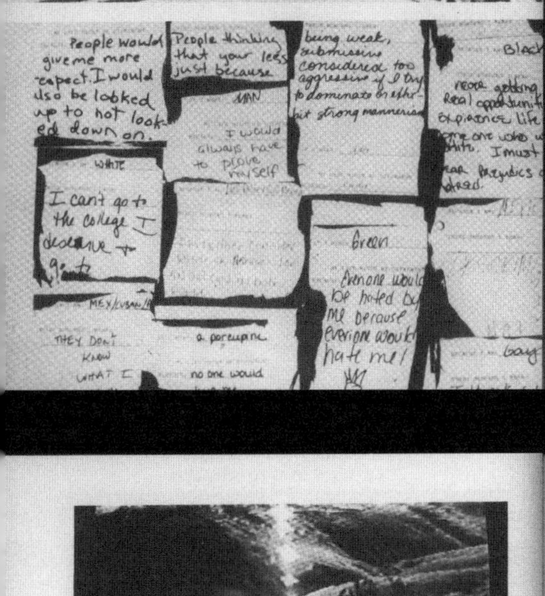
WHITE
I can't go to the college I deserve to go to
MEX/CUBAN
THEY DON'T KNOW WHAT I
People thinking that your less just because
MAN
I would always have to prove myself
a porcupine
no one would
being weak, submissive considered too aggressive if I try to dominate or either bit strong mannerism
Green
Everyone would be hated by me because everyone would hate me!
Black
people getting Real opportunity experience life someone who white. I must fear prejudice hatred.

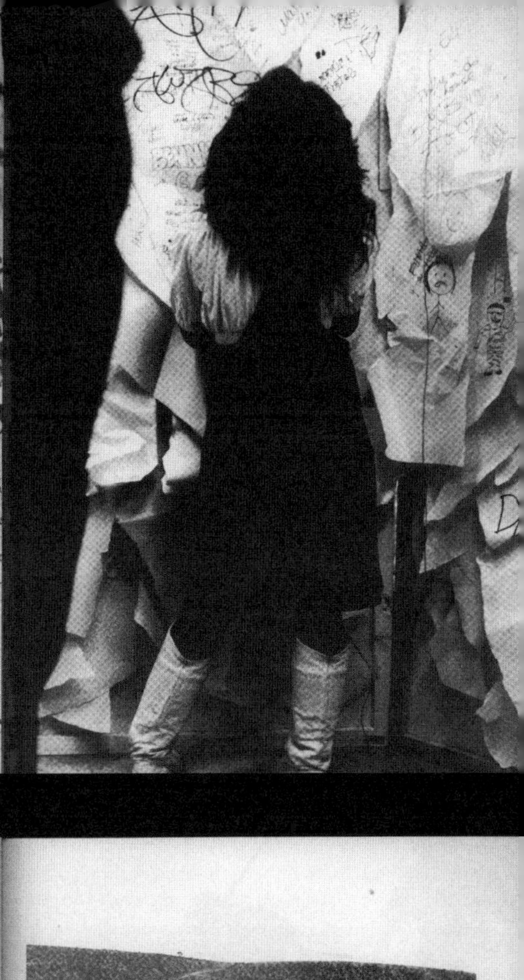

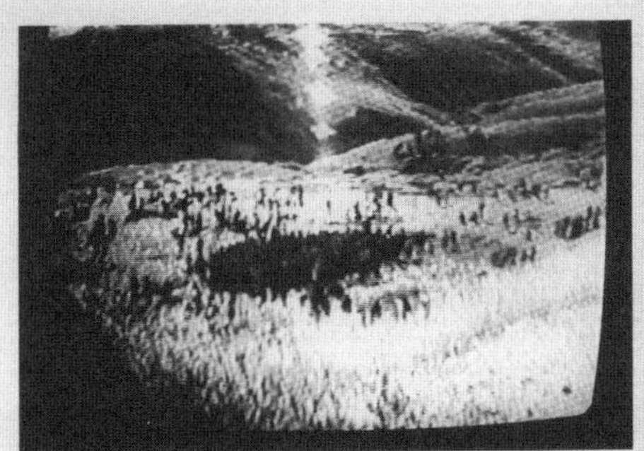

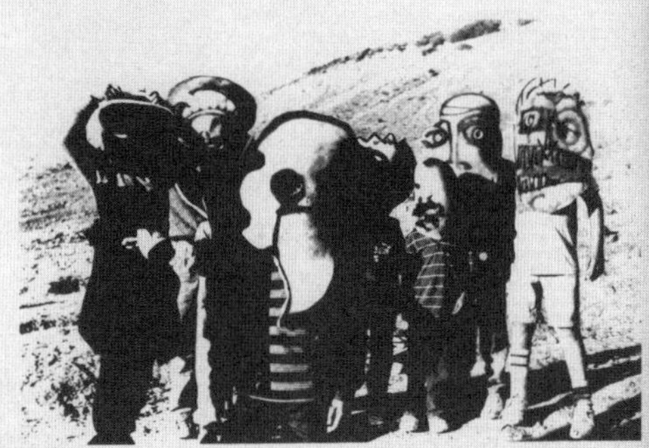

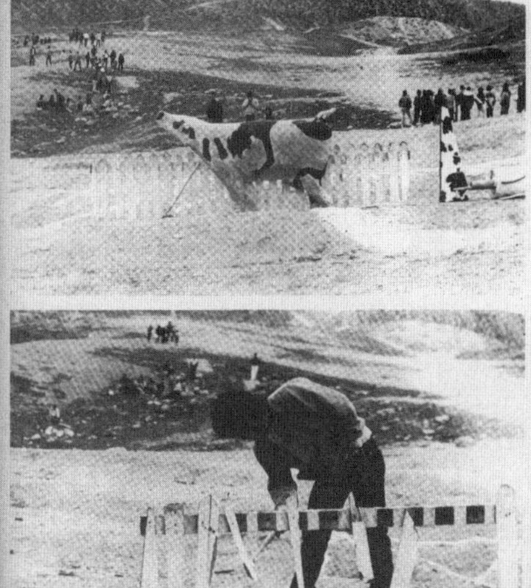

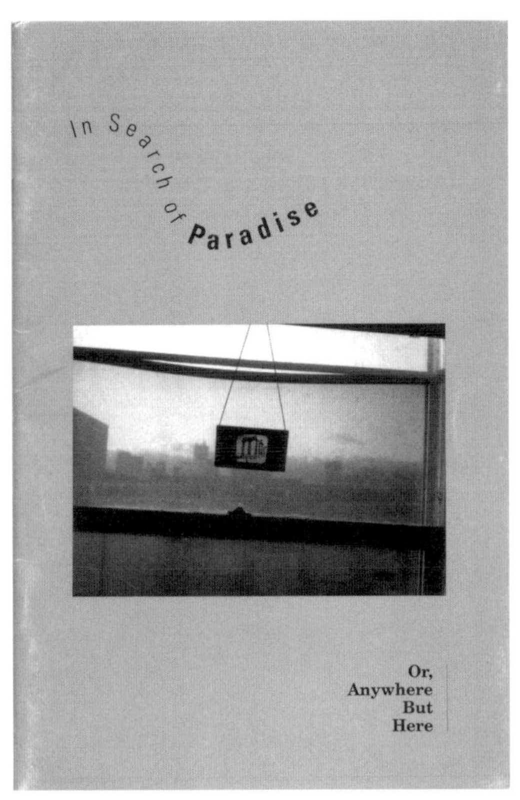

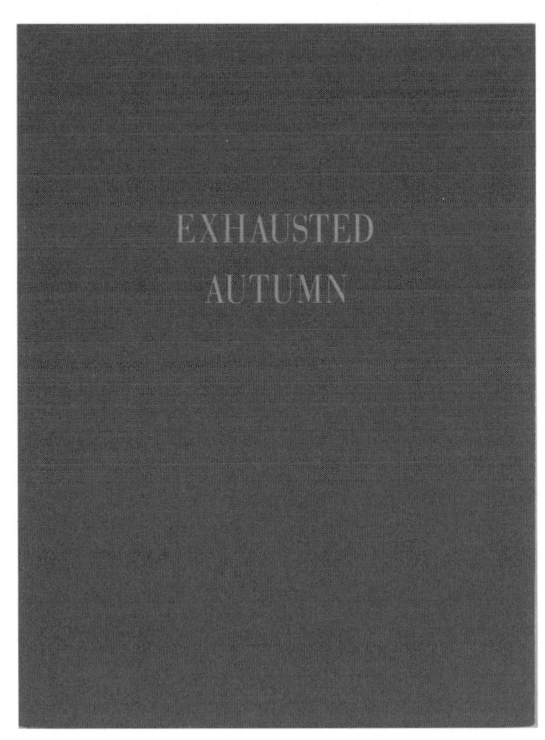

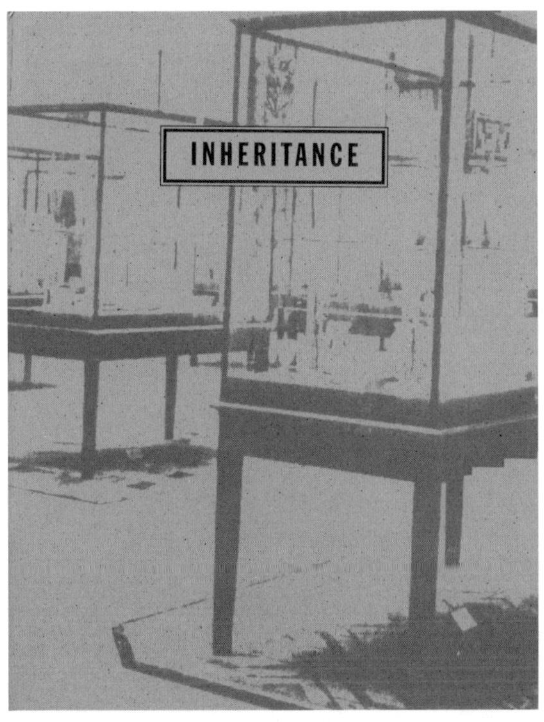

1990.02 In Search of Paradise Or, Anywhere But Here, Catalog
1990.03 how can they be so sure?, Catalog

1991.03 Exhausted Autumn, Book
1992.01 Inheritance, Catalog

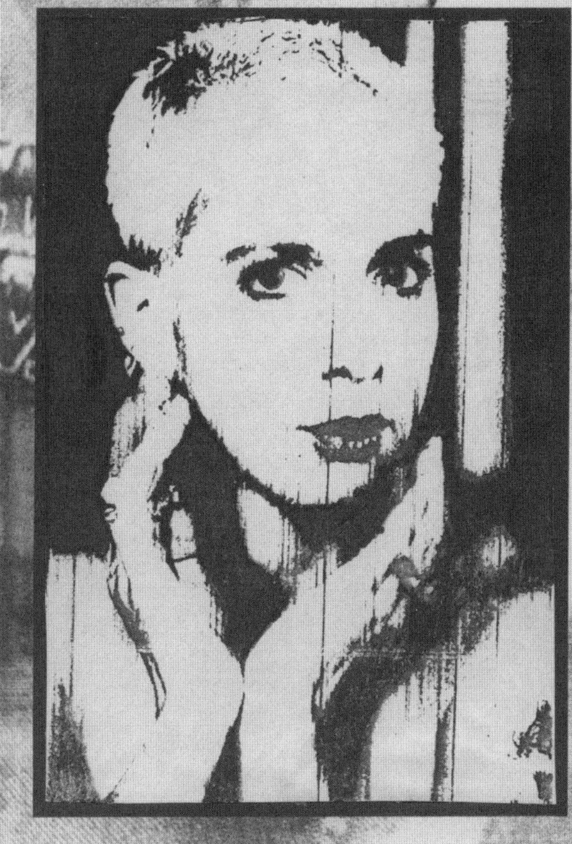

1993.01 Kathy Acker, My Mother:
Demonology, Flyer

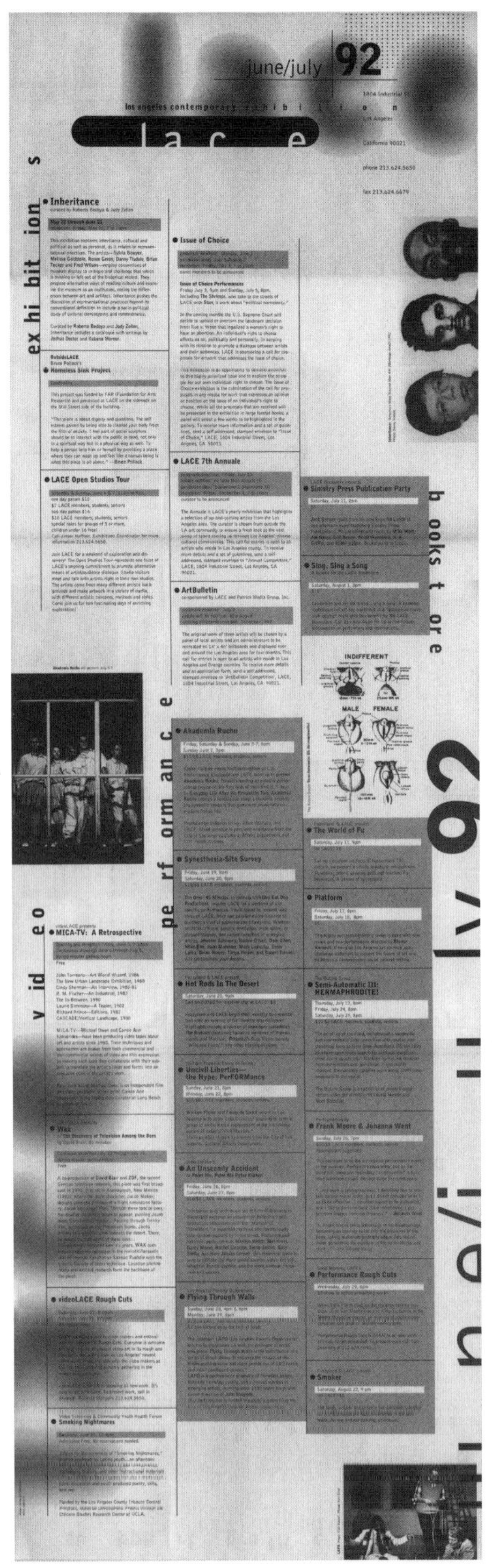

1992.02 <u>LACE</u> June/July Events, Calendar

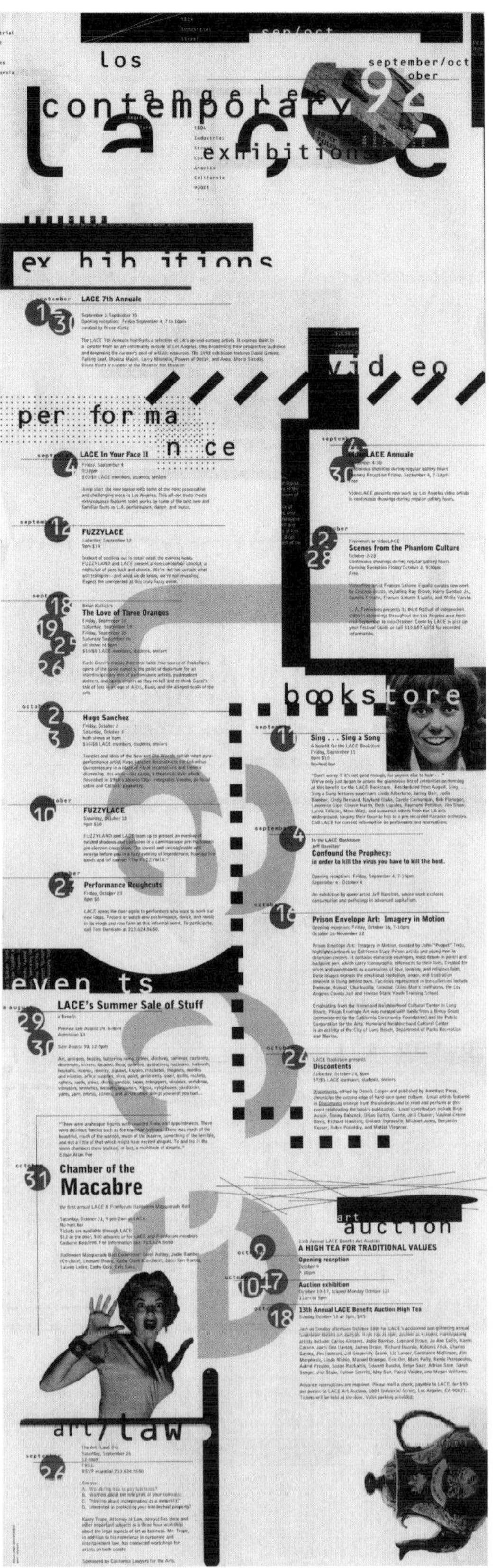

1992.03 <u>LACE</u> Sept./Oct. Events, Calendar

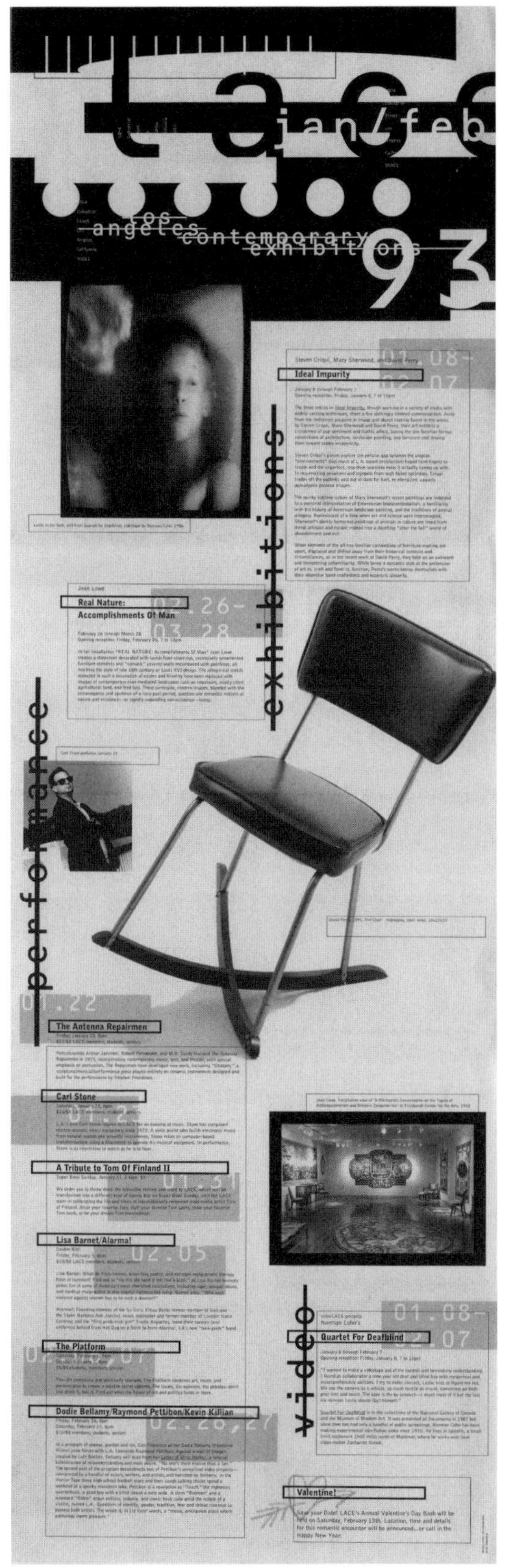

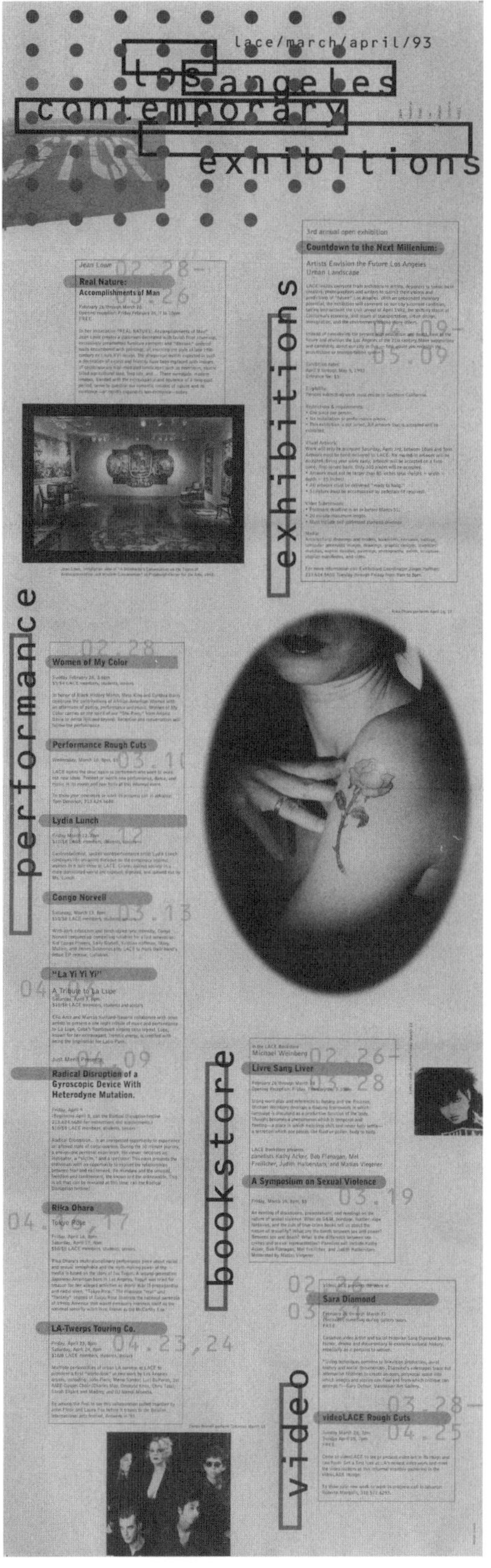

1993.02 <u>LACE</u> Jan./Feb. Events, Calendar   1993.03 <u>LACE</u> March/April Events, Calendar

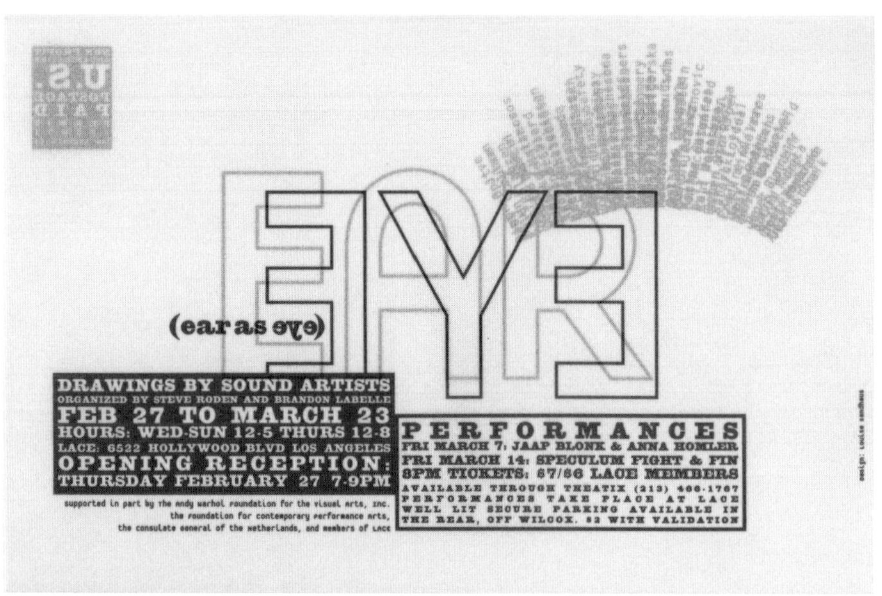

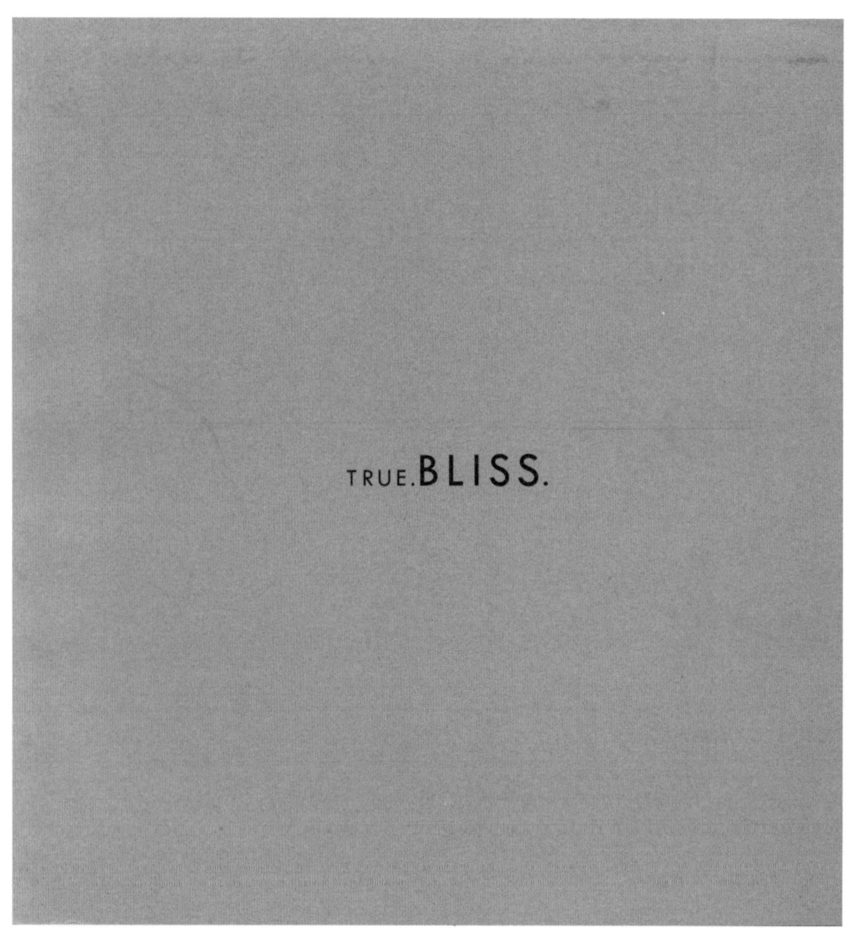

1997.01 Ear as Eye, Postcard
1996.01 True Bliss, Catalog

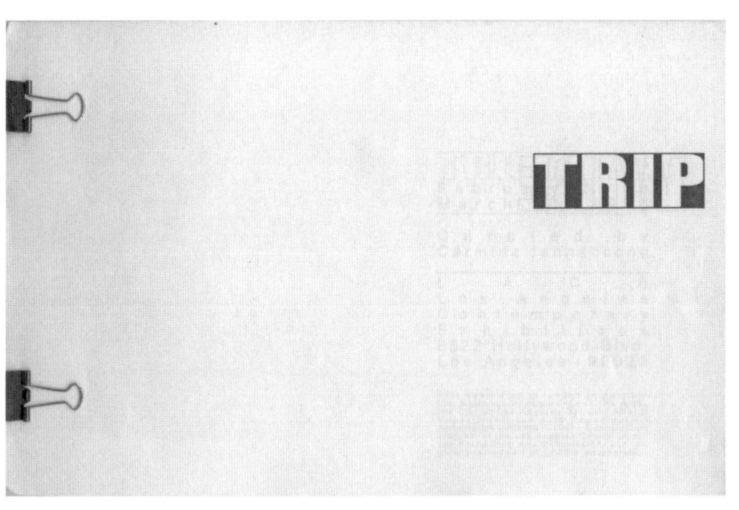

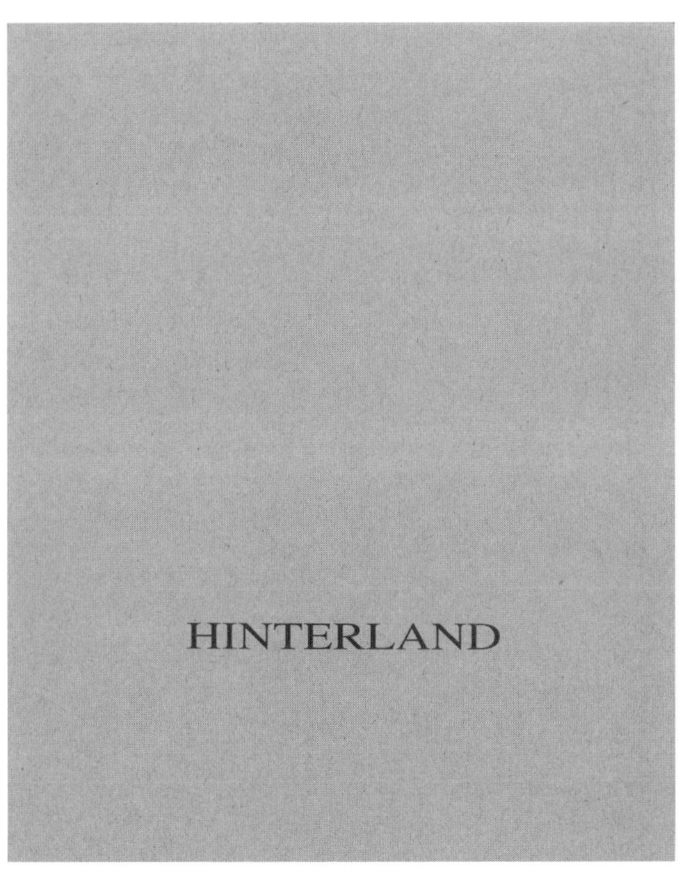

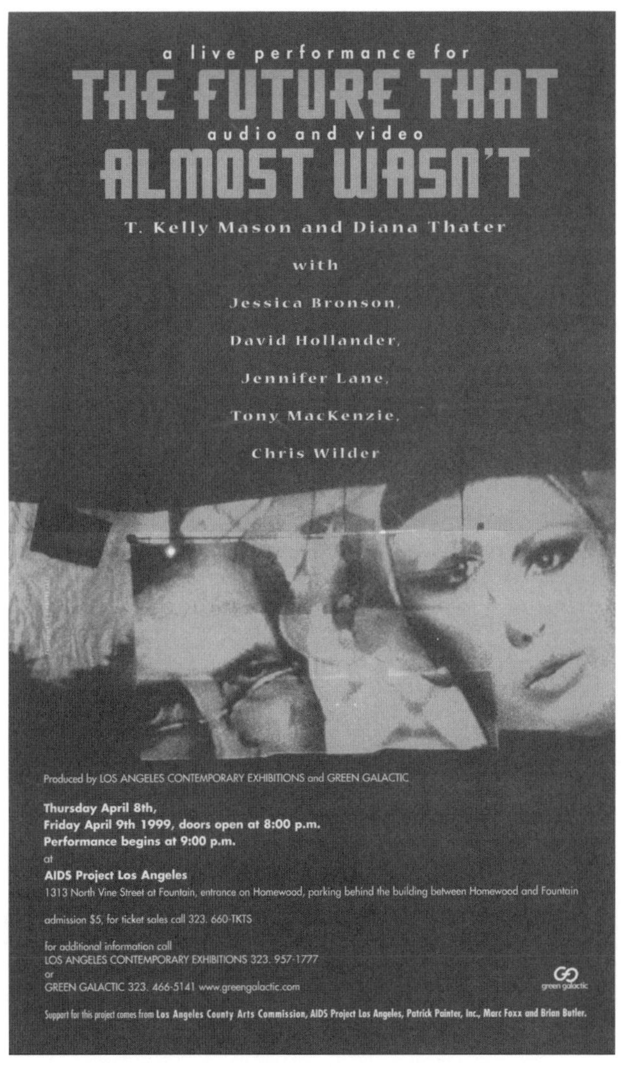

1996.02 <u>Tripwire</u>, Booklet
1997.02 <u>Hinterland</u>, Catalog

1999.01 <u>The Future that Almost Wasn't</u>,
Flyer

Tri-Annuale PART 1

Julien Bismuth, Anthony Burdin, Matthew Greene, Shawn King - guest curated by Andrea Zittel

Please join us for a Bombay Sapphire martini at the opening reception Thursday 22 July 1999

7 pm to 9 pm — Exhibition runs through Saturday 14 August 1999 Los Angeles Contemporary
Exhibitions 6522 Hollywood Boulevard Los Angeles, CA 90028 p 323 9571777

Supported by the LLWW Foundation, The Good Works Foundation, The Peter Norton Family
Foundation, The Plum Foundation, the City of Los Angeles Cultural Affairs Department,
Grant Division, and the members of Los Angeles Contemporary Exhibitions.

Tri-Annuale (Part 2): Amy Adler curates
JONI MITCHELL

OPENING RECEPTION WEDNESDAY 1 DECEMBER 1999 FROM 6-8 P.M.
EXHIBITION RUNS THROUGH THURSDAY 23 DECEMBER 1999

lās

LOS ANGELES CONTEMPORARY EXHIBITIONS
6522 Hollywood Blvd LA CA 90028 T 323.957.1777 F 323.957.9025
www.artleak.com

Supported by the LLWW Foundation, the City of Los Angeles Cultural Affairs Department Grant
Division, California Arts Council and the members of Los Angeles Contemporary Exhibitions.

TRI-ANNUALE (PART 3): PINWHEEL

Gregg Einhorn, Michele O'Marah, Brent Petersen

organized by Jason Meadows

OPENING RECEPTION SATURDAY 8 APRIL FROM 5-7 P.M.
EXHIBITION RUNS THROUGH SATURDAY 29 APRIL 2000

lās

LOS ANGELES CONTEMPORARY EXHIBITIONS
6522 Hollywood Blvd LA CA 90028 T 323.957.1777 F 323.957.9025
www.artleak.com

Supported by the LLWW Foundation, the California Arts Council, and the members of
Los Angeles Contemporary Exhibitions, with special thanks to EZTV.

1999.02 <u>Tri-Annuale (Part 1)</u>, Postcard   1999.03 <u>Tri-Annuale (Part 2)</u>, Postcard

2000.01 <u>Tri-Annuale (Part 3)</u>, Postcard

Subject: Re: No Subject
Date: Tue, 11 Apr 2000 14:50:02 EDT
From: AmyAdler@aol.com
To: irenetsatsos@artleak.com

Irene...here is a draft....please let me know what you think...also please
advise on the use of LACE or how you'd prefer it abbreviated...Amy

Gilles: Here is a more refined draft, please let me know if there appear to
be any kinks or embarrassing things, I'm back in London and more than a bit
jet lagged. Also I've included a suggestion for the preface and biography,
they're basically suggestions so please feel free to make editorial changes.
Thanks, Amy

In December 1999 an exhibition of Joni Mitchell's paintings was held at Los
Angeles Contemporary Exhibitions (LACE). The show was curated by Amy Adler
and is described here, in a letter to a friend.

Dear Tom:

Thanks for going to see the show at LACE. I do appreciate your question about
why I didn't write a "statement" to accompany the show. There was quite a
debate-whether I should write one or not- I opted not too and there are a few
reasons why.
I do want to tell you about it though, as it was quite the miraculous
experience. (I hope you have a minute)...

When Irene Tsatsos, (the director of Los Angeles Contemporary Exhibitons)
asked me to curate a show at LACE, quite honestly, a show of Joni Mitchell's
painting was the first thought that came to mind. I quickly got a hold of my
senses, however, and figured I'd choose recent graduates from this school or
that and artists I know for the show. But the Joni thing strangely haunted me.
I've always wondered about the fact that her paintings only exist within the
protected confines of her music, in her lyrics as well as on her record
covers. The only way to see them has been, for me, in reproduction and always
chaperoned by her voice.

So last spring, I presented the idea to Irene who, to my great surprise, got
totally excited. It was inspiring. The challenge then was to see if I could
actually stand face to face with Joni's paintings and then to see if it would
be even remotely possible to borrow them. I didn't know Joni Mitchell at all
so part of it at that point was whether or not I could actually do it, reach
into her music, so to speak, and have a look around.

There began an adventure I will never forget. I figured if I was gonna take
on this LACE show on top of my own insane schedule, it better be a worthy
adventure! Well, in a most miraculous chain of events a friend of mine,
Denise Railla, introduced me to the great jazz musician Wayne Shorter. Wayne
has played on many of Joni's records and is very close with her. I was able
to suggest the idea to him and he got super excited too! He called her up
and the next thing you know I was having sushi in Burbank with Joni Mitchell!

An intense summer of late night phone calls followed. She's a night owl and I
was living in London so the conversations were a bit hallucinogenic. It took

2000.02 Amy Adler E-mail correspondence.
April 11, 2000

a while for her to commit, trust me maybe, and so I didn't mention the
project to a sole until I felt that she was fully into it. Anyway we made a
date to meet to look at the work. I went over to her place one evening at 5pm
and left at 2am. We ordered in tuna melts and French-fries. She smoked
incessantly and though I'd quit earlier in the summer I smoked incessantly
too.

She showed me maybe thirty paintings all done in the past ten years. Pretty
prolific if you asked me. She doesn't sell them or give them away so they
were all there, in her private collection. I was amazed to stand there in the
room with the paintings, face to face, as a month earlier I'd only imagined!
We made the initial selection that night.

We decided to limit the selection to work done in the 90's since the show was
not meant to be a survey but rather to show her recent and current work. I
tried to be fair to her interests and accurate to her subject matter. It was
important to include landscapes, portraits, her cats, and her friends. Great
stories surround each of the works, little fragments and glimpses of a
private life of sweet and simple pleasures. My favorite story is of her cat
Nietchze who disappeared one afternoon. Joni didn't have a photo of him so
she painted his picture and passed it around to all her neighbors. Someone
recognized him from the painting and called her up and Nietchze was saved. I
just had to include that painting in the show.

We talked a lot about art school and her trials as a figurative painter in a
period heavily influenced by abstract expressionism. Her instructors tried to
send her off to study illustration. (I went to art school years later of
course but I definitely could relate.) That was the point in her life that
she chose to become a musician and she told me that her friends were
surprised by her choice to pursue a career in music instead of art. She
talked about the art world and why she has stayed out of it. It's not about
that for her. Anyway she doesn't draw the content of her painting from the
same place she draws her music. She looked at me rather intensely and said,
"Music is my sorrow, painting is my joy". She seems to paint the things she
loves and things she wants to look at. She told me she often paints lying on
the carpet with the television on, returning to the way it was when she was a
child, when drawing and painting were about pleasure and fun.

Joni often works on a painting for years, thinking of them as studies, in
pursuit of her own mastery. Her struggle is very apparent and I respect that
about the work. It is riddled with trials, but it is, in my opinion strangely
balanced by moments of subtle mastery. Interesting to look at because they
are determined, yet vulnerable.

She made three new paintings during that time that will be on her new record
which is called "Both Sides Now" that is due out this spring. A really
beautiful and haunting record I must say. Anyway I thought it was really cool
to be able to see, in this case, the paintings first before they're released
with her record. I can't wait for the record to come out, to witness the
cycle in reverse. Remember the portrait of her smoking in the green jacket?
(as you walked into the show) well that will be on the cover of her CD.
That's exciting to me, talk about "Both Sides Now".

She and I installed the show together at LACE a few days before the opening.
We had a great time. LACE seemed perfect for the show, raw, non-commercial
and kind of neutral but very real. I chose not to write a statement mostly
because I wanted her paintings to really be looked at and experienced on
their own terms. I didn't want it to be about my project, I wanted to
disappear and let her have the moment, which is pretty much what happened.
Between her celebrity and my intentions it was a miracle that the attention
could remain on her work. I don't doubt that critics will want to understand

the association and of course this interests me too but the exhibition itself
was all about Joni's paintings. That was my objective and probably the main
reason for my silence. But despite my official silence I have had endless
passionate conversations about the project with all kinds of people that have
been fascinating. It seemed people could relate on lots of different levels.

Once the show was hung I had a quiet moment to see the work alone. I found
myself going from painting to painting seeing things I had never seen. Like
the quality of light in her landscapes and the color of snow, which is
sometimes anxious, and sometimes comforting. Her compositions seem
constructed of precarious angles, which made me at times feel I was part of
the scene at other times I felt completely alienated from it. I was
disoriented suddenly by the changing positions of her self portraits, in one
painting Joni is in the canoe, then she is looking at it as it cruises by and
then her gaze is turned toward shore. I also found myself leaping from
surface to surface watching the strange build up of paint around a white sun
and unexpected colors appearing in a sort of secret conversation. It was like
the works split open for a second but then someone else walked in the gallery
and they became very private works again. When I left I knew that the next
time I saw the works would be once again, on her records and at a great
distance. I wonder if there is a connection there to her painting, for
example, these majestic Canadian landscapes from her home in Los Angeles, a
kind of longing to be in the presence of something otherwise completely
inaccessible.

Finally I have to tell you about the opening. She came in royal fashion,
looking glamorous and being very open to everyone. I introduced her to all my
friends. I wish you could've been there. We had a tiny party at Irene's and
Joni came and everyone was able to talk with her. She was very gracious and
lovely.

So Tom, that's probably the short version if you can believe it. When LACE
asked me to do this I never imagined it would become the treasured experience
that it was.
So I am, needless to say, thrilled you got a chance to see it. I hope this
helped a little to explain the project. The whole thing was very intimate
anyway so maybe the experience is best described just like this, one to one,
y'know?

Sending you lots of love,

Amy

Letter to Tom Knechtel (December 1999)

Amy Adler was born in 1966 in New York City and lives in Los Angeles. She is
an artist who has exhibited her work internationally and recently had her
first one person museum show at the Museum of Contemporary Art In Los
Angeles. She is currently an artist in residence in London at the Delfina
Studio Trust.
Tom Knechtel is an artist living in Los Angeles and a good friend of Amy's.

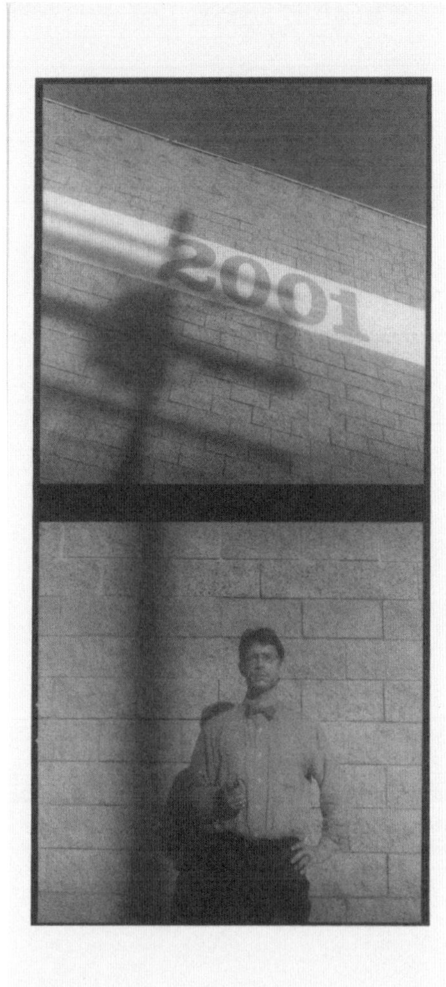

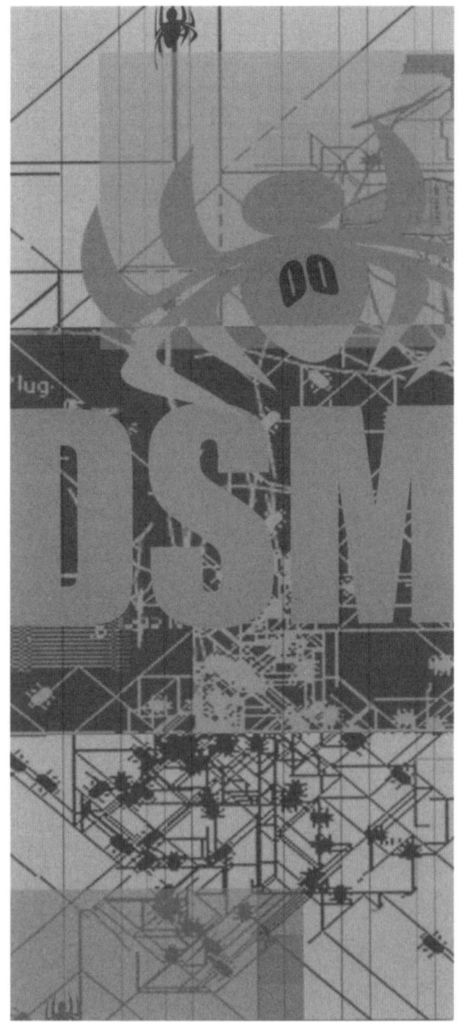

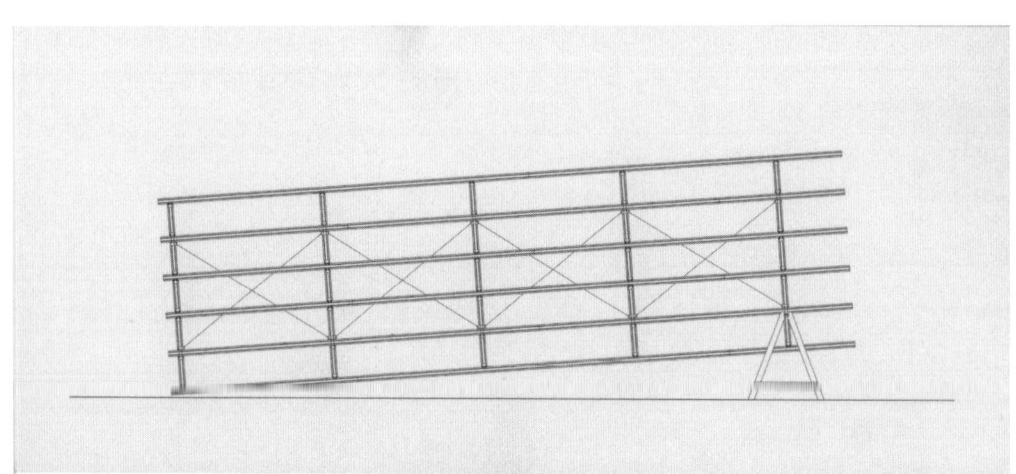

2001.01 <u>Daniel Marlos, TimeLine</u>, Postcard   2002.01 <u>Das Spyder-Man</u>, Postcard

2003.01 <u>Chris Burden, Small Skyscraper</u>, Postcard

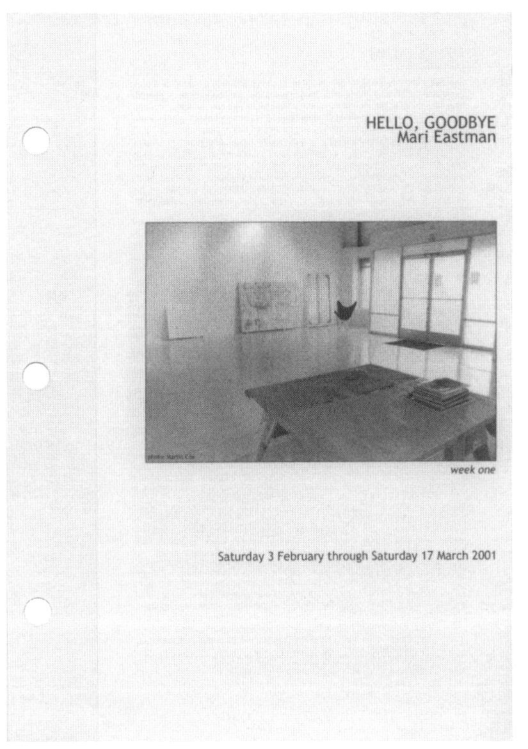

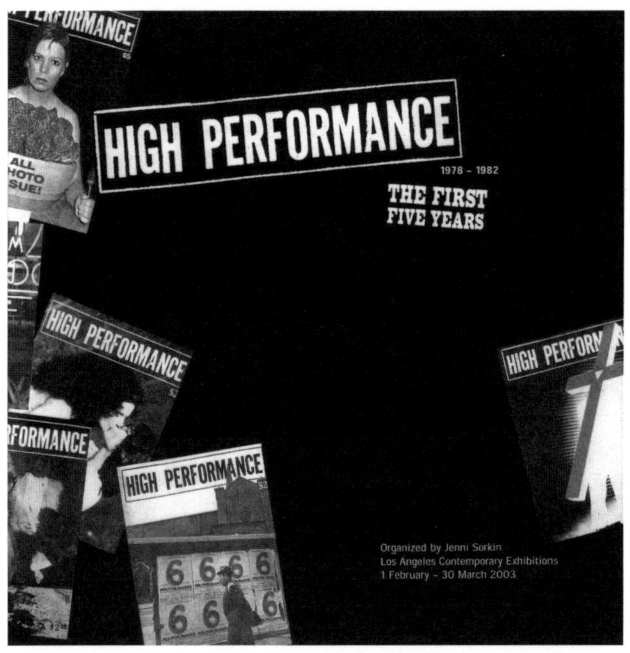

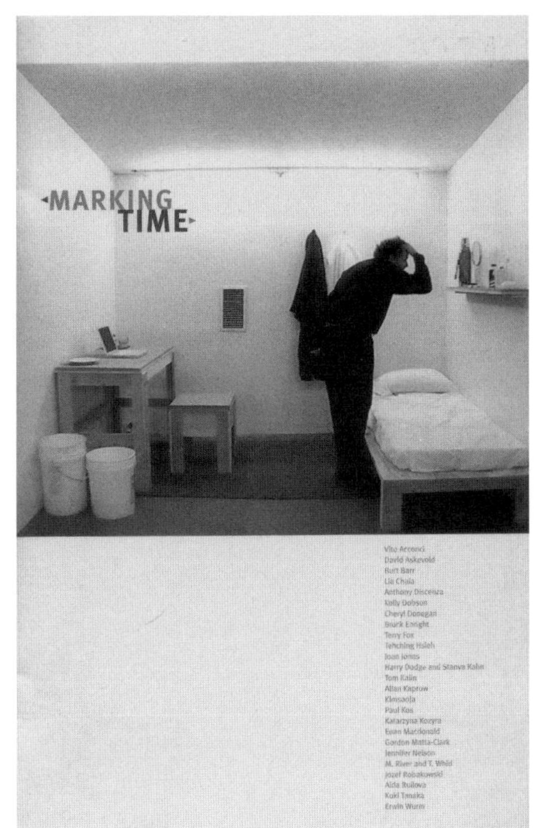

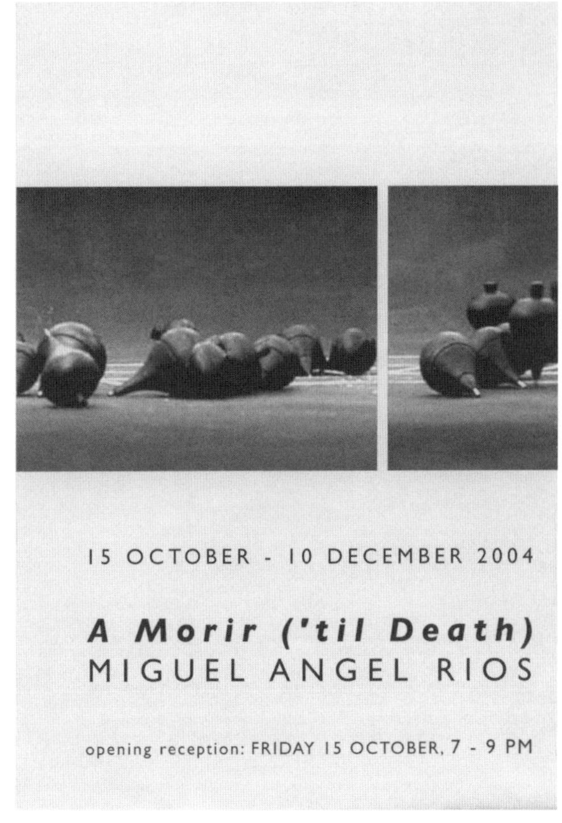

2001.02 Mari Eastman, HELLO, GOODBYE, Brochure

2005.01 Marking Time, Brochure

2003.02 High Performance: The First Five Years, 1978-1982, Brochure

2004.01 Miguel Angel Rios, A Morir ('til Death), Poster

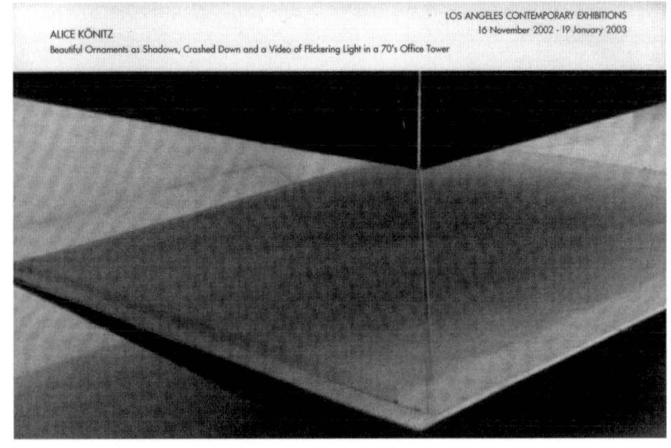

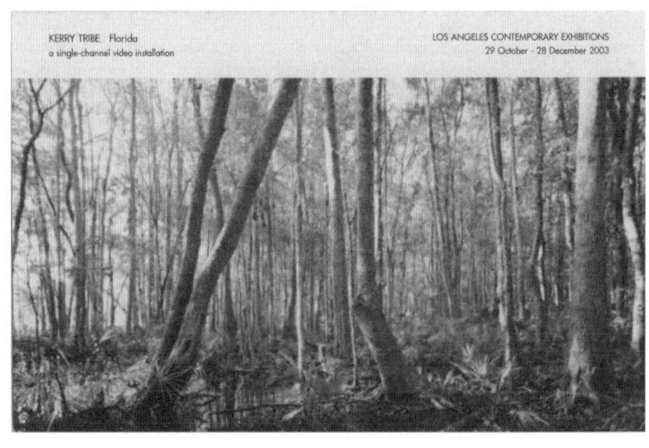

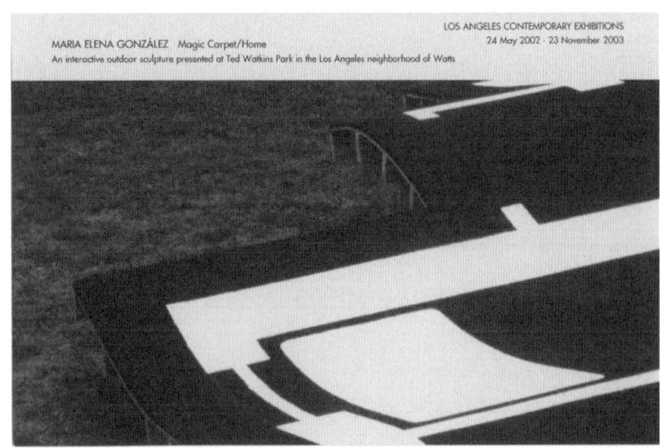

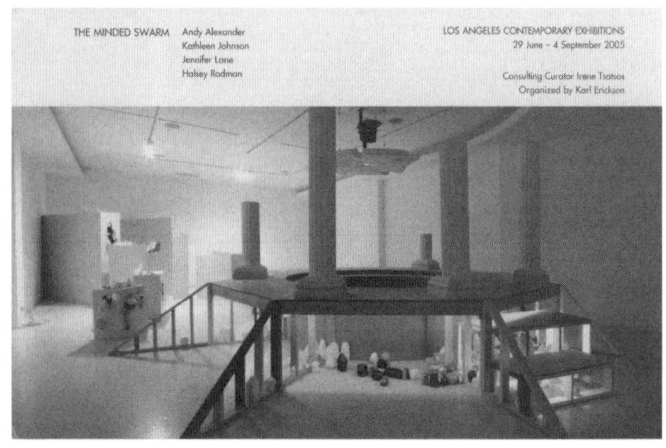

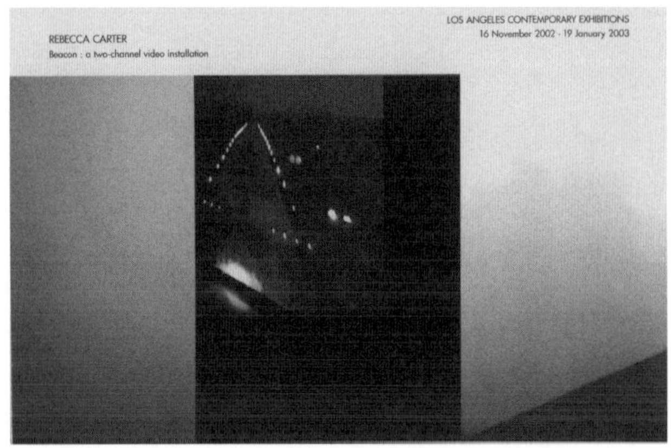

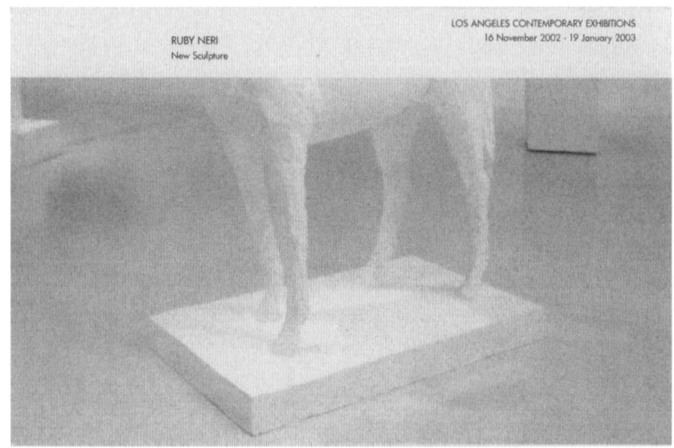

2002.02 <u>Alice Könitz</u>, Brochure

2002.03 <u>Maria Elena Gonzalez, Magic Carpet/Home</u>, Brochure

2002.04 <u>Rebecca Carter, Beacon</u>, Brochure

2003.03 <u>Kerry Tribe, Florida</u>, Brochure

2005.02 <u>The Minded Swarm</u>, Brochure

2002.05 <u>Ruby Neri, New Sculpture</u>, Brochure

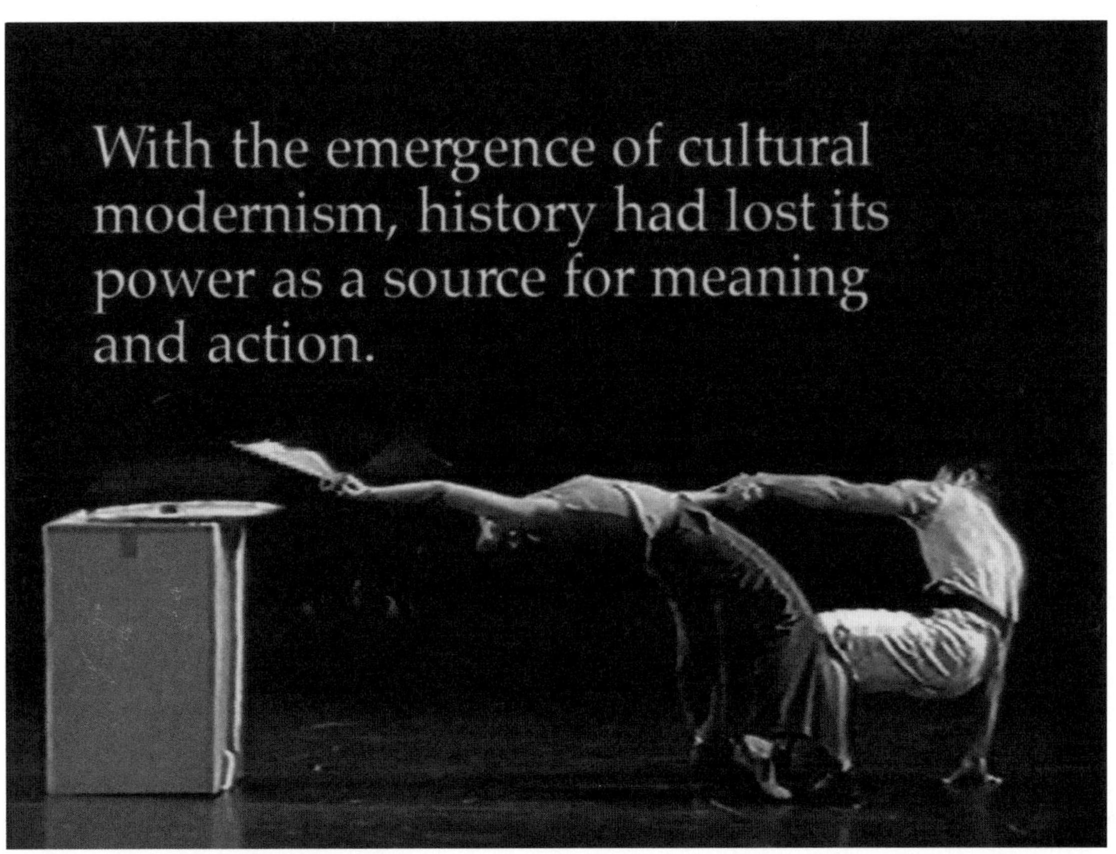

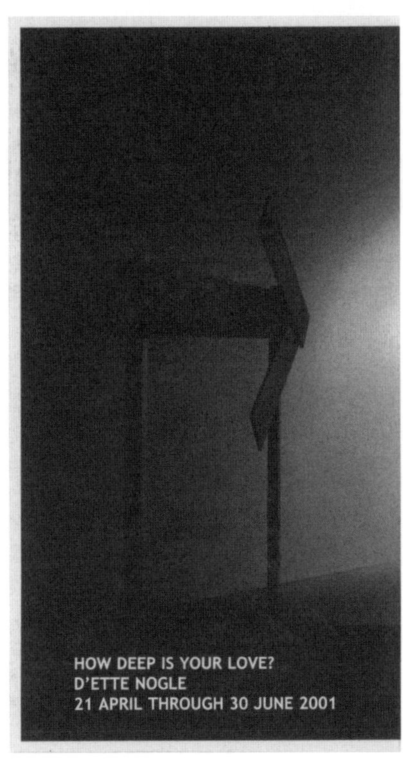

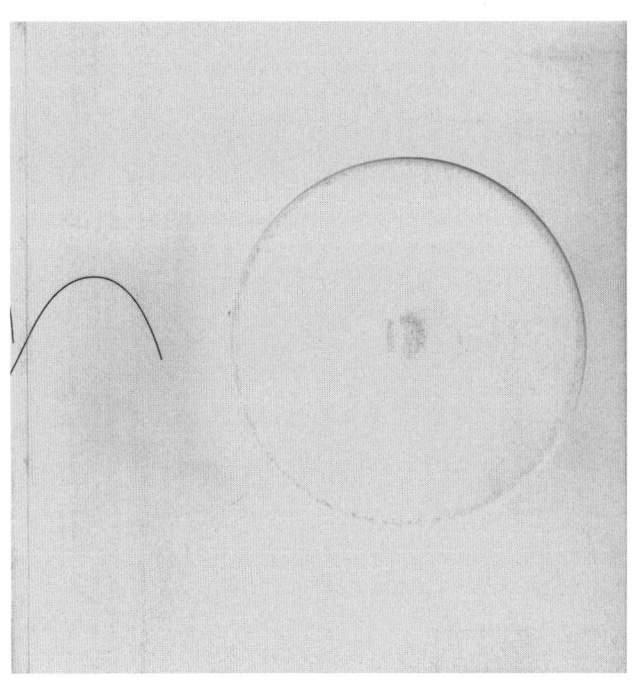

2004.02 <u>Yvonne Rainer, Radical Juxtapositions 1961-2002</u>, Poster

2001.03 <u>D'Ette Nogle, How Deep is Your Love</u>, Booklet

2002.06 <u>Michael Brewster, See Hear Now: A Sonic Drawing and Five Acoustic Sculptures</u>, Catalog

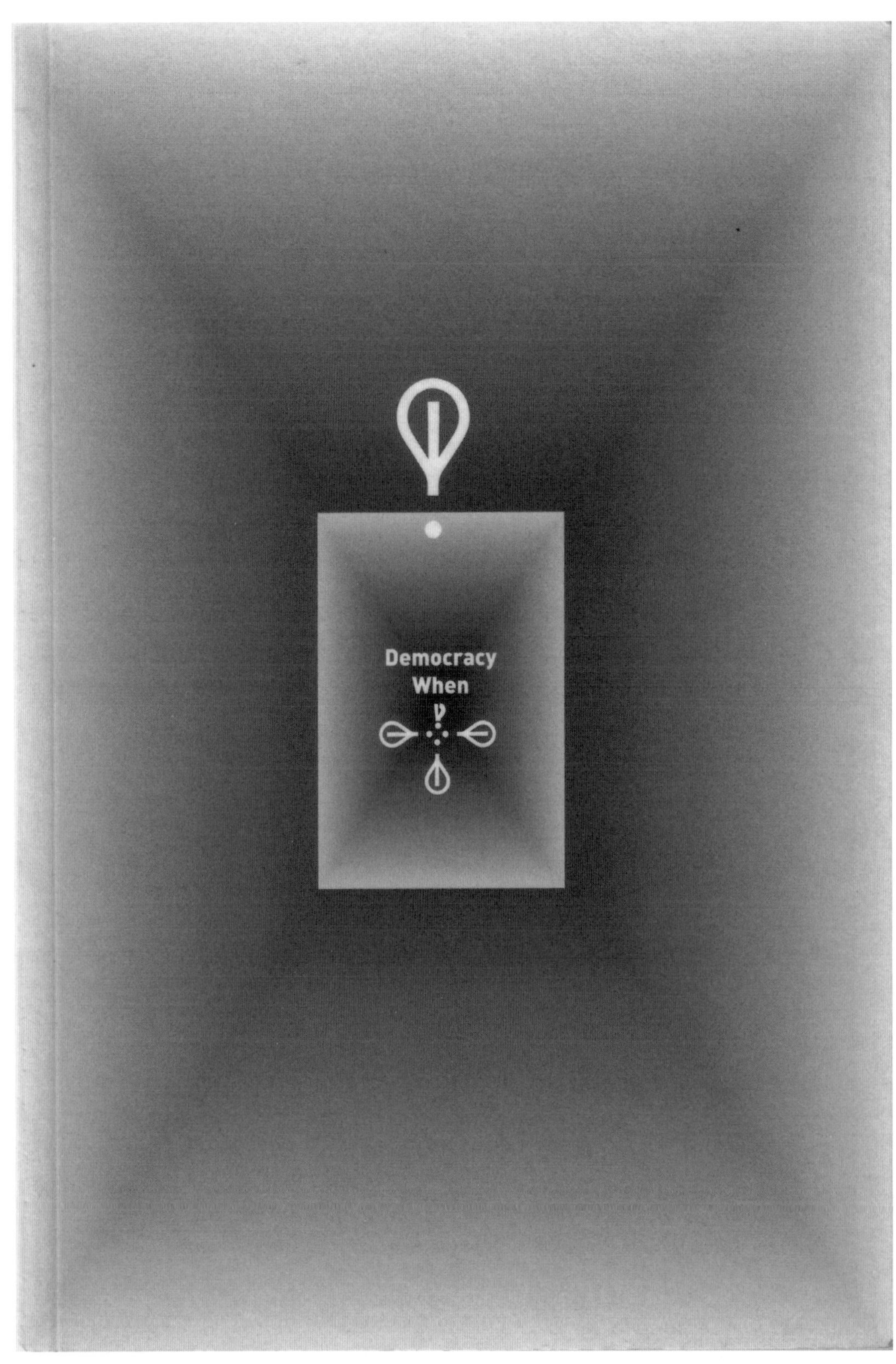

2002.07 <u>Democracy When?</u>, Catalog

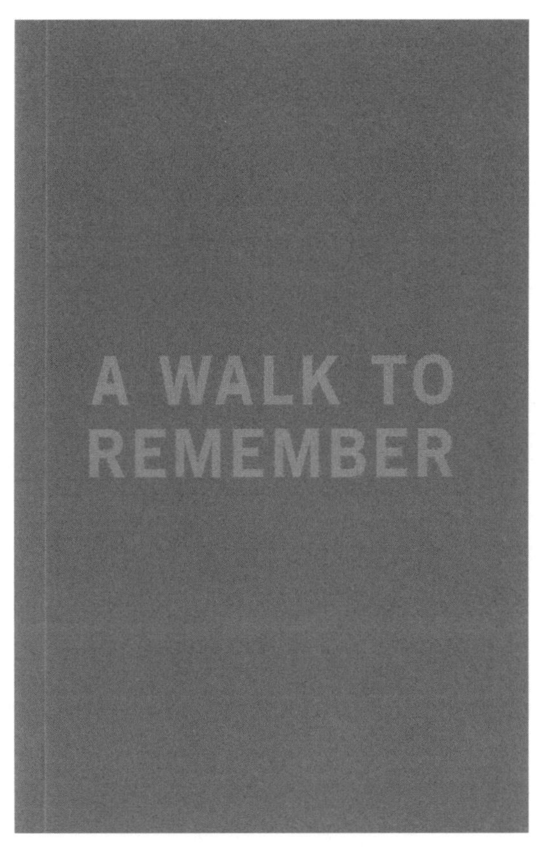

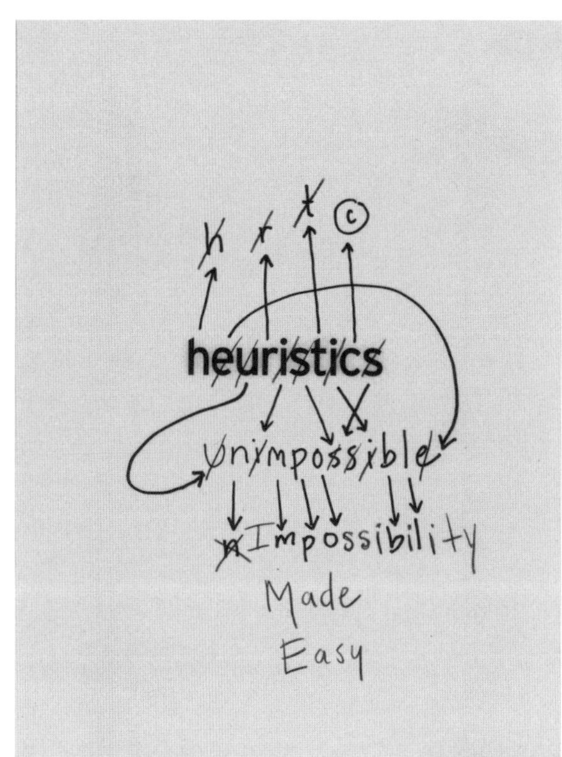

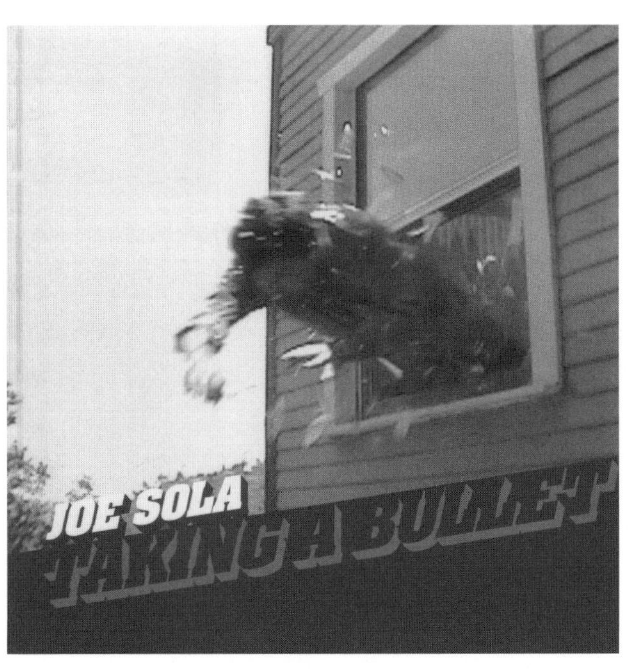

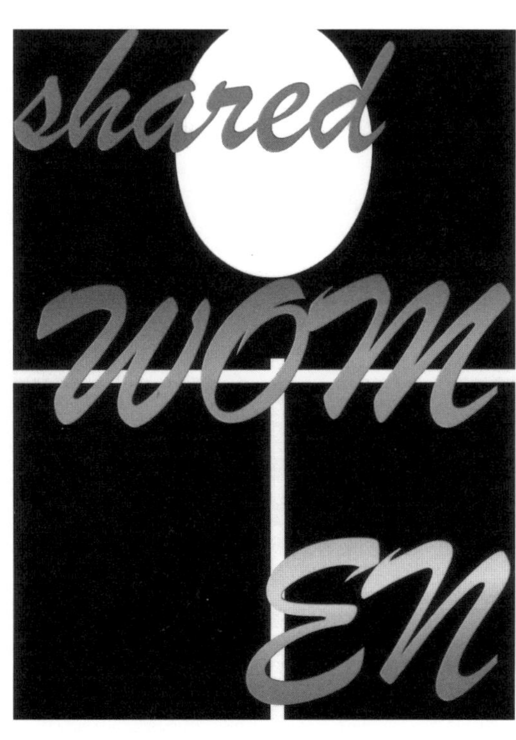

2005.03 A Walk to Remember, Catalog

2005.04 Joe Sola, Taking A Bullet, Catalog

2007.01 Impossibility Made Easy, Catalog

2007.02 Shared Women, Postcard

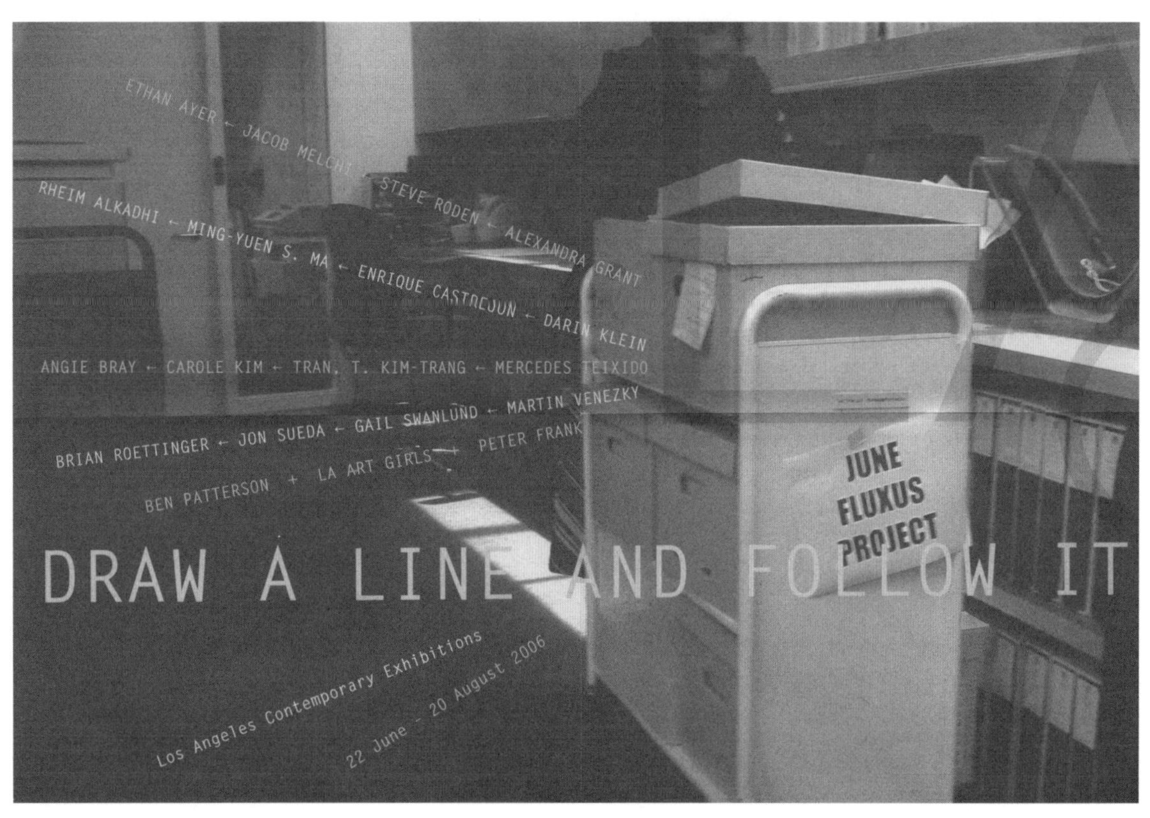

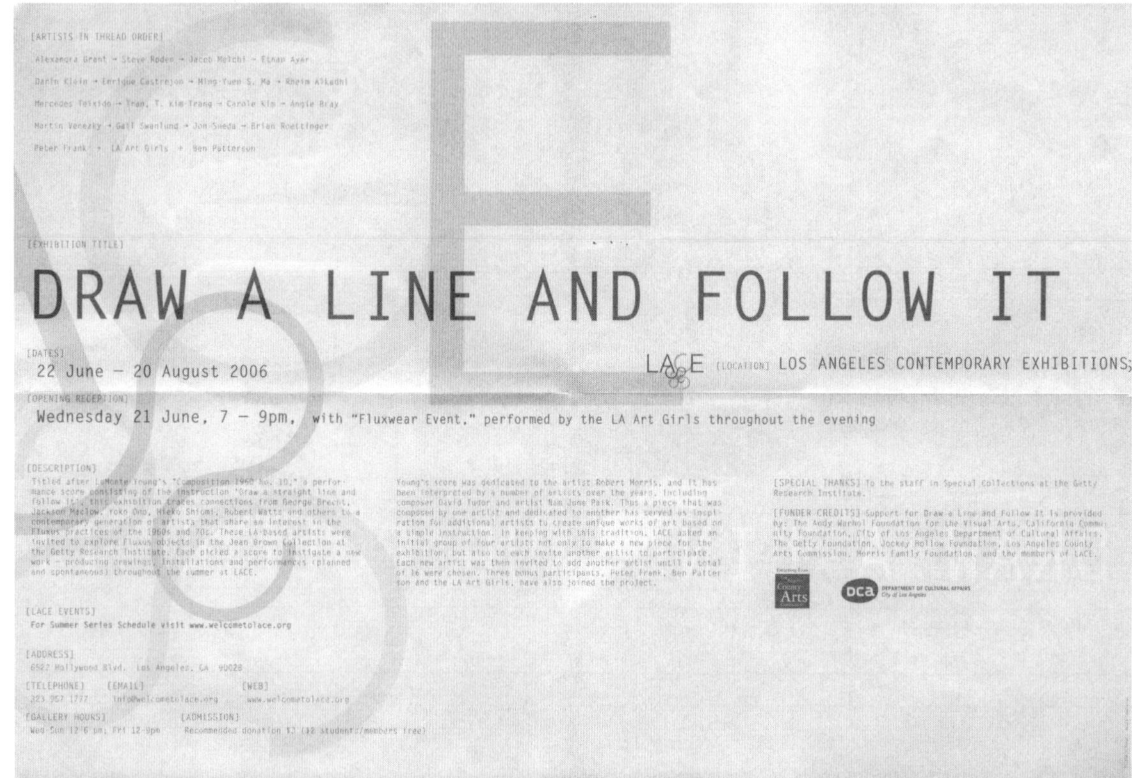

2006.01 <u>Draw a Line and Follow It</u>, Poster

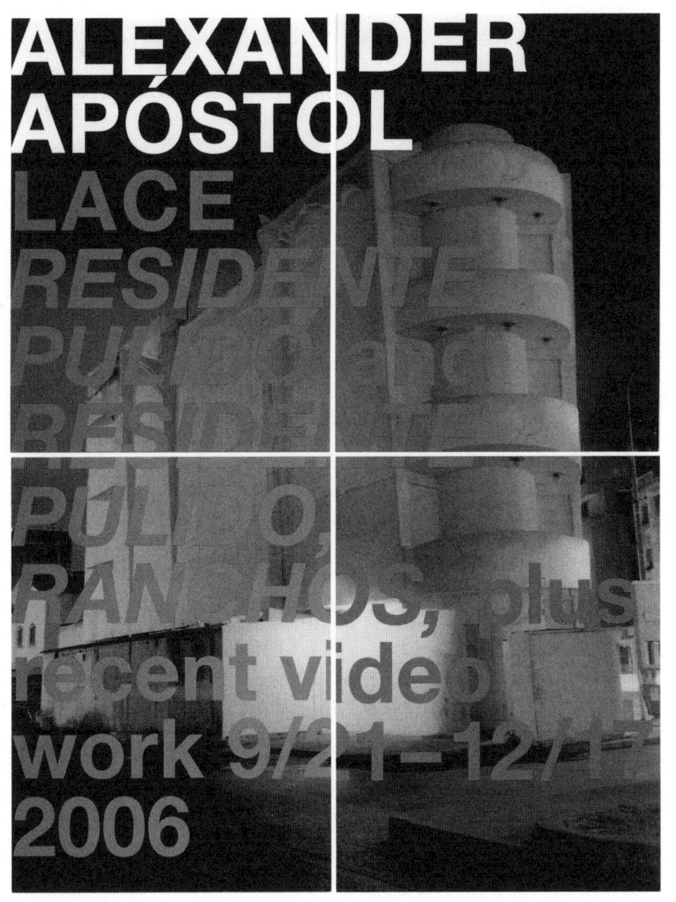

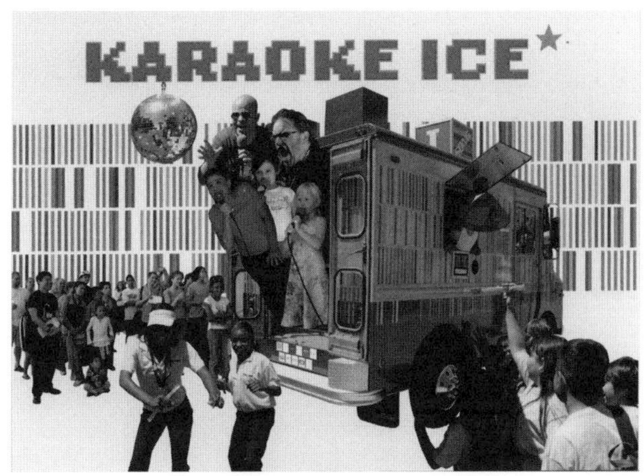

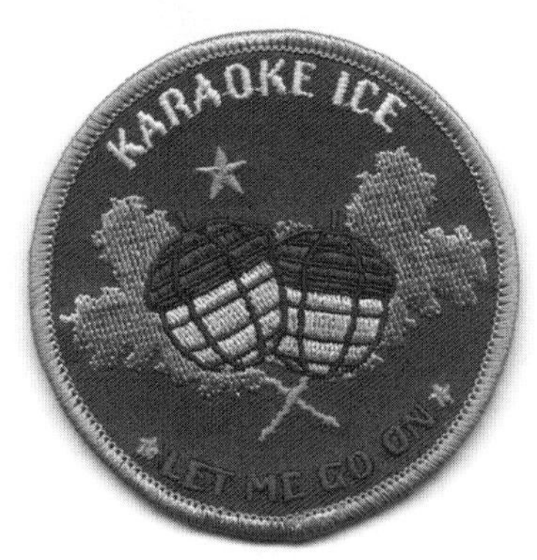

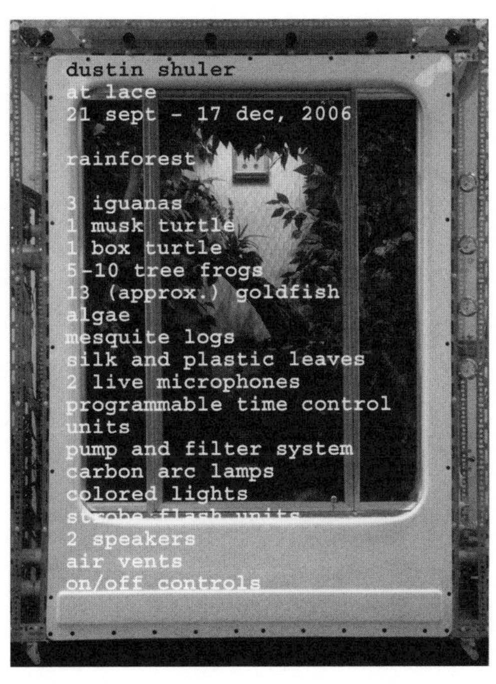

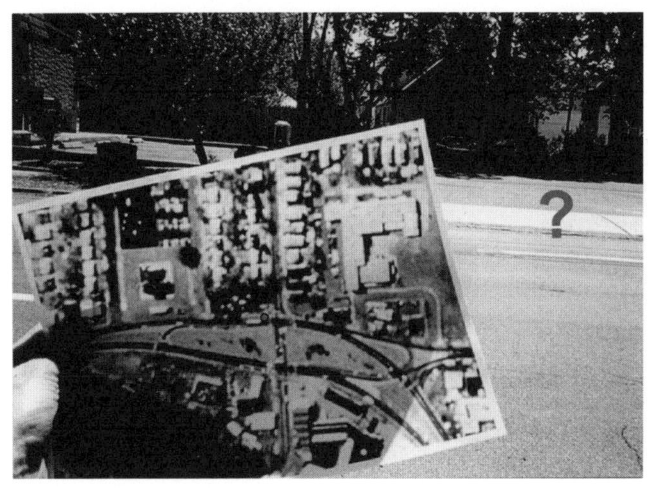

2006.02 Alexander Apóstol, Residente Pulido, Residente Pulido, Ranchos, Postcard
2006.03 Dustin Shuler, The Rainforest, A Landscape in a Shower, Postcard

2007.03 Karaoke Ice, Postcard, Patch
2007.04 Just Space(s)/AN ATLAS, Postcard

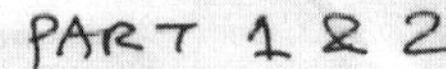

PART 1 & 2

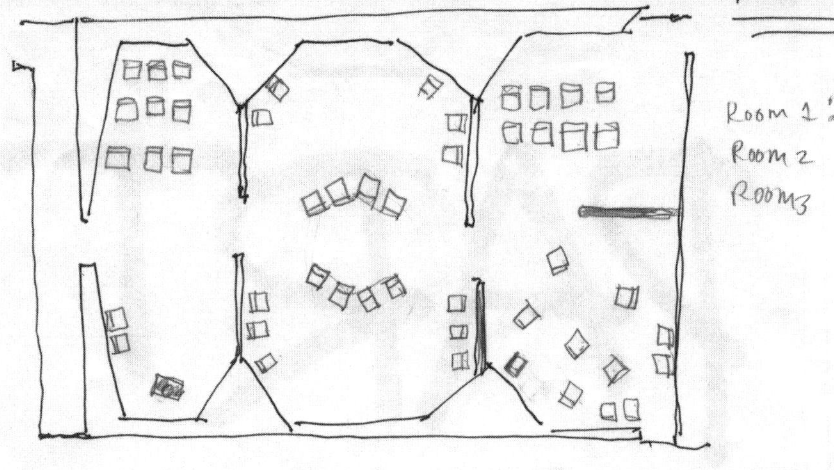

Room 1: 20
Room 2: 19
Room 3: 11
———
50

PART 3 & 4

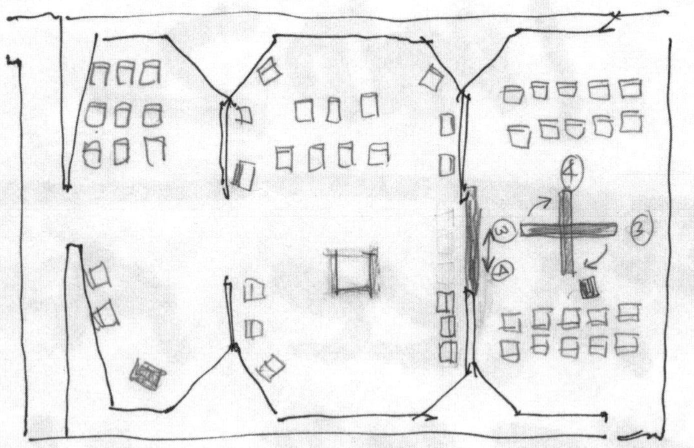

Room 1: 20
Room 2: 19
Room 3: 11
———
50

PART 5 & 6

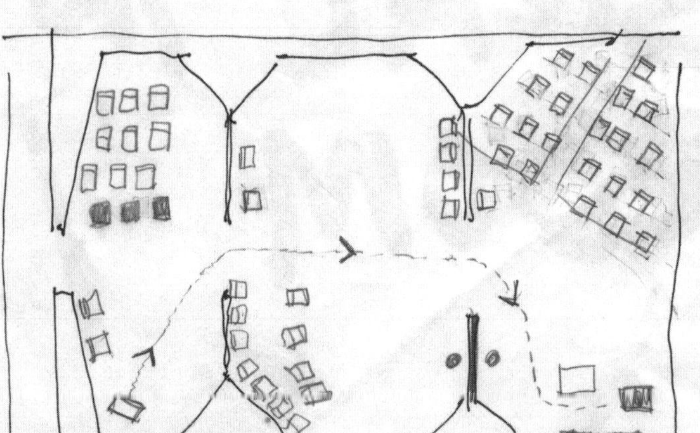

Room 1: 22
Room 2: 17
Room 3: 11
———
50

<u>Re: Happenings</u>
Michael Ned Holte

Nearly fifty years after its six-night stint at Rueben Gallery in New York City, Allan Kaprow's <u>18 Happenings in 6 Parts</u> is still a work in progress. All evidence—and the evidence is partial, fragmentary—suggests that in 1959, Kaprow's <u>18/6</u> was intended as a radical four-dimensional collage, a reflection of the modern, urban, ambulatory experience of traveling in and out of the subway, onto the street, and back again, with words, images, and sounds rapidly coming and going along the way.

<u>18/6</u> proposes a distracted subject; the audience—and the performers, for that matter—simply cannot observe, let alone digest the whole work in one sitting. Experience is rendered ephemeral. <u>18/6</u> is an attempt to make an activity-based and time-based work of art that dismantles the proscenium of theater without entirely jettisoning it, or stagecraft, or the audience. It is surely indebted to the ideas of Berthold Brecht and Antonin Artaud, but just as clearly follows from Jackson Pollock, John Cage, and pop culture. Kaprow's well-known interest in the blurring of art and life is represented here by the work's lengthy intermissions, in which life emerges from art. A devoted student of Cage (who witnessed <u>18/6</u> one evening, after paying $5 for his ticket!), Kaprow was surely as interested in the unscripted, aleatory "happenings" occurring between the six numbered parts. It should also be mentioned that this work is infused with a very healthy sense of humor—much of it aimed squarely at the pretensions of the art world and the preciousness of art.

For this realization of <u>18/6</u>, countless hours were spent with Kaprow's extensive, but incomplete and contradictory notes, yet no amount of research would have reclaimed the "original" piece as it was performed in its original context in space and time. Fittingly, given his own body of work, Steve Roden's conduction of this <u>18/6</u> reconstruction (a word that remains a placeholder) knowingly accepts translation—a complex process that combines rational methodology with intuition and playfulness—as the guiding "rule" of Kaprow's piece. Working in a group dynamic, this process of translation is multifaceted, polyvocal, and built into the structure of the work itself.

2008.02 Allan Kaprow, 18 Happenings in 6 Parts, Poster (front)

Excerpt from the original poster for "18 Happenings in 6 Parts" by Allan Kaprow, October 4, 6, 7, 8, 9, 10 1959 at The Reuben Gallery, 61 4th Avenue, New York, New York; Phone WA 9-8558

©Allan Kaprow Estate Courtesy Hauser & Wirth, Zürich London
Research Library, The Getty Research Institute, Los Angeles, California (980063)

2008.02 Allan Kaprow, 18 Happenings in
6 Parts, Poster (back)

dear mr. kaprow,

i wanted to let you know that i have been invited by carol stakenas to
direct a performance of your 1959 work "18 happenings in 6 parts".

carol and i began by visiting the getty to see your notes for 18/6. we were
very enthusiastic (and a little delusional) in that we assumed the vast
amount of material meant everything we needed was there. we wished you had
left us a better roadmap, but we figured it would easy enough to build one
ourselves. i guess you were smiling to yourself, knowing we had no idea what
we were getting into.

when we realized there was no complete score to be found, i'm not sure why
we didn't give up. it must've had something to do with your words being so
inspiring. i realize now that you didn't leave a complete score behind on
purpose. i think you believed that if we found one, we'd follow it. you knew
we'd come to know 18/6 differently if we built it ourselves. we struggled a
lot with the concept of reconstruction, and i blame you for the lengthy
discussions that missing pieces generated. eventually, we managed to build a
framework. i guess you knew we could do it; because i think your work
suggests that struggle gets you to the starting point, while an open mind is
needed to embark upon the journey.

next, we added two voices. rae was my first thought in approaching your
movement. her sensitivities towards ritual, dance, and everyday actions
seemed perfectly in line with your notes. she pieced things together, filled
holes; and, i think you will agree, brought new life to the notations. i
should also let you know that we wondered if the first performers really
memorized over 40 positions taking place during a minute and a half of
movement as you notated it... or was its near impossibility part of your
experiment?

michael also seemed a natural choice to navigate your sea of text. like rae,
his research was exhaustive, and he needed to use a very sharp knife to
whittle down material enough for a 6 day reading into what felt right for
the piece. he found connections in things; creating a reasoned, as well as
intuitive, path for what would go where. he noticed how you repeat certain
things in different forms - such as talking about time, before an image of a
clock, before reading while counting. i know you must be happy how deep our
discussions got once rae and michael were onboard, as well as the fact that
michael has never performed. sometimes, when we had no answers, we joked
about wearing bracelets that say "what would allan do?"; but of course we
knew you'd want us to consider your notes and come to our own conclusions.

when we added three more voices, the piece started to come to life. flora
brought movement that is non-traditional and continually exploratory; and
steve brought an extensive performance history that has taken numerous
forms. what can i tell you about the presence of simone. you know, of
course, that we are unbelievably lucky to have her as a collaborator,
instigator, challenger, and performer. we six built this thing together.

i suspect you knew skylar would participate, since he already worked with
apple shrine. i assume you are laughing out loud at the ways he has given
your props a new language of movement and interaction. i'd also like to
introduce you to elonda, who has added a level of intimacy to the
environment - another landscape within the landscape of audience
participation. i wonder if these forms would surprise you, and what you also
might think of the set. while managing to retain all of your original
intentionality, stephanie has created a form that is entirely new. could you
ever have imagined 18/6 happening within the framework of such a wonderful
space?

before i get to the end, i think i should mention how much i love your
original sound. being a sound maker, i simply couldn't help it... i wanted
to collaborate with you. i've left two of your compositions intact, and i've
inserted myself into the other two, one of which was missing. i hope that
the cues i took from your notes have generated something that reeks of both
of us.

mr. kaprow, at this point i think i should call you allan, because i truly
feel that the piece in its present form is as much ours as it is yours. we
have done our best to meet you on your own terms, and we've also asked you
to meet us on ours. we wanted to open the piece up, so that 50 years later
it can live connected, as well as disconnected, from its past. yes, it's
still your skeleton, but its our skin. the hope is that it can still
generate questions.

i'm sure you understand our decision not to document the performance in
video. this should ensure that the next group reaps similar benefits through
similar struggles. rather than leave them our roadmap, we felt you would be
happy if we simply added a few extra breadcrumbs to help them find their own
way.

thanks much,

steve

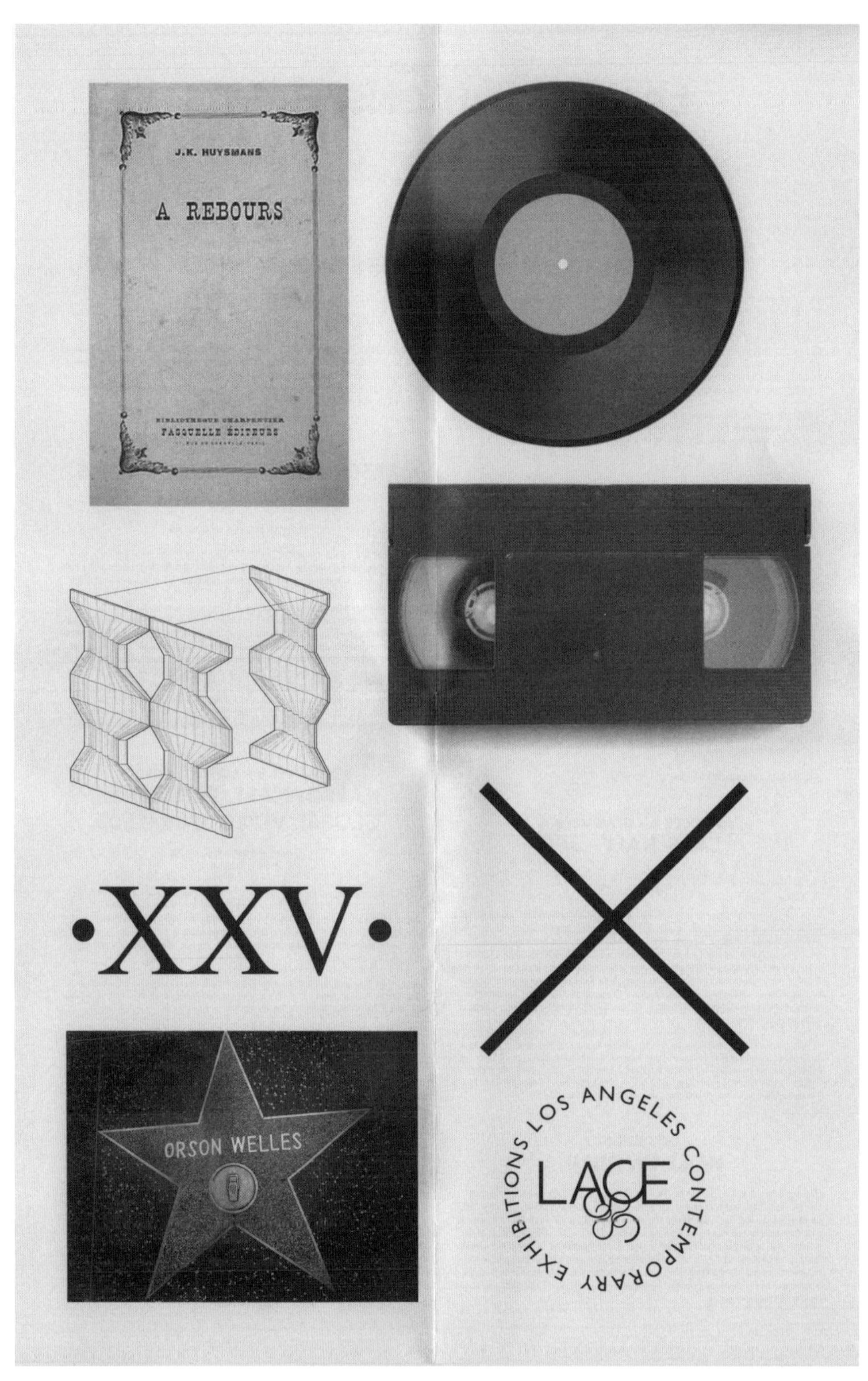

2008.06 <u>LACE Exhibitions/Events Fall 2008</u>,
        Calendar

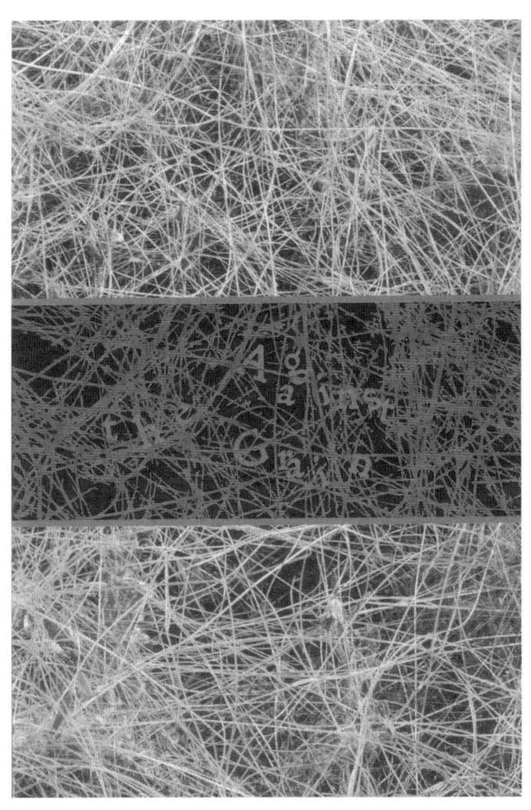

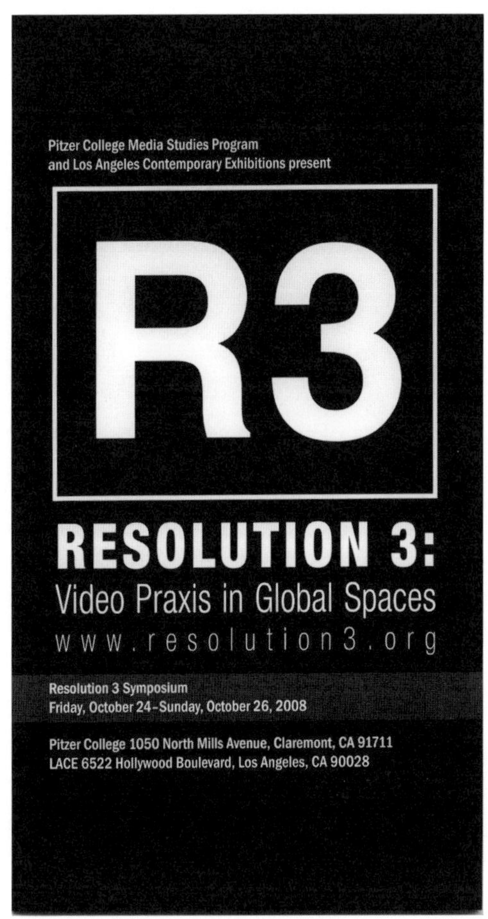

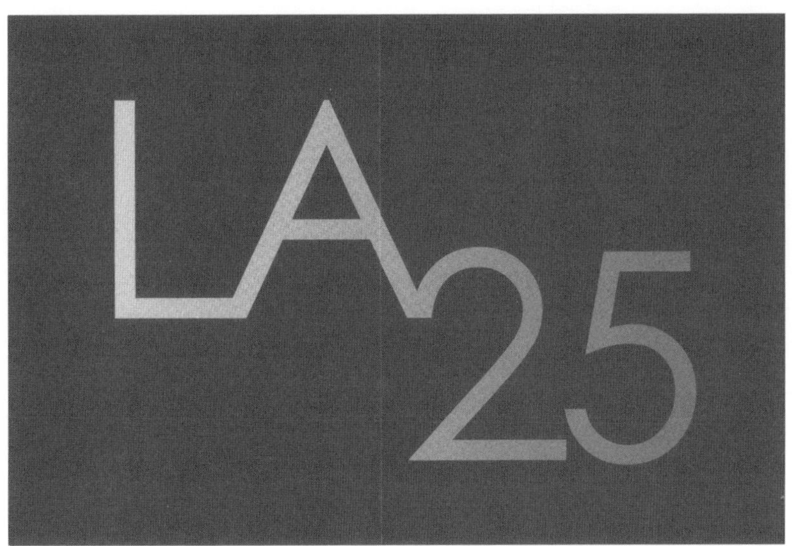

2008.07 <u>Against The Grain</u>, Catalog
2008.08 <u>LA25</u>, Postcard

2008.09 <u>Resolution 3: Video Praxis in
Global Spaces</u>, Brochure

Living the Archive:
Jane McFadden and Glenn R. Phillips
In Conversation by Email

Jane McFadden:

Hi Glenn:

Should I start our conversation about the archive? I've been thinking about how I still have a giddy sense of the archive and its potential. It's difficult to describe. Perhaps one could suggest that I am tricked into the possibility of aura —the unpublished letter as a road to authenticity—but I might think of it more as fan-like, a back stage pass. It's not so much that I think the archive will provide some hidden truth, it's just that I want to be there, behind the scenes, thinking about what it means to make a work, through materials that are inextricably intertwined with what it means to live a life—diaries, bills, love letters, rough cuts.

On a practical level, I wonder how our contemporary lives could possibly be as interesting without paper, and how we'd know it if they were. And on a theoretical level I think about how the archive preserves the notion of work of art beyond the object, at the same time that dealers are digging into archival materials to find new "works" to be sold. I suppose as a fan, I might be their perfect buyer. Thoughts?

Glenn Phillips:

But I think the archive probably does provide some hidden truth. Wouldn't it have to? But then again I certainly couldn't tell you how to find it. So much of the work I study—performance, site-specific works, ephemeral projects—don't exist as objects anymore, so the archive is often all I have left. Sometimes I think about what would happen if we put these works on trial in a court of law.

How many crimes have been photographed and captured on audiotape and videotape and witnessed by dozens of people and accompanied by carefully planned notes and sketches and statements of intent the same way so many performance works in the 1970s were?

Actually, quite a lot! But no matter what sort of archival traces we leave behind, everyone is guaranteed the chance to have it argued that the evidence does not stack up as it seems. And no matter how much evidence there is, it can be difficult to determine "what happened," even more difficult to assign "motive," and courts don't even venture into figuring out meaning. So are we getting ahead of ourselves, thinking that these documents can take us back to some original event or state of mind of the artist? What are we really trying to do? Maybe the archive just helps us clarify our own priorities, as we sift through materials and decide what we think is important?

Jane McFadden:

I've been thinking quite a bit about the question of what we, or I, am really trying to do. It is not about return or recovery. It could be about discovery. I think that we have to consider that any truth we might find would have to be a truth about us, about now, rather than a truth about then, or that. Sure, there are conversations to be had about the past, about what happened, and some sift the archive better than others, but in the end I think it has to be about challenging ourselves to think through another's process, another possibility, another time, knowing all along that we are thinking through our own. It is a way to relate to others and to ourselves.

Of course in some ways then I am positing a refiguring of art history itself, or that what an art historian of contemporary art does is something other, more akin to

criticism, but at a different pace. I find
my own use of the archive both encourages
me to argue for the value and wonder of
certain work or certain processes in the
past, while also emphasizing their
ungraspable nature.

<u>Glenn Phillips:</u>

Sometimes I think going through an archive
is just a way of forcing me to focus my
attention, to make me think about an
artist or an artwork for the length of
time it takes for me to reach whatever
conclusion I need. I get into a pleas-
antly distracted-yet-focused state, with
each new letter or photograph or piece of
ephemera making my mind jump a little bit,
but it's always jumping around the subject
at hand. I might spend some time thinking
about the graphic design on an exhibition
announcement (which is probably irrelevant) or get caught up in crazy gossip
in a letter (definitely irrelevant), but
add that to an artist's scribbled notes
and drawings for a piece, correspondence related to a work's exhibition or
construction, and after enough time has
passed I start to feel like I understand
whatever it is I'm researching.

But do I need the archive for that, or is
it just a reason to devote time to thinking? I find the same thing happens with a
lot of the long, repetitive, time-based
work from the 1970s. It's not about watching an image for an hour, it's about using
an hour as an occasion to think about an
image, perception, art, yourself. We can't
just sit and think anymore! Instead, we
have to think under the guise of viewing
art or conducting research, and conse-
quently both our art and our research has
become more tedious—so that our brain can
sneak off and do its work.

<u>Jane McFadden:</u>

Hi Glenn: so one final comment to which you
might want to respond and then perhaps I

can format into a whole and we can each
give it one last read before sending
it off?

One of the things that the archive pro-
vides is an objective set of materials
in relationship to a subjective set of
processes—both the artist's and our own.
Scholarship at its best I think is genera-
tive on both counts. An archive can be
so personal, so intimate, but in the end
it is a collection of data. The tension
between the two is productive and reflects
the exchange between the object and
subject in art in general.

Also I think the archive is so crucial
in linking art to the world at large, in
reminding us that it does not exist in
isolation, as it sometimes seems to do in
more narrow histories, and of course as
you have mentioned, at times reminding us
that the work existed at all.

<u>Glenn Phillips:</u>

I completely agree. I'm so drawn to
work that seems vague, confusing, and
enigmatic, and archival materials provide
this concrete counterpoint that helps me
get a handle on the work—even though
archives themselves are always fragmentary
and equally enigmatic. But 1) the work
and 2) the archive, and 3) our thought
processes, and 4) our need to collect
data can all come together in very productive ways, and ways that move us into the
larger questions about art that we all
hope to answer. For me, it feels like one
needs that specificity in order to figure
out a bigger picture. We spend so much of
our time isolating art works from the rest
of the world, it's nice to have something
out there to reel them back in.

Which maybe just brings us back to where
we started: giddy fans looking for a back-
stage pass to truth. Is that really what
historians are? At the very least, it's
probably how we start.

ARCHIVE INDEX

1978.01
ASCO, No Movie
May 2–31, 1978
Postcard
11" × 8.5"
p. 11

1978.02
Dreva/Gronk 1968–1978 /
Ten Years of Art of Life
March 3, 1978
Flyer
8.5" × 11"
p. 12

1979.01
First Communication
Sept. 22, 1979
Postcard
4" × 6"
p. 9

1979.02
LA Themes
May 5–26, 1979
Curator: Gil De Montes
Postcard
4.66" × 6.66"
p. 10

1979.03
The Big Dance
Nov. 3, 1979
Postcard
5.25" × 8.5"
p. 10

1979.04
La Frontera
by Ed Friedman
Mar. 8, 1979
Postcard
10.5" × 3.66"
p. 11

1979.05
Glenn Branca
Dec. 4, 1980
Flyer
13.5" × 8.5"
p. 12

1979.06
An Evening of Electronic
Music at L.A.C.E. Gallery
July 14, 1979
Flyer
8.5" × 11"
p. 12

1979.07
L.A.C.E July Events
July, 1979
Calendar
11" × 8.5"
p. 13

1979.08
Food Art for
The Animal Show
July 7,1979
Flyer
8.5" × 10"
p. 15

1979.09
Six Downtown Sculptors:
2nd Annual Downtown
Artists Exhibition
April 6–28, 1979
Curator: Melina Wortz
Exhibit organized by
Alexandra Sauer and
Gil de Montes
Flyer
5.5" × 3.5"
p. 16

1979.10
Video at L.A.C.E.
October 20–21, 1979
Flyer
8.5" × 10.75"
p. 16

1980.01
Espiña (Thorn)
Flyer
11" × 17"
p. 10

1980.02
Nancy Buchannan
If I Could Only Tell You
How Much I Love You
Oct. 10, 1980
Postcard
4" × 6"
p. 11

1980.03
John White, in performance
May 18, 1980
Flyer
17" × 11"
p. 13

1980.04
Min Tanaka, In Search of
Nature and Freedom on
Both Sides of the Bodyskin
Dec. 14, 1980
Flyer
11" × 8.5"
p. 13

1980.05
June at LACE
June 4–June 28, 1980
Curator: John Baldessari
Calendar
11" × 8.5"
p. 13

1980.06
Anne Mavor
Venus on the Half Shell
and Other Poses
May 24, 1980
Photo: Jo Goodwin
Postcard
6" × 4"
p. 14

1980.07
James Brown Revue
Band Fundraiser
July 3, 1980
Flyer
11" × 8.5"
p. 14

1980.08
Gary Lang, Weapons
Sept. 5–Sept. 22, 1980
Postcard
4.5" × 6"
p. 14

1980.09
On and Off Broadway:
3rd Annual Downtown
Artists Exhibition
April 4, 1980
Curator: John Baldessari
Mural by Kent Twitchell
Flyer
8.5" × 11"
p. 16

1980.10
Nancy Mock Dance Co.
April 4, 1980
Postcard
9" × 5.5"
p. 16

1980.11
Saibra Vickland,
Expanding the Tonal
Nov. 12–Dec. 6, 1980
Poster
4.25" × 6"
p. 17

1980.12
Ruckus Films
of Red Grooms
March 22, 1980
Flyer
8.5" × 11"
p. 19

1981.01
Constance Mallinson
Recent Work
Jan. 6–Feb. 3, 1981
Postcard
3.5" × 5.5"
p. 14

1981.02
Louie Lunetta,
Chinese Room
Feb. 24–March 27, 1981
Postcard
5.5" × 3.5"
p. 17

1981.03
B. Wurtz and
Lynne Henkel
Jan. 6–Feb. 5, 1981
Photo: Darcy Huebler
Postcard
3.5" × 5.5"
p. 17

1981.04
Bruce James,
The Road Show
Nov. 29–Dec. 20, 1981
Photo: by Janice Felgar
Postcard
3.5" × 6"
p. 17

1981.05
Joe Grant
June 3–July 3, 1981
Postcard
3.33" × 6.5"
p. 18

1981.06
The Fix-It-Up Show,
Works by Known Artists
Altered by Michael
Uhlenkott and Jeffrey
Vallance
Oct. 7–Nov. 8, 1981
Flyer
11" × 8.5"
p. 18

1981.07
Mike Kelley, Meditation
on a Can of Vernors
June 10, 1981
Postcard
3.66" × 6.5"
p. 18

1981.08
Lee Leonard:
THE CANE MAN
Oct. 7–Nov. 8, 1981
Postcard
3.66" × 6.5"
p. 19

1981.09
Hangers: A Performance
May 23, 1981
Postcard
3.5" × 6.25"
p. 19

1981.10
Site Projects:
Downtown LA
June 3–July 3, 1981
Flyer
11" × 8.5"
p. 19

1981.11
Sally Shapiro,
"an evening of video,
old and new works"
April 4, 1981
Postcard
3.5" × 8.5"
p. 19

1981.12
Tony Labat,
a performance
Sept. 13, 1981
Postcard
3.5" × 6"
p. 19

1981.13
Eat Your Heart Out
Feb. 13–14, 1981
Poster
14" × 11"
p. 21

1982.01
R.I.P. Hayman
The Phenomenology of
Aural Appearances
Flyer
April 18, 1982
11" × 8.5"
p. 14

1982.02
Lari Pittman,
Sunday Painting
June 9–July 9, 1982
Postcard
8.5" × 3.5"
p.18

1982.03
Paul McCarthy,
Humanoid
Jan. 6–Jan. 24, 1982
Postcard
3.5" × 5"
p. 20

1982.04
The American Dream:
Mediated
June 9–July 9, 1982
Curator: Kathleen Bonner
and Marga Bijvoet
Postcard
5.5" × 7"
p. 20

1982.05
Barry Campion
Jan. 6–Feb. 7, 1982
Photo by Bob Seidman
of "Sisters" by
Barry Campion
Postcard
3.5" × 5"
p. 20

1982.06
Drawings
July 22–Aug. 21, 1982
Postcard
3.5" × 8.5"
p. 20

1982.07
LACE Spring
Performance Calendar
Spring 1982
Calendar
9.25" × 15"
p. 22

1982.08
LACE Winter
Performance Calendar
Winter 1982
Calendar
9.25" × 15"
p. 22

1983.01
LACE Fall 1983
Intermedia Events
Oct. 18–Nov. 11, 1983
Calendar
14" × 9.5"
p. 23

1983.02
Los Angeles New York
Exchange
May 21–July 2, 1983 (NY)
June 8–July 16 1983 (LA)
Postcard 4" × 6"
p. 24

1983.03
Jim Pomeroy, Polarized
Projections / Special
Effects / Remote Control,
Yura Adams, Orbit on
the Hour
April 14, 1983
Postcard
3" × 6"
p. 24

1983.04
Peter Levinson,
Painted Reliefs
July 28–Aug. 27, 1983
Postcard
6" × 3.5"
p. 24

1983.05
Michael Kelley,
Confusion: A Play in
Seven Sets, Each Set
More Spectacular and
Elaborate Than the Last
Jan. 17–Jan. 18, 1983
Postcard
6.25" × 4.33"
p. 25

1983.06
Jac Mote / Foehn
July 28–Aug. 27, 1983
Postcard
6" × 3.5"
p. 27

1984.01
The Art of Spectacle
Oct. 10–Dec. 12, 1984
Design: Roy Gyongi
Catalog
12" × 5.25"
p. 25

1984.02
Emblem
Oct. 11–Sept. 11, 1984
Curator: Cam Slocum
Postcard
4" × 9.5"
p. 25

1984.03
John Sanborn
A Video Panorama
Jan. 7–Feb. 11, 1984
Design: Tim Martin and
Patti Podesta
Brochure
11" × 8.5"
p. 26

1985.01
Public Domain:
14 Video Artists
Jan. 16–Feb. 16 1985
Curator: Ilene Segalove
Design: Tom Recchion
Catalog
6.75" × 8.5"
p. 27

1985.02
Open Show
July 29–Aug. 2, 1985
Flyer
8.5" × 11"
p. 28

1986.01
Resolution: A Critique
of Video Art
April 18–May 10, 1986
Director: Patti Podesta
Edited by Patti Podesta
Catalog
8.5" × 7"
130 pages
ISBN: 0–937335–01–0
p. 27

1986.02
Video and Language,
Video as Language
Dec. 4, 1986–Jan. 18, 1987
Curator: Scott Rankin
Brochure
12" × 7.25", 6 pages
p. 27

1986.03
TV Generations
Feb. 2 1986–April 4, 1986
Curator: John Baldessari
and Bruce Yonemoto
Edited by Meg Cranston,
Jeff Mann and Tim Martin
Essays: John Baldessari,
Peter d'Agostino, John
G. Hanhardt, and Bruce
Yonemoto
Design: Haycock
Kienberger
Catalog
12.5" × 10", 71 pages
ISBN: 0–937335–00–2
p. 30–31

1986.04
TV Generations
Feb. 2 1986–April 4, 1986
Curator: John Baldessari
and Bruce Yonemoto
Letter to Bruce Yonemoto
from Jeffrey Vallance
8.27" × 11.7"
p. 32–35

1987.01
LACE 10 yrs Documented
Director, Joy Silverman
Edited by Karen Moss
Essays: Karen Moss,
Nancy Drew, Renny
Pritikin, William Olander
Design: Jeffrey Keedy
Publication
11" × 8.5", 111 pages
ISBN: 0–937335–03–7
p. 36

1987.02
Variations III
April 22–May 31, 1987
Curator: Melinda Wortz
Design: Jerry McMillan
Catalog
11" × 8.5", 79 pages
ISBN: 0–911291–13–X
p. 36

1987.03
LACE Annuale
Sept. 2–Oct. 11, 1987
Poster
p. 37

1987.04
Surveillance
Feb. 27–April 12, 1987
Curators: Branda Miller,
Deborah Irmas
Design: Terri Scarbor-
ough, Randi Ganulin,
Kimberely Baer
Catalog
11" × 8.5", 55 pages
ISBN: 0–937335–02–9
p. 38–47

1987.05
Victor Burgin,
Office At Night
June 16–July 26, 1989
Exhibition Coordinator:
Jeff Man
Design: Mr. Keedy
Brochure
7.5" × 6", 8 pages
p. 50

1987.06
Allan Sekula,
Geography Lesson:
Canadian Notes
June 10–July 26, 1989
Exhibition Coordinator:
Jeff Mann
Brochure
7.5" × 6", 8 pages
p. 50

1988.01
Re:Placement
March 2–April 17, 1988
Curators: Marc Pally and
Joy Silverman
Brochure
11.25" × 5.55", 12 pages
p. 36

1988.02
Tactical Positions
June 22–July 24, 1988
Videolace Committee:
David Bunn, Wendy
Clarke, Peter Kirby, Patti
Podesta, Bruce Yonemoto
Essays by Tim Martin,
Bill Horrigan
Design: Susan Silton
Catalog
11.75" × 5.5", 20 pages
p. 36

1988.03
Against Nature
Jan. 6–Feb. 12, 1988
Curators: Dennis Cooper
and Richard Hawkins
Edited by Dennis Cooper
and Richard Hawkins
Design: Linda Nishio
Cover Art: Tony Greene
Catalog
8.5" × 5.5", 35 pages
ISBN: 0–937335–04–05
p. 48

1988.04
Mary Kelly, Interim–
Part 1: Corpus
June 15–July 24, 1988
Curator: Rita McBride
Design: Lorraine Wild
(with Patricia Osborn)
Brochure
7.5" × 6", 8 pages
p. 50

1988.05
Connie Hatch,
FORCED TO DISAPPEAR:
A Display of Visual Inequity
and FACE VALUE: FORCED
TO SMILE
June 15–July 24, 1988
Brochure
7.5" × 6", 8 pages
p. 51

1988.06
Carole Caroompas,
Fairy Tales
Nov. 10–Dec. 24, 1988
Exhibition Coordinator:
Jinger Heffner
Design: Negastrip
Printers, Raging Fingers,
and Kim Yasuda
Brochure
7.5" × 6", 8 pages
p. 51

1988.07
Millie Wilson, FAUVE
SEMBLANT, Peter
(A Young English Girl)
Nov. 10–Dec. 24, 1988
Exhibition Coordinator:
Jinger Heffner
Photo: Catherine Opie
Brochure
7.5" × 6", 8 pages
p. 51

1988.08
Minnette Lehmann
Nov. 10–Dec. 24, 1988
Exhibition Coordinator:
Jinger Heffner
Design: Negastrip
Printers, Raging Fingers,
and Kim Yasuda
Brochure
7.5" × 6", 8 pages
p. 51

1988.09
LACE June / July Events
June–July, 1988
Design: Mr. Keedy
Calendar
11" × 16.5"
p. 52

1988.10
LACE April / May Events
April–May, 1988
Design: Mr. Keedy
Calendar
11" × 16.5"
p. 54

1988.11
LACE October /
November Events
Oct.–Nov., 1988
Design: Mr. Keedy
Calendar
11" × 16.5"
p. 55

1988.12
LACE December /
January Events
Dec.–Jan., 1989
Design: Mr. Keedy
Calendar
17" × 22.66"
p. 56

1989.01
Ana Mendieta
March 1–April 23, 1989
Curators: Petra Barreras
del Rio and John Perreault
Design: Sue Zimmerman
Catalog
11" × 5.5", 16 pages
p. 48

1989.02
Lyn Blumenthal,
Force of Vision
June 13–July 9, 1989
Curator: Kate Horsfield
Design: Susan Silton
Brochure
8" × 8", 19 pages
p. 48

1989.03
Self-Evidence
May 5–June 11, 1989
Curator: Larry Rinder
Catalog
10" × 10" × 12" × 11.75",
48 pages
ISBN: 0–937335–05–3
p. 49

1989.04
LACE February/
March Events
Feb.–March, 1989
Design: Mr. Keedy
Calendar
17" × 22.66"
p. 56

1989.05
LACE April / May Events
April–May, 1989
Design: Mr. Keedy
Calendar
17" × 22.66"
p. 57

1989.06
LACE June / July Events
June–July, 1989
Design: Mr. Keedy
Calendar
17" × 22.66"
p. 57

1990.01
All But the Obvious:
Writing, Visual Art,
Performance, Video
by Lesbians
Nov. 2–Dec. 23, 1990
Essays by Pam Gregg,
Catherine Lord, Phranc,
Cheri Gaulke, Liz Kotz,
Adriene Jenik
Design: SoS: Susan Silton
Catalog
5.5" × 9", 27 pages
p. 58–59

1990.02
In Search of Paradise, Or
Anywhere But Here
Jan. 18–Feb. 24, 1990
Curators: Steve Fagin
and Bill Horrigan
Design: Laura Miller
Catalog
9" × 6", 12 pages
p. 64

1990.03
how can they be so sure?
Feb. 23–April 8, 1990
Curator: LACE Exhibition
Committee, DougIschar
Design: Wayne Smith
Essay: Liz Kotz
Catalog
7" × 8.5", 16 pages
p. 64

1991.01
Destination L.A.
Dec. 20, 1991–Feb. 9, 1992
Curator: Patricio Chavez
Catalog
11" × 8.5", 100 pages
p. 60, 62–63

1991.02
Letter to Jinger Heffner
from Artes de Mexico
Festival Committee
Feb. 15, 1991
Correspondence
11" × 8.5"
p. 61

1991.03
Exhausted Autumn:
A companion to Sweet
Oleander, an exhibition
of works by Tony Greene
June 21–Aug. 4, 1991
Curated and Edited by:
Richard Hawkins

Contributions by Brian
Baltin, Tom Christie,
Lawrence Gipe, Fred
Fehlau, Dodie Bellamy,
John Greyson, Liz Kotz,
Millie Wilson, Hudson,
Doug Ischar, Dennis
Cooper, Matias Viegener,
Robert Gluck
Design: Wayne Smith
Book
8" × 6", 75 pages
ISBN: 0–937335–06–1
p. 64

1992.01
Inheritance
May 22–June 21, 1992
Curators: Roberto Bedoya
and Jody Zellen
Essays by Joshua Decter
and Kobena Mercer
Design: Glen Helfand
Catalog
9" × 7", 44 pages
p. 64

1992.02
LACE June / July Events
June–July, 1992
Design: Simon Johnston /
Praxis
Calendar
11" × 33"
p. 66

1992.03
LACE Sept./Oct. Events
Sept.–Oct., 1992
Design: Simon Johnston /
Praxis
Calendar
11" × 33"
p. 66

1993.01
Kathy Acker, My Mother:
Demonology
March 19, 1993
Flyer
8.5" × 11"
p. 65

1993.02
LACE Jan. / Feb. Events
Jan.–Feb., 1993
Design: Simon Johnston /
Praxis
Calendar
11" × 33"
p. 67

1993.03
LACE March /April
Events
March–April, 1993
Design: Simon Johnston /
Praxis
Calendar
11" × 33"
p. 67

1996.01
True Bliss
Dec. 5–Jan. 26, 1997
Director: Brian Karl
Edited by Sue Henger
Essays by Julie Joyce,
David A. Greene
Design: Meryl Pollen
Catalog
9" × 9", 56 pages
p. 68

1996.02
TripWire
Feb. 29–March 30, 1996
Curator: Carmine
Iannaccone
Booklet
5.5" × 8.5", 18 pages
p. 69

1997.01
Ear as Eye
Feb. 27–March 23, 1997
Curators: Steve Roden
and Brandon Labelle
Design: Louise Sandhaus
Postcard
5.5" × 8.5"
p. 68

1997.02
Hinterland
May 29–July 6, 1997
Curator: LACE Exhibition
Committee
Catalog
8" × 6.5", 100 pages
p. 69

1999.01
The Future That Almost
Wasn't
April 8–April 9, 1999
Flyer
14" × 8.5"
p. 69

1999.02
Tri-Annuale (Part 1)
July 22–August 14, 1999
Curator: Andrea Zittel
Postcard
6.25" × 4.5"
p. 70

1999.03
Tri-Annuale (Part 2)
Dec. 1, 1999–Dec. 23 1999
Curator: Amy Adler
Postcard
4.5" × 6.25"
p. 70

2000.01
Tri-Annuale (Part 3)
April 8–April 29, 2000
Curator: Jason Meadows
Postcard
4.5" × 6.25"
p. 70

2000.02
Amy Adler
Email correspondence
Nov. 15, 1999
Correspondence
p. 71–73

2001.01
Daniel Marlos, TimeLine
Dec. 8, 2001–Jan. 26, 2002
Postcard
9" × 4"
p. 74

2001.02
Mari Eastman,
HELLO, GOODBYE
Feb. 3–March 17, 2001
Curator: Irene Tsatsos
Photo: Martin Cox
Brochure
8.5" × 6", 2 pages
p. 75

2001.03
D'Ette Nogel, How
Deep Is Your Love?
Curator: Irene Tsatsos
April 21–June 30, 2001
Curator: Lora McPhail
Booklet
8.5" × 4.66"
p. 77

2002.01
Das Spyder–Man
July 6–Aug. 24, 2002
Postcard
9" × 4"
p. 74

2002.02
Alice Konitz, Beautiful
Ornaments as Shadows,
Crashed Down and a Video
of Flickering Light in a
70's Office Tower
Nov. 16, 2002–Jan. 19 2003
Irene Tsatsos
Design: K:M
Photo by Fredrick Nilson
Brochure
5.5" × 8.5", 2 pages
ISBN: 0–937335–16–9
p. 76

2002.03
Maria Elena Gonzalez,
Magic Carpet / Home
May 24, 2002–Nov. 23, 2003
Photo: Martin Cox
Brochure
5.5" × 8.5", 2 pages
p. 76

2002.04
Rebecca Carter: Beacon
Nov. 16, 2002–Jan. 19, 2003
Irene Tsatsos
Design: K:M
Photography by Joshua
White
Brochure
5.5" × 8.5", 2 pages
p. 76

2002.05
Ruby Neri: New Sculpture
Nov. 16, 2002–Jan. 19, 2003
Curator: Irene Tsatsos
Design: K:M
Photo by Fredrick Nilson
Brochure
5.5" × 8.5", 2 pages
ISBN: 0–937335–17–7
p. 76

2002.06
Michael Brewster,
See Hear Now: A Sonic
Drawing and Five
Acoustic Sculptures
Feb. 16–April 20, 2002
Curator: Irene Tsatsos
Design: Meryl Pollen
Catalog
8.5" × 8.25", 51 pages
p. 77

2002.07
Democracy When?
May 4–June 15, 2002
Curator: Tone O. Nielson
Design: Jessica Fleishmann
Catalog
8" × 6", 106 pages
ISBN: 0–937335–14–2
p. 78

2003.01
Chris Burden,
Small Skyscraper
Curators: Irene Tsatsos
with Julie Deamer
May 1–July 27, 2003
Design: KM Creative
Postcard
9" × 4"
p. 74

2003.02
High Performance,
The First Five Years,
1978–1982
Feb. 1–March 30, 2003
Curator: Jenni Sorkin
Brochure
8.5" × 8.5", 8 pages
p. 75

2003.03
Kerry Tribe, Florida
Oct. 29–Dec. 28, 2003
Curator: Irene Tsatsos
Photo: Mungo Thomson
Brochure
5.5" × 8.5", 2 pages
ISBN: 0–937335–19–3
p. 76

2004.01
Miguel Angel Rios,
A Morir ('til Death)
Oct. 15, 2004–Dec. 10, 2004
Curator: Lauri Firstenberg
Poster
8.25" × 5.75"
p. 75

2004.02
Yvonne Rainer, Radical
Juxtapositions 1961–2002
May 5–Aug. 8, 2004
Poster
6" × 8.25"
p. 77

2005.01
Marking Time
Feb. 9–May 8, 2005
Curator: Glenn R. Phillips
Brochure
8.5" × 5.5", 10 pages
p. 75

2005.02
The Minded Swarm
Curator: Karl Erickson
in consultation with
Irene Tsatsos
June 29, 2005–Sept. 4, 2005
Photo by Joshua White
Brochure
5.5" × 8.5", 2 pages
p. 76

2005.03
A Walk to Remember
Feb. 9–May 8, 2005
Curator: Jens Hoffman
Design: APFEL
Catalog
8.25" × 5.5", 56 pages
ISBN: 3–86588–224–2
p. 79

2005.04
Joe Sola, Taking a Bullet
Oct. 5–Dec.31, 2005
Curator: Irene Tsatsos
Edited by Erin Wright
Essay: Jan Tumlir
Interview: Stuart Horodner
Design: Department of
Graphic Sciences
Catalog
9" × 9", 59 pages
ISBN: 0–937335–20–7
p. 79

2006.01
Draw a Line and Follow It
June 22–August 20, 2006
Design: Helen Sanematsu
Poster
11.75" × 16.5"
p. 80

2006.02
Akexander Apóstol,
Residente Pulido Residente
Pulido, Ranchos
Sept. 21, 2006–Dec. 17, 2006
Postcard
7.25" × 5.5"
p. 81

2006.03
Dustin Shuler, The
Rainforest. A Landscape
in a Shower
Sept. 21–Dec. 17, 2006
Postcard
7.25" × 5.5"
p. 81

2007.01
Impossibility Made Easy
June 13–June 19, 2001
Curator: Elaine Tin Nyo
Design: dB Foundation
and Carl J. Ferrero
Catalog
8" × 11", 36 pages
ISBN: 0–937335–22–3
p. 79

2007.02
Shared Women
Feb. 28–April 8, 2007
Curators: Eve Fowler,
Emily Roysdon and
A.L. Steiner
Postcard
7.25" × 5.5"
p. 79

2007.03
Karaoke Ice
Aug. 31–Sept. 3, 2007;
Sept. 6–9, 2007
Curator: San Jose State
Cadre Laboratory for
New Media
Postcard, Memorabilia
5" × 7", 3" × 3"
p. 81

2007.04
Just Space(s)
Curator: Ava Bromberg
and Nicholas Brown
Sept. 26–Nov.18, 2007
Postcard
4.25" × 6"
p. 81

2008.01
Allan Kaprow, 18
Happenings in 6 Parts
Organized by Steve Roden
Re-staging diagram
8.5" × 11"
p. 82

2008.02
Allan Kaprow, 18
Happenings in 6 Parts
Organized by Steve Roden
Design: Mark Owens
Poster
11" × 17"
p. 84–85

2008.04
Allan Kaprow, 18
Happenings in 6 Parts
Organized by Steve Roden
Steve Roden, "dear mr.
kaprow" program insert
8.25" × 7"
p. 86–87

2008.06
LACE Exhibitions /
Events, Fall 2008
Fall 2008
Design: Mark Owens
Calendar
11" × 17"
p. 88

2008.07
Against the Grain
Curator: Christopher
Russell
Design: Christopher
Russell
7.5" × 10"
p. 89

2008.08
LA25: Half-Life
Oct. 8–Nov. 16, 2008
Curator: Thomas Solomon
Design: Meryl Pollen,
Josh White, F.A. Daniels,
Tony Payne
Postcard
7" × 5"
p. 89

2008.09
Resolution 3: Video Praxis
in Global Spaces
Curators: Ciara Ennis
and Ming-Yuen S. Ma
Dec. 9, 2008–March 1, 2009
Brochure
11" × 6", 8 pages
p. 89

ARTIST INDEX

Living the Archive:
LACE In Print, Volume 1

Project Director/Co-editor:
Carol A. Stakenas

Co-Editor: Lisa Carlson
Designer: Mark Owens
Research Assistants: Zemula Barr, Ingrid
Cruz, Anne Libby, and Joanne Mitchell

© 2010 LACE
(Los Angeles Contemporary Exhibitions)
6522 Hollywood Blvd.
Los Angeles, CA 90028
www.welcometolace.org

Printer:
Oceanic Graphic Printing Inc.
Printed in China

Distribution:
RAM Publications + Distribution Inc.
2525 Michigan Ave., Bldg #A2
Santa Monica, CA 90404
tel: (310)453-0043 / fax: (310)264-4888
www.rampub.com

Living the Archive: Box Edition
also available with artist portfolio
projects and original LACE ephemera.
For more information contact LACE
(323)957-1777, www.welcometolace.org

This publication has been made
possible by generous support from
the Peter Norton Family Foundation
and The Andy Warhol Foundation for
the Visual Arts, Lawrence Barth,
Gary and Tracy Mezzatesta, and
Elinor and Ruben Turner.

ISBN—10: 0937335215
ISBN—13: 9780937335215